The Craft of Research

Chicago Guides
to *Writing*, Editing,
and Publishing

The Craft of Research

THIRD EDITION

WAYNE C. BOOTH

GREGORY G. COLOMB

JOSEPH M. WILLIAMS

THE UNIVERSITY OF CHICAGO PRESS

Chicago & London

WAYNE C. BOOTH was the George M. Pullman Distinguished Service Professor Emeritus at the University of Chicago. His many books include *The Rhetoric of Fiction, For the Love of It: Amateuring and Its Rivals,* and *The Essential Wayne Booth,* each published by the University of Chicago Press. Professor Booth died in 2005.

GREGORY G. COLOMB is professor of English at the University of Virginia. He is the author of *Designs on Truth: The Poetics of the Augustan Mock-Epic.*

JOSEPH M. WILLIAMS was professor emeritus in the Department of English Language and Literature at the University of Chicago. His books include *Style: Toward Clarity and Grace,* currently in its ninth edition. Professor Williams died in 2008.

The University of Chicago Press, Chicago 60637
The University of Chicago Press, Ltd., London
© 1995, 2003, 2008 by The University of Chicago
All rights reserved. Published 2008
Printed in the United States of America

17 16 15 14 13 12 11 10 09 08   1 2 3 4 5

ISBN-13: 978-0-226-06565-6 (cloth)
ISBN-10: 0-226-06565-0 (cloth)
ISBN-13: 978-0-226-06566-3 (paper)
ISBN-10: 0-226-06566-9 (paper)

Library of Congress Cataloging-in-Publication Data

Booth, Wayne C.
    The craft of research / Wayne C. Booth, Gregory G. Colomb, Joseph M. Williams. — 3rd ed.
        p.   cm. — (Chicago guides to writing, editing, and publishing)
    Includes bibliographical references and index.
    ISBN-13: 978-0-226-06565-6 (cloth: alk. paper)
    ISBN-10: 0-226-06565-0 (cloth: alk. paper)
    ISBN-13: 978-0-226-06566-3 (pbk.: alk. paper)
    ISBN-10: 0-226-06566-9 (pbk.: alk. paper) 1. Research—Methodology. 2. Technical writing. I. Colomb, Gregory G. II. Williams, Joseph M. III. Title.
    Q180.55.M4B66 2008
    001.4′2—dc22
                                                                    2007042761

♾ The paper used in this publication meets the minimum requirements of the American National Standard for Information Sciences—Permanence of Paper for Printed Library Materials, ANSI Z39.48-1992.

Contents

Preface: The Aims of This Edition

The aim of the third edition of *The Craft of Research* is the same as the first two: to meet the needs of all researchers, not just first-year undergraduates and advanced graduate students, but even those in business and government who do and report research on any topic, academic, political, or commercial. We wrote it to

- guide you through the complexities of turning a topic or question into a research problem whose significance matches the effort that you put into solving it

- help you organize and draft a report that justifies the effort

- show you how to read your report as your readers will so that you can revise it into one that they will read with the understanding and respect it deserves

Other handbooks touch on these matters, but this one, we think, is different. Most current guides acknowledge that researchers rarely move in a straight line from finding a topic to stating a thesis to filling in note cards to drafting and revision. Experienced researchers loop back and forth, move forward a step or two before going back in order to move ahead again, change directions, all the while anticipating stages not yet begun. But so far as we know, no other guide tries to explain how each part of the process influences all the others—how asking questions about a topic prepares the researcher for drafting, how drafting can reveal problems in an argument, how writing an introduction can send you back to a search for more sources.

In particular, we have tried to be explicit about matters that other guides treat as a mysterious creative process beyond analysis and explanation, including:

- how to turn a vague interest into a problem readers think is worth posing and solving

- how to build an argument that motivates readers to take your claim seriously

- how to anticipate the reservations of thoughtful but critical readers and then respond appropriately

- how to create an introduction and conclusion that answer that toughest of questions from readers, *So what?*

- how to read your own writing as readers will, and thereby know when and how to revise it

Central in every chapter is our advice to side with your readers, to imagine how they will judge what you have written.

The approval of readers, however, is not our only reward for mastering the formal elements of a research report. When we understand not just the superficial shape of those elements but how they help us *think* about our research and its reporting, we are better able to plan, evaluate, and, most important, use the process not just to produce a good report but to think better about our entire project. The elements of a report—its structure, style, and methods of proof—are not empty formulas for convincing readers to accept our claims: they help us test our work and even discover new lines of thought.

As you might guess, we believe that the skills of doing and reporting research are not just for the elite; they can be learned by all students. Though some aspects of advanced research can be learned only in the context of a specific community of researchers, the good news is that even if you don't yet belong to one, you can create something like it on your own. To that end, our "Postscript for Teachers" suggests ways that you (and your teachers) can do that.

WHAT THIS EDITION DOES NOT ADDRESS

We should note what we do not address. We do not discuss how to incorporate into your argument narratives, "thick descriptions," or audiovisual forms of evidence. They are important issues, but too large for us to do justice to them here. Nor do we cover those techniques of research that are unique to particular fields. Researchers must now also learn advanced techniques for Internet searches and other ways of gathering data that we do not have space to cover. Our bibliography suggests a number of sources for guidance in those areas, but so fast are advances in online research that our advice would be dated the minute we offered it.

WHAT'S NEW IN THIS EDITION

In revising the second edition, we have been grateful to all those who praised it, but especially to those who have used it. We hoped for a wide audience but didn't expect it to be as wide as it turned out to be, ranging from first-year students in composition classes to advanced graduate students to advanced researchers (including more than a few tenured professors, if we can believe our e-mail). And we are especially pleased by the fact that *The Craft of Research* has been translated into Russian, Spanish, Portuguese, and Korean and is being translated into Japanese and Chinese.

Since the reception of the first and second editions was so positive, we were cautious about doing a third. We didn't want to lose whatever it was that readers found useful. Yet we had learned some things, and we knew the book could be improved. (Besides, we'd never pass up a chance for one more draft.)

- We divided chapter 12, "Planning and Drafting," into two chapters, and we switched the order of chapter 15, "Introductions and Conclusions," and chapter 16, "Communicating Evidence Visually." So if your syllabus assigns those chapters, you'll have to revise it a bit.

- We revised our comments about online research. Rather than warning that *all* online resources should be viewed with caution, we now emphasize the need to distinguish between the many reliable sources based in libraries and those other less reliable sources that indiscriminate Web searches turn up.

- We have once again revised the chapter on warrants, a matter that has been difficult to explain ever since Stephen Toulmin introduced the concept fifty years ago.

- Throughout, we have tightened things up, cut repetitions, and fixed sentences that were less than felicitous.

In doing all that, we have tried to preserve the amiable voice, the sense of directness, and the stance of colleagues working together that so many of you thought were important in the first and second editions. We revised this book to improve it, but we know that revisions can sometimes make one worse. Let us know what you think.

Finally, a brief tribute to a friend. The following is from the second edition, in just this place in the preface.

> ### A True Story
> As we were preparing the second edition, Booth got a call from a former student who, as had all of his students, been directed again and again by Booth to revise his work. Now a professional in his mid-forties, he called to tell Booth about a dream he had had the night before: "You were standing before Saint Peter at the Pearly Gates," he said, "hoping for admission. He looked at you, hesitant and dubious, then finally said, 'Sorry, Booth, we need another draft.'"

Well, maybe Wayne did get sent back on October 10, 2005, but we doubt it. In life, after all, the only draft any of us can offer is the first one. And in any event, his was well more than good enough. Despite his passing, this book still bears his name, because so much of him is in it.

Greg Colomb
Joe Williams

Our Debts

We want again to thank the many without whose help the first and second editions could never have been realized, especially Steve Biegel, Jane Andrew, and Donald Freeman. The chapter on the visual presentation of data was improved significantly by the comments of Joe Harmon and Mark Monmonier. We would also like to thank those who helped us select and edit the "Appendix: Bibliographic Resources": Jane Block, Sara Bryant, Diane Carothers, Tina Chrzastowski, James Donato, Kristine Fowler, Clara Lopez, Bill McClellan, Nancy O'Brien, Kim Steele, David Stern, Ellen Sutton, and Leslie Troutman. We are also indebted to those at the University of Chicago Press who, when we agreed to undertake this project almost a decade ago, kept after us until we finally delivered. For the second edition, we'd like to thank those whose thoughtful reviews of the first edition and our early revisions of it helped us see opportunities we would otherwise have missed: Don Brenneis, University of California, Santa Cruz; John Cox, Hope College; John Mark Hansen, University of Chicago; Richard Hellie, University of Chicago; Susannah Heschel, Dartmouth College; Myron Marty, Drake University; Robert Sampson, University of Chicago; Joshua Scodel, University of Chicago; W. Phillips Shively, University of Minnesota; and Tim Spears, Middlebury College. We are also grateful to Alec MacDonald and Sam Cha for their invaluable help tracking down details of all sorts.

We would also like to thank those many colleagues whom we asked for advice and who generously shared their suggestions for this third edition.

We are again indebted to those at the University of Chicago Press who supported the writing of this revision.

From WCB (composed for the second edition): I am amazed as I think back on my more than fifty years of teaching and research by how many students and colleagues could be cited here as having diminished my ignorance. Since that list would be too long, I'll thank mainly my chief critic, my wife, Phyllis, for her many useful suggestions and careful editing. She and my daughters, Katherine Stevens and Alison Booth, and their children, Robin, Emily, and Aaron, along with all those colleagues, have helped me combat my occasional despair about the future of responsible inquiry.

From GGC: I, too, have been blessed with students and colleagues who have taught me much—first among them the hundreds of grad students who shared with me their learning to be teachers. They, above all, have shown me the possibilities in collaborative inquiry. What I lean on most, though, are home and family: Sandra, Robin, Kikki, Karen, and Lauren. Through turbulent times and calm, they gave point and purpose to it all. Before them was another loving family, whose center, Mary, still sets an example to which I can only aspire.

From JMW: The family has tripled in size since the first edition, and I am ever more grateful for their love and support: Ol, Michele, and Eleanor; Chris and Ingrid; Dave, Patty, Matilde, and Owen; Megan, Phil, Lily, and Calvin; Joe, Christine, Nicholas, and Katherine. And at beginning and end, Joan, whose patience, love, and good sense flow still more bountifully than I deserve.

In Memoriam

WAYNE C. BOOTH
(1921–2005)

*His dedication to the spirit of research is a lesson to us all.
At its moral center was his belief that*

"intellectual understanding is one of the best versions of the Golden Rule: Listen to others as you would have others listen to you. Precise demonstration of truth is important but not as important as the communal pursuit of it. Put in terms of Kant's categorical imperative, When addressing someone else's ideas, your obligation is to treat them as you believe all human beings *ought* to treat one another's ideas."

WAYNE C. BOOTH,
My Many Selves: The Quest for a Plausible Harmony

PART I

Research,
Researchers,
and
Readers

Prologue

WHO NEEDS RESEARCH?

When you think of a researcher, what do you imagine? Someone in a lab coat peering into a microscope? A white-bearded professor taking notes in a silent library? That's what most people think. But you might also have pictured Oprah, Yahoo creator Jerry Yang, or the manager of every major league baseball, football, and basketball team in the world. Like just about every successful person, they are not only experts in doing research, but in using the research of others. In fact, that's part of what makes them successful. In an aptly named "age of information" (or, too often, *misinformation*), every one of them has learned not only how to find information, but how to evaluate it, then to report it clearly and accurately. More than ever, those skills are essential to anyone who wants to succeed in just about any profession you can think of.

You may not yet be one of those practicing professionals, but learning to do research now will help you today and prepare you for what's to come. First, it will help you understand what you read as nothing else will. You can accurately judge the research of others only after you've done your own and can understand the messy reality behind what is so smoothly and confidently presented in your textbooks or by experts on TV. The Internet and cable TV flood us with "facts" about government, the economy, the environment, the products we buy. Some are sound; most are not. That's why, as you learn to do research, you'll also learn to value reliable research reported clearly and accurately.

You'll also discover how new knowledge depends on what questions you ask—and don't; how the way you present your research shapes the questions you can ask and how you answer them. Most important, you will understand how the knowledge we all rely on depends on the quality of the research that supports it and the accuracy of its reporting. Although some might think it idealistic, another reason for doing research is the sheer pleasure of solving a puzzle, of discovering something that no one else knows.

But learning to do research is not like learning to ride a bike, the sort of thing you learn once and never forget. Each of the three of us has started projects that forced us to rethink how we do our work. Whenever we've addressed a new research community, we've had to learn its ways to help us understand what its members think is important. But even then, we could still rely on principles that all researchers follow, principles that we describe in this book. We think you will find them useful as your projects and readers become more demanding, both in school and after.

FLOODS OF MISINFORMATION

Since 9/11, our government has had to counter bizarre claims that have circulated around the world: No Muslims were among the hijackers; Jews had advance notice and stayed home; the attacks were the work of the CIA. These claims have been widely believed, even though no evidence backs them up. But we should also recall some bizarre stories believed by many Americans: The CIA started the AIDS epidemic to kill homosexuals and African Americans; the government still hides the bodies of aliens in Area 51; bar codes are a UN conspiracy. Every society falls for outlandish claims, but we can learn to see through them once we understand how to make a good case for what we should believe, based not on fear or paranoia, but on reliable evidence and a sound argument.

We must be candid, though: doing research carefully and reporting it clearly are hard work, consisting of many tasks, often competing for your attention at the same time. And no matter how carefully you plan, research follows a crooked path, taking unexpected turns, sometimes up blind alleys, even looping back on itself. As complex as that process is, we will work through it step-by-step so that you can see how its parts work together. When you can manage its parts, you can manage the often intimidating whole and look forward to doing more research with greater confidence.

STARTING A RESEARCH PROJECT

If you are beginning your first project, the task may seem overwhelming. *How do I find a topic? Where do I find information on it? What do I do when I find it?* Even if you've done a research paper in a writing class, the idea of another may be even more intimidating if this time it's *the real thing.* If so, you're not alone. Even experienced researchers feel anxious when they tackle a new kind of project for a new audience. So whatever anxiety you feel, most researchers have felt it too. (It's a feeling that the three of us know well.*) The difference is that experienced researchers know what lies ahead—hard work, but also the pleasure of the hunt; some frustration, but more satisfaction; periods of confusion, but confidence that, in the end, it will all come together and that the result is worth the effort. Most of all, experienced researchers know how to get from start to finish not easily, perhaps, but as efficiently as the complexity of their task allows. That's the aim of this book.

WORKING WITH A PLAN

You will struggle with your project if you don't know what readers look for in a final report or how to help them find it. Experienced researchers know that they most often produce a sound report when they have a plan, no matter how rough, even if only in their heads. In fact, they create two kinds of plans: One helps them prepare and conduct their research; the second helps them draft their report of it.

They usually begin with a question and a plan to guide their search for an answer. They may not know exactly what they'll find,

---

*Careful readers may notice that in this third edition we still speak in the voice of three authors, even though Wayne Booth was no longer with us to participate in the revisions. We two (Colomb and Williams) chose to keep Wayne's voice because we could not imagine the book without it.

but they know generally what it will look like, even if it surprises them. They also know that once they have an answer, they don't just start writing, any more than an experienced carpenter just starts sawing. They draw up a second plan, a rough blueprint for a first draft—maybe no more than a sketch of an outline. Shrewd researchers, though, don't let that plan box them in: they change it if they run into a problem or discover something that leads them in a new direction. But before they start a first draft, they begin with *some* plan, even when they know they'll almost certainly change it.

That plan for a draft helps researchers write, but created with their readers in mind, it also helps readers read. In fact, researchers of all kinds use standard forms to anticipate what readers look for:

- A newspaper reporter writes her story in the traditional "pyramid" form, with the salient information first, not just to make her job of drafting easier, but also so that her readers can find the gist of the news quickly, then decide whether to read on.

- An accountant follows a standard form for her audit report not just to organize her own writing, but so that investors can find the information they need to decide whether the company is another Enron or the next Apple.

- A Food and Drug Administration scientist follows the predictable form for a scientific report—Introduction, Methods and Materials, Results, Discussion, Conclusion—not just to order his own thoughts coherently, but to help readers find the specific issues they have to consider before they accept his findings.

Within these forms or *genres*, writers are free to emphasize different ideas, to put a personal stamp on their work. But they know that a plan helps them write efficiently and, no less important, helps their readers read productively.

This book will help you create and execute a plan for doing your research and another for reporting it in ways that not only encourage your best thinking, but help your readers see its value.

HOW TO USE THIS BOOK

The best way to deal with the complexity of research (and its anxieties) is to read this book twice. First skim it to understand what lies ahead (flip past what seems tedious or confusing). But then as you begin your work, read carefully the chapters relevant to your immediate task. If you are new to research, reread from the beginning. If you are in an intermediate course but not yet at home in your field, skim part I, then concentrate on the rest. If you are an experienced researcher, you will find chapter 4 and parts III and IV most useful.

In part I, we address what those undertaking their first project must think about deliberately: why readers expect us to write up our research in particular ways (chapter 1), and why you should think of your project not as solitary work but as a conversation with sources whose work you read and with those who will in turn read your work (chapter 2).

In part II, we discuss how to frame and develop your project. We explain

- how to find a topic in an interest, then how to focus and question it (chapter 3)

- how to transform those questions into a research problem (chapter 4)

- how to find sources to guide your search for answers (chapter 5)

- how to engage sources in ways that encourage your own best thinking (chapter 6)

In part III, we discuss how to assemble a sound case in support of your claim. That includes

- an overview of a research argument (chapter 7)

- how to evaluate your claim for its significance (chapter 8)

- how to judge what count as good reasons and sound evidence (chapter 9)

- how to acknowledge and respond to questions, objections, and alternative views (chapter 10)

- how to make clear the logic of your argument (chapter 11)

  In part IV, we lay out the steps in producing your report:

- how to plan a first draft (chapter 12)

- how to draft it quickly and efficiently (chapter 13)

- how to test and revise it (chapter 14)

- how to present complex quantitative evidence clearly and pointedly (chapter 15)

- how to write an introduction and conclusion that convince readers your report is worth their time (chapter 16)

- how to edit your style to make it clear, direct, and readable (chapter 17)

Between some of the chapters you will find "Quick Tips," brief sections that complement the chapters with practical advice.

In an afterword, "The Ethics of Research," we reflect on a matter that goes beyond professional competence. Doing and reporting research is a social activity with ethical implications. We often read about the dishonest research of historians, scientists, stock analysts, and others. And we see plagiarism among writers at all levels of achievement, from secondary-school students to leaders of their professions. Such events highlight the importance of *ethical* research and its reporting.

In a concluding essay, we address those who teach research. At the end of the book is a bibliography of sources for beginning researchers and for advanced researchers in particular fields.

Research is hard work, but like any challenging job done well, both its process and its results can bring great satisfaction. No small part of that satisfaction comes from knowing that your work sustains the fabric of a community of people who share your interests, especially when you discover something that you believe can improve your readers' lives by changing what and how they think.

CHAPTER ONE

Thinking in Print

THE USES OF RESEARCH, PUBLIC AND PRIVATE

In this chapter we define research, then discuss how you benefit from learning to do it well, why we three value it, and why we hope you will too.

Whenever we read about a scientific breakthrough or a crisis in world affairs, we benefit from the research of those who report it, who in turn benefited from the research of countless others. When we walk into a library, we are surrounded by more than twenty-five centuries of research. When we log on to the Internet, we can read millions of reports written by researchers who have posed questions beyond number, gathered untold amounts of information from the research of others to answer them, then shared their answers with the rest of us so that we can carry on their work by asking new questions and, we hope, answering them.

Teachers at all levels devote their lives to research. Governments spend billions on it, businesses even more. Research goes on in laboratories and libraries, in jungles and ocean depths, in caves and in outer space, in offices and, in the information age, even in our own homes. Research is in fact the world's biggest industry. Those who cannot do it well or evaluate that of others will find themselves sidelined in a world increasingly dependent on sound ideas based on good information produced by trustworthy inquiry and then presented clearly and accurately.

In fact, research reported by others, in writing, is the source of most of what we believe. Of your three authors, only Williams has ever set foot in Australia, but Booth and Colomb believe it exists, because for a lifetime they have read about it in reports they trust and have seen it on reliable maps (and heard reports about it from Williams). None of us has been to Venus, but we believe that it is hot, dry, and mountainous, because that's what we've read. But we trust that research only because we think it was done carefully and reported accurately.

Without trustworthy *published* research, we all would be locked in the opinions of the moment, prisoners of what we alone experience or dupes to whatever we're told. Of course, we want to believe that our opinions are sound, yet mistaken ideas, even dangerous ones, flourish because too many people accept too many opinions based on too little evidence. And as recent events have shown, those who act on unreliable evidence can lead us—indeed have led us—into disaster.

That's why in this book we will urge you to be amiably skeptical of the research you read, to question it even as you realize how much you depend on it. Are we three authors 100 percent drop-dead certain of reports that Venus is hot, dry, and mountainous? No, but we trust the researchers who have published reports about it, as well as the editors, reviewers, and skeptical readers who have tested those reports and published their own results. So we'll go on thinking that Venus is hot and dry, at least until we see better evidence that it's not.

1.1 WHAT IS RESEARCH?

In the broadest terms, we do research whenever we gather information to answer a question that solves a problem:

PROBLEM: Where do I find a new head gasket for my '65 Mustang?
RESEARCH: Look in the yellow pages for an auto-parts store, then call to see if it has one in stock.

PROBLEM: To settle a bet, I need to know when Michael Jordan was born.
RESEARCH: You Google "Michael Jordan birthday."

PROBLEM: I'm just curious about a new species of fish.
RESEARCH: You search the Internet for articles in newspapers
and academic journals.

We all do that kind of research every day, and though we rarely write it up, we rely on those who wrote up theirs: Jordan's biographers, the fish discoverers, the publishers of the yellow pages and the catalogs of the auto-parts suppliers—they all wrote up their research because they knew that one day someone would have a question that they could answer.

If you're preparing to do a research project not because you want to but because it's been assigned, you might think that it is just make-work and treat it as an empty exercise. We hope you won't. Done well, your project prepares you to join the oldest and most esteemed of human conversations, one conducted for millennia among philosophers, engineers, biologists, social scientists, historians, literary critics, linguists, theologians, not to mention CEOs, lawyers, marketers, investment managers—the list is endless.

Right now, you may feel that the conversation is one-sided, that you have to listen more than you can speak, and that in any event you have little to contribute and only one reader. That may be true, for the moment. But at some point, you will join a conversation that, at its best, can help you and your community free us from ignorance, prejudice, and the half-baked ideas that so many charlatans try to impose on us. It is no exaggeration to say that, maybe not today or tomorrow but one day, your research and your reports of it can improve if not the whole world, at least your corner of it.

1.2 WHY WRITE IT UP?

For some of you, though, the invitation to join this conversation may still seem easy to decline. If you accept it, you'll have to find a good question, search for sound data, formulate and support a good answer, and then write it all up. Even if you turn out a first-rate report, it may be read not by an eager world but only by your teacher.

And, besides, you may think, *my teacher knows all about my topic. What do I gain from writing up my research, other than proving I can do it?*

One answer is that we write not just to share our work, but to improve it before we do.

1.2.1 Write to Remember

Experienced researchers first write just to remember what they've read. A few talented people can hold in mind masses of information, but most of us get lost when we think about what Smith found in light of Wong's position, and compare both to the odd data in Brunelli, especially as they are supported by Boskowitz—*but what was it that Smith said?* When you don't take notes on what you read, you're likely to forget or, worse, misremember it.

1.2.2 Write to Understand

A second reason for writing is to see larger patterns in what you read. When you arrange and rearrange the results of your research in new ways, you discover new implications, connections, and complications. Even if you could hold it all in mind, you would need help to line up arguments that pull in different directions, plot out complicated relationships, sort out disagreements among experts. *I want to use these claims from Wong, but her argument is undercut by Smith's data. When I put them side by side, I see that Smith ignores this last part of Wong's argument. Aha! If I introduce it with this part from Brunelli, I can focus on Wong more clearly.* That's why careful researchers never put off writing until they've gathered all the data they need: they write from the beginning of their project to help them assemble their information in new ways.

1.2.3 Write to Test Your Thinking

A third reason to write is to get your thoughts out of your head and onto paper, where you'll see what you really *can* think. Just about all of us, students and professionals alike, believe our ideas are more compelling in the dark of our minds than they turn out to be in the cold light of print. You can't know how good your ideas are until you separate them from the swift and muddy flow of thought and fix them in an organized form that you—and your readers—can study.

In short, we write to remember more accurately, understand better, and evaluate what we think more objectively. (And as you will discover, the more you write, the better you read.)

1.3 WHY A FORMAL REPORT?

But even when they agree that writing is an important part of learning, thinking, and understanding, some still wonder why they can't write up their research in their own way, why they have to satisfy demands imposed by a community that they have not joined (or even want to) and conform to conventions they did nothing to create. *Why should I adopt language and forms that are not mine? Aren't you just trying to turn me into an academic like yourself? If I write as you expect me to, I risk losing my identity.*

Such concerns are legitimate (most teachers wish students would raise them more often). But it would be a feeble education that did not change you at all, and the deeper your education, the more it will change the "you" that you are or want to be. That's why it's so important to choose carefully what you study and with whom. But it would be a mistake to think that learning to write sound research reports must threaten your true identity. It will change the way you think, but only by giving you more ways of thinking. You will be different by being freer to choose who you want to be and what you want to do with the rest of your life.

But the most important reason for learning to report research in ways readers expect is that when you write for others, you demand more of yourself than when you write for yourself alone. By the time you fix your ideas in writing, they are so familiar to you that you need help to see them not for what you want them to be but for what they really are. You will understand your own work better when you try to anticipate your readers' inevitable and critical questions: *How have you evaluated your evidence? Why do you think it's relevant? What ideas have you considered but rejected?*

All researchers, including the three of us, can recall moments when in writing to meet their readers' expectations, they found a flaw or blunder in their thinking or even discovered a new insight that escaped them in a first draft written for themselves. You can do that only when you imagine and then meet the needs and expectations of informed and careful readers. When you do that, you create what we call a *rhetorical community* of shared values.

You might think, *OK, I'll write for readers, but why not in my own way?* The traditional forms that readers expect are more than empty vessels into which you must squeeze your ideas. They have evolved to help writers question their thinking in ways they might not otherwise; they also embody the shared values of a research community. Whatever community you join, you'll be expected to show that you understand its practices by reporting your research as its members do. Once you know its standard forms, you'll be better able to answer your particular community's predictable questions and understand what its members care about and why.

But regardless of these differences among communities, what counts as good work is the same, whether it's in the academic world or the world of government, commerce, or technology. If you learn to do research well now, you gain an immense advantage in the kind of research you will do later, no matter where you do it.

1.4 WRITING IS THINKING

Writing a research report is, finally, thinking with and for your readers. When you write for others, you disentangle your ideas from your memories and wishes, so that you—and others—can explore, expand, combine, and understand them more fully. Thinking for others is more careful, more sustained, more insightful—in short, more thoughtful—than just about any other kind of thinking.

You can, of course, take the easy way: do just enough to satisfy your teacher. This book will help you do that, but you'll shortchange yourself if you do. If instead you find a topic that *you* care about, ask a question that *you* want to answer, then pursue that answer as best you can, your project can have the fascination of a mystery whose solution richly rewards your efforts. Nothing contributes more to successful research than your commitment to it, and nothing teaches you more about how to think than a successful (or even unsuccessful) report of its product.

We wish we could tell you how to balance your belief in the worth of your project with the need to accommodate the demands of teachers and colleagues, but we cannot. If you believe in what you're doing and cannot find anyone else who shares your beliefs, all you can do is put your head down and press on. With our admiration.

Some of the world's most important research has been done by those who persevered in the face of indifference or even hostility, because they never lost faith in their vision. The geneticist Barbara McClintock struggled for years unappreciated because her research community considered her work uninteresting. But she believed in it and pressed on. When her colleagues finally realized that she had already answered questions that they were just starting to ask, she won science's highest honor, the Nobel Prize.

CHAPTER TWO

Connecting with Your Reader

(RE-)CREATING YOURSELF AND YOUR READERS

~~Research counts for little if few read it~~. *Yet even experienced researchers sometimes forget to keep their readers in mind as they plan and draft their report. In this chapter we show you how to think about readers even before you begin your project.*

Most of the important things we do, we do with others. Some students think research is different. They imagine that solitary scholar reading in a hushed library. But no place is more filled with imagined voices than a library or lab. Whether you read a book or a lab report, you silently converse with its writer—and through her with everyone else she has read. In fact, every time you go to a written source for information, you join a conversation between writers and readers that began more than five thousand years ago. And when you report your own research, you add your voice and can hope that other voices will respond to you, so that you can in turn respond to them. So it goes and, we hope, will continue for a long time to come.

2.1 CREATING ROLES FOR YOURSELF AND YOUR READERS

All conversations are social activities in which we are expected to play our parts. In face-to-face conversations, we can judge how well we and others do that by sensing how the conversation is going. Do we treat each other as equals, speaking and listening civilly, answering each other's questions directly? Or does one of us seem to be playing the role of expert, dismissing others as a mere audience? We can judge how well a conversation is going as we have it, and we can adjust our roles and behavior to repair mistakes and misunderstandings as they occur. But in an imagined conversation in writing, once we decide what role to play and what role to assign to readers, those roles are fixed. If as we read we think, *Well, Abrams acknowledges Stanik's evidence, but he's dogmatic in criticizing it and ignores obvious counterexamples,* Abrams can't change what we read next to recover from our judgment. (Right now, we three expect that you're judging us.)

Of course, judgments go both ways: just as we judge a writer as we read, so a writer must judge his readers, but before he writes. For example, the writers of these next two passages imagined different readers, with different questions based on different levels of knowledge about the chemistry of heart muscles. So they wrote in different ways:

> 1a. The control of cardiac irregularity by calcium blockers depends on calcium's activation of muscle groups through its interaction with the regulatory proteins actin, myosin, tropomyosin, and troponin in the sarcomere, the basic unit of muscle contraction.

> 1b. Doctors can control irregular heartbeats with the drugs called calcium blockers. When the heart contracts, its muscles are activated by calcium. The calcium in a heart muscle cell interacts with four proteins that regulate contraction. The proteins are actin, myosin, tropomyosin, and troponin. That interaction happens in the basic unit of muscle contraction, the sarcomere.

The writer of (1a) casts herself and her readers as colleagues who know how muscles work. The writer of (1b) casts himself in the role of an expert, patiently explaining a complicated matter to readers who know little. If they judged their readers correctly, their readers will judge them favorably.

But suppose they switched passages. Someone ignorant of the way muscles work would read (1a) thinking the writer was indifferent to his needs; those who knew how muscles work would read (1b) thinking the writer was talking down to them. In either case, the writers would lose their readers because they misjudged them and their relationship.

In writing this book, we tried to imagine you—what you're like, what you know about research, whether you even care about it. We imagined a *persona* for you, a role we hoped you would adopt: someone interested in learning how to do and report research and who shares our belief in its importance (or at least is open to being persuaded). Then we imagined a persona of our own: writers committed to the value of research, interested in sharing how it works, not talking *at* you like a lecturer or *down* to you like a pedant, but working *with* the "you" that we hoped you would be willing to be. At times we struggled trying to speak as easily to those of you starting your first project as to those doing advanced work. We hoped that new researchers would not be frustrated when we discussed issues they haven't yet faced and that more experienced readers would be patient as we covered familiar ground. Only you can judge how well we've succeeded.

In fact, we can't avoid creating *some* role for ourselves and our readers: they will infer them from our writing whether we plan them or not. So roles are worth thinking about before you write a word. If from the outset, you ignore or miscast your readers, you'll leave so many traces of that mistake in your early drafts that you won't easily fix them in the final one.

2.2 UNDERSTANDING YOUR ROLE

Since few people read research reports for entertainment, you have to create a relationship that encourages them to see why it's in their interest to read yours. That's not easy. Too many beginning researchers offer readers a relationship that caricatures a bad classroom: *Teacher, I know less than you. So my role is to show you how many facts I can dig up. Yours is to say whether I've found enough to give me a good grade.* Big mistake. Do that and you turn your project into a pointless drill that demeans both you and your teacher. Worse, you cast yourself in a role exactly opposite to that of a true researcher.

In a research report, you must switch the roles of student and teacher. When you do research, you learn something that others don't know. So when you report it, you must think of your reader as someone who doesn't know it *but needs to* and yourself as someone who will *give her reason to want to know it.* You must imagine a relationship that goes beyond *Here are some facts I've dug up about medieval Tibetan weaving. Are they enough of the right ones?*

There are three better reasons for offering those facts: the third is most common in academic research.

2.2.1 I've Found Some New and Interesting Information

You take the first step beyond data-grubbing when you say to your reader, *Here are some facts about medieval Tibetan weaving that you do not know and may find interesting.* This offer assumes, of course, that your reader wants to know, but even if not, you must still cast yourself in the role of someone who has found something your reader will find interesting and your reader as someone who wants to know, *whether she really will or not.* Down the road, you'll be expected to find (or create) a community of readers who not only share an interest in your topic (or can be convinced to), but also have questions about it that you can answer. But even if you don't have that audience right now, you must write as if you do. You must present yourself as interested in, even enthusiastic about wanting to share something new, because the interest you show in your work roughly predicts the interest your reader will take in it. And in you.

2.2.2 I've Found a Solution to an Important Practical Problem

You take big a step toward more significant research when you can say to readers not just *Here are some facts that should interest you,* but *These facts will help you do something to solve a problem you care about. That is the kind of research that people do every day in business, government, and the professions.* They confront practical problems whose solutions require research into the facts of the matter, first to understand the problem, then to figure out how to solve it—problems ranging from spam to falling profits to terrorism.

To help new researchers learn that role, teachers sometimes invent "real world" scenarios: an environmental science professor might assign you to write a report for the director of the state Environmental Protection Agency on how to clean up a local lake.

In this scenario you are not playing the role of a student dumping data on a teacher, but of a professional giving practical advice to someone who needs it. To make your report credible, however, you must use the right terminology, cite the right sources, find and present the right evidence, all in the right format. But most important, you have to design your report around a specific *intention* that defines your role: to advise a decision maker on what to *do* to solve a problem. That kind of research is typical in the world at large but is less common in academic research than the next one.

2.2.3 I've Found an Answer to an Important Question

Although academic researchers sometimes advise EPA directors on what to do, their more common role is that of scholars who help their research community simply understand something better. Others might use their findings to solve a practical problem—a discovery about the distribution of prime numbers, for example, helped cryptologists design an unbreakable code. But that research itself was aimed at solving not the practical problem of keeping secrets, but the *conceptual* problem of not entirely understanding prime numbers. Some researchers call this kind of research "pure" as opposed to "applied."

Teachers occasionally invent "real world" scenarios involving conceptual problems: a political science professor asks you to play the role of a senator's intern researching how violent TV affects children's behavior. But more typically they expect you to imagine yourself as what you are learning to be—a researcher addressing a community of other researchers interested in issues that they want to understand better. Your report on medieval Tibetan weaving, for example, might help rug designers sell more rugs, but its basic aim is to help scholars better understand something about Tibetan art, such as *How did medieval Tibetan rugs influence the art of modern China?*

2.3 IMAGINING YOUR READER'S ROLE

You establish your side of the relationship with your readers when you adopt one of those three roles—*I have information for you; I* can help you fix a problem; I can help you understand something better. You must, however, cast your readers in a complementary role by offering them a social contract: I'll play my part if you play yours. But that means you have to understand their role. If you cast them in a role they won't accept, you're likely to lose them entirely. In this case, the old advice to "consider your audience" means that you must report your research in a way that motivates your readers to play the role you have imagined for them.

For example, suppose you're an expert on blimps and zeppelins. You've been asked to share your research with three different groups with three different reasons for wanting to hear about it. How they receive you will depend on how accurately you imagine the role they intend to play and how well you match your role to theirs. For that, you must understand what they want and what they are in return willing *and able* to do for you.

2.3.1 Entertain Me

Imagine the first group that invited you to speak is the local Zeppelin Club. Its members are not experts, but they know a lot about zeppelins. They read about them, visit historic sites, and collect zeppelin memorabilia. You decide to share some new facts you've found in a letter from your great-uncle Otto describing his transatlantic zeppelin flight in 1936, along with some photographs and a menu he saved. His letter comments on the grilled oysters he had for dinner and tells a funny story about why he happened to take the trip in the first place.

In planning your talk, you judge that what's at stake is just a diverting hour of zeppelin trivia. You meet your side of the bargain when you share whatever you think might interest them—hunches, speculation, even unsubstantiated rumors. You won't show PowerPoint slides, present data, or cite scholarly sources to substantiate your claims. Your audience will play its role by listening with interest, asking questions, maybe sharing their own anecdotes. You don't expect them to challenge the authenticity of the letter from Great-Uncle Otto or question how the photos are relevant to the social history of zeppelins, much less of lighter-than-air travel in general. Your job is to give an engaging talk; theirs is to be amiably engaged.

Some beginning researchers imagine their readers belong to a Zeppelin Club, already fascinated by their topic and eager to hear anything new about it. While that sometimes works for experts with the right audience (see the box below), it rarely works for students learning to do and report serious research. Your teachers expect you to report not just *what* you find, but what you can *do* with it.

2.3.2 Help Me Solve My Practical Problem

Imagine that your next meeting is with True-to-Life Films. It plans to make a movie about a zeppelin flight in 1936 and wants you to help them get the historical details right, including a scene in the dining cabin. They want to know how the cabin was furnished, what people ate, what the menus looked like, and so on. They don't care whether your facts are new, only whether they are right, so that they can make the scene authentic. You show them your photos and the menu and describe the oysters Great-Uncle Otto ate, but you don't bother with why he took the trip. To succeed in this role, you must help them solve a practical problem whose solution you base not on *all* the data you can find, no matter how new, but on just those *particular* facts that are relevant to the problem of authenticity and whose sources you can show are reliable. Your audience will listen intently and critically, because they want to get the details right.

That's the kind of task you're likely to face if your teacher invents a "real world" assignment—write to an EPA official who needs to *do* something about a polluted lake. Academic researchers sometimes address practical problems like these, but for them another kind of problem is far more common. So pose a practical problem *only if* your teacher creates one; otherwise, check with her first. (We'll discuss practical problems in more detail in chapter 4.)

2.3.3 Help Me Understand Something Better

Now imagine that your audience is the faculty of Zeppo University's Department of Lighter-than-Air Studies (with the same standing as, say, your English department). They study all aspects of blimps and zeppelins, do research on their economics and aerodynamics, and participate in a worldwide conversation about their history and social significance. They compete with other lighter-than-air scholars to produce new lighter-than-air knowledge and theories that they publish in lighter-than-air journals and books read by everyone in their lighter-than-air field.

These scholars have invited you to talk about your specialty: the social history of zeppelin travel in the 1930s. They don't want you just to amuse them with new facts (though they'll be happy if you do) or to help them *do* something (though they'd be pleased if you got them consulting work with True-to-Life Films). They want you to use whatever new facts you have to help them better *understand* the social history of zeppelin travel or, better still, of lighter-than-air culture in general.

Because these lighter-than-air scholars are intensely committed to finding the Truth about zeppelins, you know they expect you to be objective, rigorously logical, able to examine every issue from all sides. You also know that if you don't nail down your facts, they'll hammer you during the question period, and if you don't have good answers, slice you up afterward over the wine and cheese, not just to be contentious or even nasty (though some will be), but to get as close as they can to the Truth about zeppelins in the 1930s. If you offer new data, like Great-Uncle Otto's photos, letter, and menu, they'll be glad to see them, but they'll want to know why they matter and might even question their authenticity.

Above all, they will care about your documents *only if* you can show how they serve as *evidence* that helps you answer a question important to understanding something about zeppelins that is *more important* than your uncle's trip. They will receive you especially well if you can convince them that they do not understand the social history of zeppelins as well as they thought and that your new data will improve their flawed understanding. If you can't do that, they'll respond not with *I don't agree*—we all learn to live with that; some of us even thrive on it—but with a response far more devastating: *I don't care.*

So you begin your talk:

As we all have been led to believe by a number of studies on the food service on transatlantic zeppelin flights in the 1930s (especially Schmidt 1986 and Kloepfer 1998), items were never cooked over an open flame because of the danger of explosions. However, I have recently discovered a menu from the July 12, 1936, crossing of the *Hindenburg* indicating that oysters grilled over charcoal were served. . . . [You then go on to show why that new knowledge matters.]

That is the kind of conversation you join when you report research to a community of scholars, lighter-than-air or not. You must imagine them imagining this conversation with you: *Never mind whether your style is graceful (though I will admire your work more if it is); don't bother me with amusing anecdotes about your great-uncle Otto (though I like hearing them if they help me understand your ideas better); ignore whether what you know will make me rich (though I would be happy if it did). Just tell me something I don't know so that I can better understand our common interest.*

Your academic readers will almost always adopt this third role. They will think you've fulfilled your side of the social contract only when you treat them as who they think they are: scholars interested in greater knowledge and better understanding. To be sure, the faculty over in chemistry or philosophy care little about zeppelins, much less their meal service. (*Can you believe the trivia they study over in Helium Hall?*) But then you don't much care about their issues, either. You are concerned with your *particular* community of readers, with *their* interests and expectations, with improving *their* understanding, based on the best evidence you can find. That's the social contract that all researchers must establish with their readers.

Who Cares about That?

Academic researchers are often scoffed at for studying esoteric topics that matter to no one but themselves. The charge is usually unfair, but some researchers do become fascinated with matters that seem to have little significance. Williams once attended the dissertation defense of a PhD candidate who had discovered reels and reels of film shot by European anthropologists in Africa and Asia in the early twentieth century. This previously unknown footage fascinated the film scholars on the committee. But when Williams asked the candidate, "How do these new films improve our understanding of movies then or now?" she could answer only that "no one has ever seen this footage before." Williams put his question in different ways but never got a better answer. The film scholars, on the other hand, were untroubled (and found Williams's questions naive), because they were already imagining how the footage might change their thinking about early film. And in any event, they all loved old film for its own sake. So sometimes new data alone are enough to interest the right readers. But if that candidate hopes to write anything that interests anyone but a tiny coterie of specialists, she will have to make an offer better than *Here's some new stuff.*

☞ QUICK TIP: *A Checklist for Understanding Your Readers*

Think about your readers from the start, knowing that you'll understand them better as you work through your project. Answer these questions early on, then revisit them when you start planning and again when you revise.

1. Who will read my report?

   - Professionals who expect me to follow every academic convention and use a standard format?

   - Well-informed general readers?

   - General readers who know little about the topic?

2. What do they expect me to do? Should I

   - entertain them?

   - provide new factual knowledge?

   - help them understand something better?

   - help them do something to solve a practical problem in the world?

3. How much can I expect them to know already?

   - What do they know about my topic?

   - Is the problem one that they already recognize?

   - Is it one that they have but haven't yet recognized?

   - Is the problem not theirs, but only mine?

   - Will they take the problem seriously, or must I convince them that it matters?

4. How will readers respond to the solution/answer in my main claim?

   • Will it contradict what they already believe? How?

   • Will they make standard arguments against my solution?

   • Will they want to see the steps that led me to the solution?

PART II

Asking
Questions,
Finding
Answers

Prologue

If you've skimmed this book once, you're ready to begin your project. If you have a research question and know how to look for its answer, review the next two chapters quickly; then read the remaining ones carefully as they become relevant to your task. You may, however, feel bewildered if you're starting from scratch, without even a topic to guide you. But you can manage if you have a plan and take one step at a time.

If you are starting from scratch, your first task is to find a research problem that might be worth solving. Here are four steps to that end:

1. Find a topic specific enough to let you master a reasonable amount of information on it in the time you have: not, for example, *the history of scientific writing*, but *essays in the* Proceedings of the Royal Society *(1675–1750) as precursors to the modern scientific article*; not *doctors in seventeenth-century drama*, but *Molière's mockery of doctors in three early plays*.

2. Question that topic until you find questions that catch your interest. For example, *How did early Royal Society authors demonstrate that their evidence was reliable?* Or, *Why did Molière mock doctors?*

3. Determine the kind of evidence your readers will expect you to offer in support of your answer. Will they accept reports of

facts from secondary sources, or will they expect you to consult primary sources (see 5.1.1)? Will they expect quantitative data, quotations from authorities, or firsthand observations?

4. Determine whether you can find those data. There's no point starting research on a topic until you know you have a good chance of finding data on it.

WHAT ARE YOUR DATA?

No matter their field, researchers collect information to use as evidence to support their claims. But researchers in different fields call that information by different names. We call it *data*. By *data* we mean not just the numbers that natural and social scientists collect, but anything you find "out there" relevant to answering your rsearch question. The term is used less often by researchers in the humanities, but they, too, gather data in the form of quotations, historical facts, and so on. Data are inert, however, until you use them to support a claim that answers your research question. At that point, your data become *evidence*. If you don't have more data than you can use as evidence, you haven't collected enough. (Incidentally, *data* is plural; a single bit of data is a *datum*.)

Once you think you have enough data to support at least a plausible answer to your question, you'll be ready to assemble an argument that makes your case (see part III), then to plan, draft, and revise it (part IV).

You'll discover, however, that you can't march through those steps in the neat order we present them. You'll think of a tentative answer to your research question before you have all the evidence you need to support it. And when you think you have an argument worth making, you may discover that you need more and maybe different evidence from new sources. You may even modify your topic. Doing research is not like strolling along an easy, well-marked path to a familiar destination; it's more like zigzagging up and down a rocky hill through overgrown woods, sometimes in a fog, searching for something you won't recognize until you see it. But no matter how indirect your path, you can make progress if at each step of the way you plan for predictable detours (and maybe even avoid some of them).

Resolve to do lots of writing along the way. Much of it will be routine note-taking, but you should also write reflectively, to understand: make outlines; explain why you disagree with a source; draw diagrams to connect disparate facts; summarize sources, positions, and schools; record even random thoughts. Many researchers find it useful to keep a journal for hunches, new ideas, random thoughts, problems, and so on. You might not include much of this writing-to-discover-and-understand in your final draft. But when you *write as you go, every day,* you encourage your own best critical thinking, understand your sources better, and, when the time comes, draft more productively.

A downside of academic research is its isolation. Except for group projects, you'll read and write mostly alone. But it doesn't have to be that way. Look for someone other than your instructor or adviser who will talk with you about your progress, review your drafts, even pester you about how much you've written. That might be a generous friend, but better is another writer so that you can comment on each other's ideas and drafts.

Best of all is a group of four or five people working on their own projects who meet regularly to read and discuss one another's work. Early on, each meeting should start with a summary of each person's project in this three-part sentence: *I'm working on X because I want to find out Y, so that I (and you) can better understand Z* (more about this in 3.4). As your projects advance, develop an opening "elevator story," a short summary of your project that you could give someone on the way to a meeting. It should include your research question, your best guess at an answer, and the kind of evidence you expect to use to support it. The group can then follow up with questions, responses, and suggestions.

Don't limit your talk to just your story, however. Talk about your readers: Why should they be interested in your question? How might they respond to your argument? Will they trust your evidence? Will they have other evidence in mind? Such questions help you plan an argument that anticipates what your readers expect. Your group can even help you brainstorm when you bog down. Later the group can read one another's outlines and drafts to imagine how their final readers will respond. If your group has a problem with your draft, so will those readers. But for most writers, a writing group is most valuable for the discipline it imposes. It is easier to meet a schedule when you know you must report to others.

Writing groups are common for those writing theses or dissertations. But the rules differ for a class paper. Some teachers think that a group or writing partner provides more help than is appropriate, so be clear what your instructor allows.

CHAPTER THREE

From Topics to Questions

In this chapter we discuss how to find a topic among your interests, narrow it to a manageable scope, then question it to find the makings of a problem that can guide your research. If you are an experienced researcher or know the topic you want to pursue, skip to chapter 4. But if you are starting your first project, you will find this chapter useful.

If you are free to research any topic that interests you, that freedom might seem frustrating—so many choices, so little time. At some point, you have to settle on a topic. But you can't jump from picking a topic to collecting data: your readers want more than a mound of random facts. You have to find a reason better than a class assignment not only for you to devote weeks or months to your research, but for your readers to spend any time reading about it. You'll find that better reason when you can ask a *question* whose answer solves a *problem* that you can convince readers to care about. That question and problem are what will make readers think your report is worth their time. They also focus your research and save you from collecting irrelevant data.

In all research communities, some questions are "in the air," widely debated and researched, such as whether traits like shyness or an attraction to risk are learned or genetically inherited. But other questions may intrigue only the researcher: *Why do cats rub their faces against us? Why does a coffee spill dry up in the shape of a ring?* That's how a lot of research begins—not with a big question that attracts everyone in a field, but with a mental itch about a small one that only a single researcher wants to scratch. If you feel that itch, start scratching. But at some point, you must decide whether the answer to your question solves a problem significant to a teacher, to other researchers, or even to a public whose lives your research could change.

Now that word *problem* is itself a problem. Commonly, a problem means trouble, but among researchers it has a meaning so special that we devote the next chapter to it. But before you can frame your research problem, you have to find a topic that might lead to one. So we'll start there, with finding a topic.

QUESTION OR PROBLEM?

You may have noticed that we've been using the words *question* and *problem* almost interchangeably. But they are not quite the same. Some questions raise problems; others do not. A question raises a problem if not answering it keeps us from knowing something more important than its answer. For example, if we cannot answer the question *Are there ultimate particles?* we cannot know something even more important: the nature of physical existence. On the other hand, a question does not raise a problem if not answering it has no apparent consequences. For example, *Was Abraham Lincoln's right thumb longer than his nose?* We cannot think of what we would gain by knowing. At least at the moment.

3.1 FROM AN INTEREST TO A TOPIC

Most of us have more than enough interests, but beginners often find it hard to locate among theirs a topic focused enough to support a substantial research project. A research topic is an interest stated specifically enough for you to imagine becoming a local expert on it. That doesn't mean you already know a lot about it or that you'll have to know more about it than your teacher does. You just want to know a lot more about it than you do now.

If you can work on any topic, we offer only a cliché: start with what most interests you. Nothing contributes to the quality of your work more than your commitment to it.

3.1.1 Finding a Topic in a General Writing Course

Start by listing as many interests as you can that you'd like to explore. Don't limit yourself to what you think might interest a teacher or make him think you're a serious student. Let your ideas flow. Prime the pump by asking friends, classmates, even your teacher about topics that interest them. If no good topics come to mind, consult the Quick Tip at the end of this chapter.

Once you have a list of topics, choose the one or two that interest you most. Then do this:

- In the library, look up your topic in a general bibliography, such as the *Readers' Guide to Periodical Literature* and skim the subheadings. If you have a more narrow focus, look into specialized guides such as the *American Humanities Index*. Most libraries have copies on the shelf; many subscribe to their online equivalents, but not all of them let you skim subject headings. (We discuss these resources in chapter 5 and list several in the appendix.)

- On the Internet, Google your topic, but don't surf indiscriminately. Look first for Web sites that are roughly like sources you would find in a library, such as online encyclopedias. Read the entry on your general topic, and then copy the list of references at the end for a closer look. Use Wikipedia to find ideas and sources, but always confirm what you find in a reliable source. Few experienced researchers trust Wikipedia, so *under no circumstances cite it as a source of evidence* (unless your topic is the Wikipedia itself).

- You can also find ideas in blogs, which discuss almost every contentious issue, usually ones too big for a research paper. But look for posts that take a position on narrow aspects of the larger issues: if you disagree with a view, investigate it.

3.1.2 Finding a Topic for a First Research Project in a Particular Field

Start by listing topics relevant to your particular class *and that interest you,* then narrow them to one or two promising ones. If the topic is general, such as *religious masks,* you'll have to do some random reading to narrow it. But read with a plan:

- Skim encyclopedia entries in your library or online. Start with standard ones such as the *Encyclopaedia Britannica.* Then consult specialized ones such as the *Encyclopedia of Religion* or the *Stanford Encyclopedia of Philosophy.*

• Skim headings in specialized indexes, such as the *Philosopher's Index, Psychological Abstracts,* or *Women's Studies Abstracts.* Use subheadings for ideas of how others have narrowed your topic.

• Google your topic, but not indiscriminately. Use Google Scholar, a search engine that focuses on scholarly journals and books. Skim the articles it turns up, especially their lists of sources.

When you know the general outline of your topic and how others have narrowed it, try to narrow yours. If you can't, browse through journals and Web sites until it becomes more clearly defined. That takes time, so start early.

3.1.3 Finding a Topic for an Advanced Project

Most advanced students already have interests in topics relevant to their field. If you don't, focus on what interests you, but remember that you must eventually show why it should also interest others.

• Find what interests other researchers. Look online for recurring issues and debates in the archives of professional discussion lists relevant to your interests. Search online and in journals like the *Chronicle of Higher Education* for conference announcements, conference programs, calls for papers, anything that reflects what others find interesting.

• Skim the latest issues of journals on your library's new arrivals shelf, not just for articles, but also for conference announcements, calls for papers, and reviews. Skim the most recent articles in your library's online database.

• Investigate the resources that your library is particularly rich in. If, for example, it (or one nearby) holds a collection of rare papers on an interesting topic, you have not only found a topic but a way into it. Before you settle on a topic, on the other hand, be sure your library has at least some relevant sources. If not, you may have to start over.

3.2 FROM A BROAD TOPIC TO A FOCUSED ONE

At this point, your biggest risk is settling on a topic so broad that it could be a subheading in a library catalog: *spaceflight; Shakespeare's problem plays; natural law.* A topic is probably too broad if you can state it in four or five words:

Free will in Tolstoy

The history of commercial aviation

A topic so broad can intimidate you with the task of finding, much less reading, even a fraction of the sources available. So narrow it:

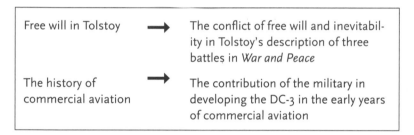

| Free will in Tolstoy | ⟶ | The conflict of free will and inevitability in Tolstoy's description of three battles in *War and Peace* |
| The history of commercial aviation | ⟶ | The contribution of the military in developing the DC-3 in the early years of commercial aviation |

We narrowed those topics by adding words and phrases, but of a special kind: *conflict, description, contribution,* and *developing.* Those nouns are derived from verbs expressing actions or relationships: *to conflict, to describe, to contribute,* and *to develop.* Lacking such "action" words, your topic is a static thing.

Note what happens when we restate static topics as full sentences. Topics (1) and (2) change almost not at all:

(1) Free will in Tolstoy$_{topic}$ → There is free will in Tolstoy's novels.$_{claim}$

(2) The history of commercial aviation$_{topic}$ → Commercial aviation has a history.$_{claim}$

But when (3) and (4) are revised into full sentences, they are closer to claims that a reader might find interesting.

(3) The *conflict* of free will and inevitability in Tolstoy's *description* of three battles in *War and Peace*$_{topic}$ → In *War and Peace*, Tolstoy *describes* three battles in which free will and inevitability *conflict*.$_{claim}$

(4) The *contribution* of the military in *developing* the DC-3 in the early years of commercial aviation$_{topic}$ → In the early years of commercial aviation, the military *contributed* to the way the DC-3 *developed*.$_{claim}$

Such claims may at first seem thin, but you'll make them richer as you work through your project.

~~Caution: Don't narrow your topic so much that you can't find data on it.~~ Too many data are available on *the history of commercial aviation* but too few (at least for beginning researchers) on *the decision to lengthen the wingtips on the DC-3 prototype for military use as a cargo carrier.*

3.3 FROM A FOCUSED TOPIC TO QUESTIONS

Once they have a focused topic, many new researchers make a beginner's mistake: they immediately start plowing through all the sources they can find on a topic, taking notes on everything they read. With a promising topic such as *the political origins of legends about the Battle of the Alamo,* they mound up endless facts connected with the battle: what led up to it, histories of the Texas Revolution, the floor plan of the mission, even biographies of generals Santa Anna and Sam Houston. They accumulate notes, summaries, descriptions of differences and similarities, ways in which the stories conflict with one another and with what historians think really happened, and so on. Then they dump it all into a report that concludes, *Thus we see many differences and similarities between . . .*

Many high school teachers would reward such a report with a good grade, because it shows that the writer can focus on a topic, find data on it, and assemble those data into a report, no small achievement—for a first project. But in *any* college course, such a report falls short if it is seen as just a pastiche of vaguely related facts. ~~If a writer asks no specific *question* worth asking, he can offer no specific *answer* worth supporting.~~ And without an answer to support, he cannot select from all the data he *could* find on a topic just those relevant to his answer. To be sure, those fascinated by Elvis Presley movie posters or early Danish anthropological films will read *anything* new about them, no matter how trivial. Serious researchers, however, do not report data for their own sake, but to support the answer to a question that they (and they hope their readers) think is worth asking.

So the best way to begin working on your specific topic is not to find all the data you can on your general topic, but to formulate questions that point you to just those data that you need to answer them.

You can start with the standard journalistic questions: *who, what, when,* and *where,* but focus on *how* and *why.* To engage your best critical thinking, systematically ask questions about your topic's history, composition, and categories. Then ask any other question you can think of or find in your sources. Record all the questions, but don't stop to answer them even when one or two grab your attention. (And don't worry about keeping these categories straight; their only purpose is to stimulate questions and organize your answers.) Let's take up the example of masks mentioned earlier.

3.3.1 Ask about the History of Your Topic

- How does it fit into a **larger developmental context**? Why did your topic come into being? *What came before masks? How were masks invented? Why? What might come after masks?*

- What is its own **internal history**? How and why has the topic itself changed through time? *How have Native American masks changed? Why? How have Halloween masks changed? How has the role of masks in society changed? How has the booming market for kachina masks influenced traditional design? Why have masks helped make Halloween the biggest American holiday after Christmas?*

3.3.2 Ask about Its Structure and Composition

- How does your topic fit into the context of a larger structure or function as part of a larger system? *How do masks reflect the values of different societies and cultures? What roles do masks play in Hopi dances? In scary movies? In masquerade parties? How are masks used other than for disguise?*

- How do its parts fit together as a system? *What parts of a mask are most significant in Hopi ceremonies? Why? Why do some masks cover only the eyes? Why do few masks cover just the bottom half of the face? How do their colors play a role in their function?*

3.3.3 Ask How Your Topic Is Categorized

- How can your topic be grouped into kinds? *What are the different kinds of masks? Of Halloween masks? Of African masks? How are they categorized by appearance? By use? By geography or society? What are the different qualities of masks?*

- How does your topic compare to and contrast with others like it? *How do Native American ceremonial masks differ from those in Japan? How do Halloween masks compare with Mardi Gras masks?*

3.3.4 Turn Positive Questions into Negative Ones

- Why have masks not become a part of other holidays, like President's Day or Memorial Day? How do Native American masks not differ from those in Africa? *What parts of masks are typically not significant in religious ceremonies?*

3.3.5 Ask *What If?* and Other Speculative Questions

- How would things be different if your topic never existed, disappeared, or were put into a new context? *What if no one ever wore masks except for safety? What if everyone wore masks in public? What if it were customary to wear masks on blind dates? In marriage ceremonies? At funerals? Why are masks common in African religions but not in Western ones? Why don't hunters in camouflage wear masks? How are masks and cosmetic surgery alike?*

3.3.6 Ask Questions Suggested by Your Sources

You won't be able to do this until you've done some reading on your topic. Ask questions that **build on agreement**:

- If a source makes a claim you think is persuasive, ask questions that might extend its reach. *Elias shows that masked balls became popular in eighteenth-century London in response to anxieties about social mobility. Did the same anxieties cause similar developments in Venice?*

- Ask questions that might support the same claim with new evidence. *Elias supports his claim about masked balls with published sources. Is it also supported by letters and diaries?*

- Ask questions analogous to those that sources have asked about similar topics. *Smith analyzes costumes from an economic point of view. What would an economic analysis of masks turn up?*

Now ask questions that reflect **disagreement**:

- *Martinez claims that carnival masks uniquely allow wearers to escape social norms. But could there be a larger pattern of all masks creating a sense of alternative forms of social or spiritual life?*

(We discuss in more detail how to use disagreements with sources in 6.4.)

If you are an experienced researcher, look for questions that other researchers ask but don't answer. Many journal articles end with a paragraph or two about open questions, ideas for more research, and so on (see p. 63 for an example). You might not be able to do all the research they suggest, but you might carve out a piece of it. You can also look for Internet discussions on your topic, then "lurk," just reading the exchanges to understand the kinds of questions those on the list debate. Record questions that spark your interest. You can post questions on the list if they are specific and narrowly focused. But first see whether the list welcomes questions from students. (If you can't find a list using a search engine, ask a teacher or visit the Web site of professional organizations in your field.)

3.3.7 Evaluate Your Questions

When you run out of questions, evaluate them, because not all questions are equally good. Look for questions whose answers might make you (and, ideally, your readers) think about your topic in a new way. Avoid questions like these:

- Their answers are settled fact that you could just look up. *Do the Inuit use masks in their wedding ceremonies?* Questions that ask *how* and *why* invite deeper thinking than *who, what, when,* or *where,* and deeper thinking leads to more interesting answers.

- Their answers would be merely speculative. *Would church services be as well attended if the congregation all wore masks?* If you can't imagine finding hard data that might settle the question, it's a question you can't settle.

- Their answers are dead ends. *How many black cats slept in the Alamo the night before the battle?* It is hard to see how an answer would help us think about any larger issue worth understanding better, so it's a question that's probably not worth asking.

You might, however, be wrong about that. Some questions that seemed trivial, even silly, have answers more significant than expected. One researcher wondered why a coffee spill dries up in the form of a ring and discovered things about the properties of fluids that others in his field thought important—and that paint manufacturers found valuable. So who knows where a question about cats in the Alamo might take you? You can't know until you get there.

Once you have a few promising questions, try to combine them into larger ones. For example, many questions about the Alamo story ask about the interests of the storytellers and their effects on their stories: *How have politicians used the story? How have the storytellers' motives changed? Whose purposes does each story serve?* These can be combined into a single more significant question:

> How and why have users of the Alamo story given the event a mythic quality?

With only a topic to guide your research, you can find endless data and will never know when you have enough (much less what to do with it). To go beyond fact-grubbing, find a question that will narrow your search to just those data you need to answer it.

3.4 FROM A QUESTION TO ITS SIGNIFICANCE

Even if you are an experienced researcher, you might not be able to take the next step until you are well into your project, and if you are a beginner, you may find it deeply frustrating. Even so, once you have a question that holds your interest, you must pose a tougher one *about* it: *So what? Beyond your own interest in its answer, why would others think it a question worth asking?* You might not be able to answer that *So what?* question early on, but it's one you have to start thinking about, because it forces you to look beyond your own interests to consider how your work might strike others.

Think of it like this: What will be lost if you *don't* answer your question? How will *not* answering it keep us from understanding something else better than we do? Start by asking *So what?* at first of yourself:

> So what if I don't know or understand how butterflies know where to go in the winter, or how fifteenth-century musicians tuned their instruments, or why the Alamo story has become a myth? So what if I can't answer my question? What do we lose?

Your answer might be *Nothing. I just want to know.* Good enough to start, but not to finish, because eventually your readers will ask as well, and they will want an answer beyond *Just curious.* Answering *So what?* vexes all researchers, beginners and experienced alike, because when you have only a question, it's hard to predict whether others will think its answer is significant. But you must work toward that answer throughout your project. You can do that in three steps.

3.4.1 Step 1: Name Your Topic
If you are beginning a project with only a topic and maybe the glimmerings of a good question or two, start by naming your project:

> I am trying to learn about (working on, studying) _____.

Fill in the blank with your topic, using some of those nouns derived from verbs:

> I am studying the *causes* of the *disappearance* of large North American mammals . . .

> I am working on Lincoln's *beliefs* about *predestination* and their *influence* on his *reasoning* . . .

3.4.2 Step 2: Add an Indirect Question
Add an indirect question that indicates what you do not know or understand about your topic:

> 1. I am studying/working on _____
>   2. **because I want to find out who/what/when/where/whether/ why/how** _____.

> 1. I am studying the causes of the disappearance of large North American mammals
>   2. **because I want to find out whether they were hunted to extinction . . .**

> 1. I am working on Lincoln's beliefs about predestination and its influence on his reasoning
>   2. **because I want to find out how his belief in destiny influenced his understanding of the causes of the Civil War . . .**

When you add that *because I want to find out how/why/whether* clause, you state why *you* are pursuing your topic: to answer a question important to you.

If you are a new researcher and get this far, congratulate yourself, because you have moved beyond the aimless collection of data. But now, if you can, take one step more. It's one that advanced researchers know they must take, because they know their work will be judged not by its significance to them but by its significance to others in their field. They must have an answer to *So what?*

3.4.3 Step 3: Answer *So What?* by Motivating Your Question

This step tells you whether your question might interest not just you but others. To do that, add a second indirect question that explains why you asked your first question. Introduce this second implied question with *in order to help my reader understand how, why, or whether*:

1. I am studying the causes of the disappearance of large North American mammals
   2. because I want to find out whether the earliest peoples hunted them to extinction
      3. **in order to help my reader understand whether native peoples lived in harmony with nature or helped destroy it.**

1. I am working on Lincoln's beliefs about predestination and their influence on his reasoning
   2. because I want to find out how his belief in destiny and God's will influenced his understanding of the causes of the Civil War,
      3. **in order to help my reader understand how his religious beliefs may have influenced his military decisions.**

It is the indirect question in step 3 that you hope will seize your readers' interest. If it touches on issues important to your field, even indirectly, then your readers should care about its answer.

Some advanced researchers begin with questions that others in their field already care about: *Why did the giant sloth and woolly mammoth disappear from North America?* Or: *Is risk taking genetically based?* But many researchers, including at times the three of us, find that they can't flesh out the last step in that three-part sentence until they finish a first draft. So you make no mistake *begin-*

ning your research without a good answer to that third question—
Why does this matter?—but you face a problem when you *finish* it
without having thought through those three steps at all. And if
you are doing advanced research, you *must* take that step, because
answering that last question is your ticket into the conversation of
your community of researchers.

Regularly test your progress by asking a roommate, relative, or
friend to force you to flesh out those three steps. Even if you can't
take them all confidently, you'll know where you are and where
you still have to go. To summarize: Your aim is to explain

1. what you are writing about—*I am working on the topic of . . .*
    2. what you don't know about it—*because I want to find out . . .*
        3. why you want your reader to know and care about it—*in
           order to help my reader understand better . . .*

In the following chapters, we return to those three steps and
their implied questions, because they are crucial not just for finding questions, but for framing the research problem that you want
your readers to value.

If you are a beginner, start with our suggestions about skimming bibliographical guides (3.1). If you still draw a blank, try these steps.

FOR GENERAL TOPICS

1. What special interest do you have—sailing, chess, finches, old comic books? The less common, the better. Investigate something about it you don't know: its origins, its technology, how it is practiced in another culture, and so on.

2. Where would you like to travel? Surf the Internet, finding out all you can about your destination. What particular aspect surprises you or makes you want to know more?

3. Wander through a museum with exhibitions that appeal to you—artworks, dinosaurs, old cars. If you can't browse in person, browse a "virtual museum" on the Internet. Stop when something catches your interest. What more do you want to know about it?

4. Wander through a shopping mall or store, asking yourself, *How do they make that?* Or, *I wonder who thought up that product?*

5. Leaf through a Sunday newspaper, especially its features sections. Skim reviews of books or movies, in newspapers or on the Internet.

6. Browse a large magazine rack. Look for trade magazines or those that cater to specialized interests. Investigate whatever catches your interest.

7. If you can use an Internet news reader, look through the list of "alt" newsgroups for one that interests you. Read the posts, looking for something that surprises you or that you disagree with.

8. Tune into talk radio or interview programs on TV until you hear a claim you disagree with. Or find something to disagree with on the Web sites connected with well-known talk shows. See whether you can make a case to refute it.

9. Use an Internet search engine to find Web sites about something people collect. (Narrow the search to exclude dot-com sites.) You'll get hundreds of hits, but look only at the ones that surprise you.

10. Is there a common belief that you suspect is simplistic or just wrong? A common practice that you find pointless or irritating? Do research to make a case against it.

11. What courses will you take in the future? What research would help you prepare for them?

FOR TOPICS FOCUSED ON A PARTICULAR FIELD
If you have experience in your field, review 3.1.2–3.

1. Browse through a textbook of a course that is one level beyond yours or a course that you know you will have to take. Look especially hard at the study questions.

2. Attend a lecture for an advanced class in your field, and listen for something you disagree with, don't understand, or want to know more about.

3. Ask your instructor about the most contested issues in your field.

4. Find an Internet discussion list in your field. Browse its archives, looking for matters of controversy or uncertainty.

5. Surf the Web sites of departments at major universities, including class sites. Also check sites of museums, national associations, and government agencies, if they seem relevant.

CHAPTER FOUR

From Questions to a Problem

In this chapter we explain how to turn a question into a problem that readers think is worth solving. If you are an advanced researcher, you know how essential this step is. But if you are new to research, understanding its importance may prove challenging. If you feel lost, skip to chapter 5, but we hope you'll stay with us, because what you learn here will be essential to all your future projects.

In the last chapter, we suggested that you can identify the significance of your research question by fleshing out this three-step formula:

1. **Topic:** I am studying _____
   2. **Question:** because I want to find out what/why/how _____,
   3. **Significance:** in order to help my reader understand

   _____.

These steps describe not only the development of your project, but your own as a researcher.

- When you move from step 1 to 2, you are no longer a mere data collector but a researcher interested in understanding something better.

- When you then move from step 2 to 3, you focus on why that understanding is *significant*.

That significance might at first be just for yourself, but you join a community of researchers when you can state that significance *from your readers' point of view.* In so doing, you create a stronger relationship with readers because you promise something in return for their interest in your report—a deeper understanding of something that matters to *them*. At that point, you have posed a *problem* that they recognize needs a solution.

4.1 DISTINGUISHING PRACTICAL AND RESEARCH PROBLEMS

Finding the significance of a problem is hard, even for experienced researchers. Too many researchers at all levels write as if their only task is to answer a question that interests them alone. They fail to understand that their answer must solve a problem that others in their community think needs a solution. To understand how to find that question and its significance, though, you first have to know what research problems look like.

4.1.1 Practical Problems: What Should We Do?

Everyday research usually begins not with dreaming up a topic to think about but with a practical problem that, if you ignore it, means trouble. When its solution is not obvious, you have to find out how to solve it. To do that, you must pose and solve a problem of another kind, a *research* problem defined by what you do not *know* or *understand* about your practical problem.

It's a familiar task that typically looks like this:

PRACTICAL PROBLEM: My brakes are screeching.

RESEARCH PROBLEM: Can I find a brake shop in the yellow pages to fix them?

RESEARCH SOLUTION: Here it is. The Car Shoppe, 1401 East 55th Street.

PRACTICAL SOLUTION: Drive over to get them fixed.

Problems like that are in essence no different from more complicated ones.

- The National Rifle Association is lobbying me to oppose gun control. *How many votes do I lose if I refuse?* Do a survey. *Most of my constituents support gun control.* I can reject the request.

- Costs are up at the Omaha plant. *What changed?* Send Sally to find out. *Increase in turnover.* If we improve training and morale, our workers will stick with us.

To solve either of those *practical* problems, someone first had to solve a research problem that improved their *understanding*. Then on the basis of that better understanding, someone had to decide what to *do* to solve the practical problem, then report their research so that their solution could be shared and studied.

Graphically, the relationship between practical and research problems looks like this:

4.1.2 Academic Research Problems: What Should We Think?

Solving a practical problem usually requires that we first solve a research problem, but it's crucial to distinguish *practical* research problems from *conceptual* ones:

- A *practical* problem is caused by some condition in the world (from spam to losing money in Omaha to terrorism) that makes us unhappy because it costs us time, respect, security, pain, even our lives. We solve a practical problem by *doing* something (or by encouraging others to do something) that eliminates the cause of the problem or at least ameliorates its costs.

- In academic research, a *conceptual* problem arises when we simply do not *understand* something about the world as well as we would like. We solve a conceptual problem not by doing something to change the world but by answering a question that helps us understand it better.

The term *problem* thus has a special meaning in the world of research, one that sometimes confuses beginners. In our everyday world, a problem is something we try to avoid. But in academic research, a problem is something we seek out, even invent if we have to. Indeed, a researcher without a good conceptual problem to work on faces a bad practical problem, because without a research problem, a researcher is out of work.

There is a second reason inexperienced researchers sometimes struggle with this notion of a research problem. Experienced researchers often talk about their work in shorthand. When asked what they are working on, they often answer with what sounds like one of those general topics we warned you about: *adult measles, mating calls of Wyoming elk, zeppelins in the 1930s*. As a result, some beginners think that having a topic to read about is the same as having a problem to solve.

When they do, they create a big practical problem for themselves, because without a research question to answer, with only a topic to guide their work, they gather data aimlessly and endlessly, with no way of knowing when they have enough. Then they struggle to decide what to include in their report and what not, usually throwing in everything, just to be on the safe side. So it's not surprising they feel frustrated when a reader says of their report, *I don't see the point here; this is just a data dump*.

To avoid that judgment, you need a research problem that focuses you on finding just those data that will help you solve it. It might take awhile to figure out what that problem is, but from the outset, you have to think about it. That begins with understanding how conceptual problems work.

4.2 UNDERSTANDING THE COMMON STRUCTURE OF PROBLEMS

Practical problems and conceptual problems have the same two-part structure:

- a situation or *condition*, and

- undesirable *consequences* caused by that condition, *costs* that you (or, better, your readers) don't want to pay

What distinguishes them is the nature of those conditions and costs.

4.2.1 The Nature of Practical Problems

A flat tire is a typical practical problem, because it is (1) a condition in the world (the flat) that imposes (2) a tangible cost that you don't want to pay, like missing a dinner date. But suppose you were bullied into the date and would rather be anywhere else. In that case, the benefit of the flat is more than its cost, so the flat is not a problem but a solution to the bigger problem of an evening spent with someone you don't like. Low cost, big benefit, no problem.

To be part of a practical, tangible problem, a condition can be anything, so long as it imposes intolerable costs. Suppose you win a million dollars in the lottery but owe a loan shark two million and your name gets in the paper. He finds you, takes your million, and breaks your leg. Winning the lottery turns out to be a Big Problem.

To state a practical problem so that others understand it clearly, you must describe both its parts.

1. Its condition:

   I missed the bus.

   The hole in the ozone layer is growing.

2. The **costs** of that condition that make you (or your reader) unhappy:

   I'll be late for work and lose my job.

   Many will die from skin cancer.

But a caution: It's not you who judges the significance of your problem by the cost *you* pay, but your readers who judge it by the cost *they* pay if you don't solve it. So what *you* think is a problem, they might not. To make your problem their problem, you must frame it from *their* point of view, so that they see its costs to *them*. To do that, imagine that when you pose the condition part of your problem, your reader responds, *So what?*

The hole in the ozone layer is growing.
So what?

You answer with the cost of the problem:

A bigger hole exposes us to more ultraviolet light.

Suppose he again asks, *So what?*, and you respond with the cost of more ultraviolet light:

Too much ultraviolet light can cause skin cancer.

If, however improbably, he again asks, *So what?*, you have failed to convince him that *he* has a problem. We acknowledge a problem only when we stop asking *So what?* and say instead, *What do we do about it?*

Practical problems like cancer are easy to grasp because when people have it, we don't ask *So what?* In academic research, however, your problems will usually be conceptual ones, which are harder to grasp because both their conditions and costs are not palpable but abstract.

4.2.2 The Nature of Conceptual Problems

Practical and conceptual problems have the same two-part structure, but they have different kinds of conditions and costs.

- The condition of a practical problem can be *any* state of affairs whose cost makes you (or better, your reader) unhappy.

- The condition of a conceptual problem, however, is *always* some version of *not knowing* or *not understanding* something.

You can identify the condition of a conceptual problem by completing that three-step sentence (3.4): The first step is *I am studying/working on the topic of* _____. In the second step, the indirect question states the condition of a conceptual problem, what you do not know or understand:

I am studying stories of the Alamo, because I want to understand **why voters responded to them in ways that served the interests of Texas politicians.**

That's why we emphasize the value of questions: they force you to state what you don't know or understand but want to.

The two kinds of problems also have two different kinds of costs.

- The **cost** of a practical problem is always some degree of unhappiness.

A conceptual problem does not have such a tangible cost. In fact, we'll call it not a cost but a *consequence*.

- The **consequence** of a conceptual problem is a *second* thing that we don't know or understand because we don't understand the first one, *and that is more significant, more consequential than the first.*

You express that bigger lack of understanding in the indirect question in step 3 of that formula:

> I am studying stories of the Alamo, because I want to understand why voters responded to them in ways that served the interests of local Texas politicians, in order to help readers understand the bigger and more important question **of how regional self-images influence national politics.**

All this may sound confusing, but it's simpler than it seems. The condition and the consequence of a conceptual problem are both questions: Q1 and Q2. But there are two differences: (1) the answer to the first question helps you answer the second, and (2) the answer to the second question is more important than the answer to the first.

Q1 *helps you answer* ▸ **Q2**

Here it is again: The first part of a research problem is something you don't know but want to. You can phrase that gap in knowledge or understanding as a direct question: *How have romantic movies changed in the last fifty years?* Or as an indirect question, as in: *I want to find out how romantic movies have changed in the last fifty years.*

Now imagine someone asking, *So what if you can't answer that question?* You answer by stating *something else more important* that you can't know until you answer the first question. For example:

If we can't answer the question of how romantic movies have changed in the last fifty years,*condition/first question* **then we can't answer a more important question: How have our cultural depictions of romantic love changed?***consequence/larger, more important second question*

If you think that it's important to answer that second question, you've stated a consequence that makes your problem worth pursuing, and if your readers agree, you're in business.

But what if you imagine a reader again asking, *So what if I don't know whether we depict romantic love differently than we did?* You have to pose a yet larger question that you hope your readers will think is significant:

If we can't answer the question of how our depictions of romantic love have changed,*second question* **then we can't answer an even more important one: How does our culture shape the expectations of young men and women about marriage and families?***consequence/larger, more important question*

If you imagine that reader again asking, *So what?*, you might think, *Wrong audience.* But if that's the audience you're stuck with, you just have to try again: *Well, if we don't answer that question, we can't . . .*

Those outside an academic field often think that its specialists ask ridiculously trivial questions: *How did hopscotch originate?* But they fail to realize that researchers want to answer a question like that so that they can answer a *second*, more important one. For those who care about the way folk games influence the social development of children, the conceptual consequences of not knowing justifies the research. *If we can discover how children's folk games originate, we can better understand how games socialize children, and before you ask, once we know that, we can better understand . . .*

4.2.3 Distinguishing "Pure" and "Applied" Research

We call research *pure* when the solution to a problem does not bear on any practical situation in the world, but only improves the understanding of a community of researchers. When the solution to a research problem does have practical consequences, we call the research *applied*. You can tell whether research is pure or applied by looking at the last of the three steps defining your project. Does it refer to knowing or doing?

1. **Topic:** I am studying the electromagnetic radiation in a section of the universe
   2. **Question:** because I want to find out how many stars are in the sky,
      3. **Significance:** in order to help readers *understand* whether the universe will expand forever or collapse into a new big bang.

That is pure research, because step 3 refers only to understanding.

In an applied research problem, the second step refers to knowing, but that third step refers to *doing*:

1. **Topic:** I am studying how readings from the Hubble telescope differ from readings for the same stars measured by earthbound telescopes
   2. **Question:** because I want to find out how much the atmosphere distorts measurements of electromagnetic radiation,
      3. **Practical Significance:** so that astronomers can use data from earthbound telescopes *to measure* more accurately the density of electromagnetic radiation.

That is an applied problem because only when astronomers *know* how to account for atmospheric distortion can they *do* what they want to—measure light more accurately.

4.2.4 Connecting a Research Problem to Practical Consequences

Some inexperienced researchers are uneasy with pure research because the consequence of a conceptual problem—merely not knowing something—is so abstract. Since they are not yet part of a community that cares deeply about understanding its part of the world, they feel that their findings aren't good for much. So they try to cobble a practical cost onto a conceptual question to make it seem more significant:

1. **Topic:** I am studying differences among nineteenth-century versions of the Alamo story
2. **Research Question:** because I want to find out how politicians used stories of such events to shape public opinion,
   3. **Potential Practical Significance:** in order to protect ourselves from unscrupulous politicians.

Most readers would think that the link between steps 2 and 3 is a bit of a stretch.

To formulate a useful applied research problem, you have to show that the answer to the indirect question in step 2 *plausibly* helps answer the indirect question in step 3. Ask this question:

(a) If my readers want to achieve the goal of _____ [state your objective from step 3],
(b) would they think that they could do it if they found out _____? [state your question from step 2]

Try that test on this applied astronomy problem:

(a) If my readers want to use data from earthbound telescopes to measure more accurately the density of electromagnetic radiation,
(b) would they think that they could if they knew how much the atmosphere distorts measurements?

The answer would seem to be *Yes*.

Now try the test on the Alamo problem:

(a) If my readers want to protect themselves from unscrupulous politicians,
(b) would they think they could if they knew how nineteenth-century politicians used stories about the Alamo to shape public opinion?

We may see a connection, but it's a stretch.

If you think that the solution to your conceptual problem *might* apply to a practical one, formulate your problem as the pure research problem it is, then *add* your application as a *fourth* step:

1. **Topic:** I am studying how nineteenth-century versions of the Alamo story differ

    2. **Conceptual Question:** because I want to find out how politicians used stories of great events to shape public opinion,

        3. **Conceptual Significance:** in order to help readers understand how politicians use popular culture to advance their political goals,

            4. **Potential Practical Application:** so that readers *might* better protect themselves from unscrupulous politicians.

When you state your problem in your introduction, however, formulate it as a purely conceptual research problem whose significance is in its conceptual consequences. Then wait until your conclusion to suggest its practical application. (For more on this, see chapter 16.)

Most research projects in the humanities and many in the natural and social sciences have no direct application to daily life. But as the term *pure* suggests, many researchers value such research more than they do applied. They believe that the pursuit of knowledge "for its own sake" reflects humanity's highest calling—to know more, not for the sake of money or power, but for the transcendental good of greater understanding and a richer life of the mind. As you may have guessed, the three of us are deeply committed to pure research, but also to applied—so long as the research is done well and is not corrupted by malign motives. For example, there is a threat to both pure and applied research in the biological sciences, where profits not only determine the choice of some research problems, but color how some researchers reach their solutions: *Tell us what to look for, and we'll provide it!* That raises an ethical question that we touch on in our afterword on ethics.

ANTICIPATING A TYPICAL BEGINNER'S MISTAKE

No one can solve the world's great problems in a five- or even a fifty-page paper. But you might help us better understand a *small part* of one, and that can move us closer to a practical solution. So if you care deeply about a practical problem, such as destructive forest fires, carve out of it a conceptual question that is small enough to answer but whose answer might ultimately contribute to a practical solution: *How important are fires to the ecological health of a forest? How do local fire codes affect the spread of forest fires?* The right answer to a small question moves us closer to solving a big problem than a big answer that doesn't work.

4.3 FINDING A GOOD RESEARCH PROBLEM

What distinguishes great researchers from the rest of us is the brilliance, knack, or just dumb luck of stumbling over a problem whose solution makes all of us see the world in a new way. It's easy to recognize a good problem when we bump into it, or it bumps into us. But researchers often begin a project without being clear about what their real problem is. Sometimes they hope just to define a puzzle more clearly. Indeed, those who find a new problem or clarify an old one often make a bigger contribution to their field than those who solve a problem already defined. Some researchers have even won fame for *disproving* a plausible hypothesis that they had set out to prove.

So don't be discouraged if you can't formulate your problem fully at the outset of your project. Few of us can. But thinking about it early will save you hours of work along the way (and perhaps panic toward the end). It also gets you into a frame of mind crucial to advanced work. Here are some ways you can aim for a problem from the start and along the way.

4.3.1 Ask for Help

Do what experienced researchers do: talk to teachers, classmates, relatives, friends, neighbors—anyone who might be interested. Why would anyone want an answer to your question? What would they do with it? What new questions might an answer raise?

If you are free to work on any problem, look for a small one that is part of a bigger one. Though you won't solve the big one, your small piece of it will inherit some of its larger significance. (You will also educate yourself about the problems of your field, no small benefit.) Ask your teacher what she is working on and whether you can work on part of it. But a warning: Don't let her suggestions define the limits of your research. Nothing discourages a teacher more than a student who does *exactly* what is suggested *and no more.* Teachers want you to use their suggestions to *start* your thinking, not *end* it. Nothing makes a teacher happier than when you use her suggestions to find something she never expected.

4.3.2 Look for Problems as You Read

You can also find a research problem in your sources. Where in them do you see contradictions, inconsistencies, incomplete explanations? Tentatively assume that other readers would or should feel the same. Many research projects begin with an imaginary conversation while reading another's report: *Wait a minute, he's ignoring . . .* But before you set out to correct a gap or misunderstanding, be sure it's real, not your own misreading. Countless research papers have refuted a point that no one ever made. Before you correct a source, reread it carefully. (In 6.4 we list several common "moves" that writers make to find a problem in a source, variations on *Source thinks X, but I think Y.*)

Once you think you've found a real puzzle or error, do more than just point to it. If a source says X and you think Y, you may have a research problem, but only if you can show that those who misunderstand X misunderstand some larger issue, as well.

Finally, read the last few pages of your sources closely. That's where many researchers suggest more questions that need answers. The author of the following paragraph had just finished explaining how the life of nineteenth-century Russian peasants influenced their performance as soldiers:

> And just as the soldier's peacetime experience influenced his battlefield performance, so must the experience of the officer corps have influenced theirs. Indeed, a few commentators after

the Russo-Japanese War blamed the Russian defeat on habits acquired by officers in the course of their economic chores. In any event, to appreciate the service habits of Tsarist officers in peace and war, *we need a structural—if you will, an anthropological—analysis of the officer corps like that offered here for enlisted personnel.* [our emphasis]

That last sentence offers a new problem waiting for you to tackle.

4.3.3 Look at Your Own Conclusion

Critical reading can also help you discover a good research problem in your own drafts. We usually do our best thinking in the last few pages we write. It is often only then that we begin to formulate a final claim that we did not anticipate when we started. If in an early draft you arrive at an unanticipated claim, ask yourself what question it might answer. Paradoxical as it might seem, you may have answered a question that you have not yet asked, and thereby solved a problem that you have not yet posed. Your task is to figure out what it might be.

4.4 LEARNING TO WORK WITH PROBLEMS

Experienced researchers dream of finding new problems to solve. A still bigger dream is to solve a problem that no one even knew they had. But that new problem isn't worth much until others think (or can be persuaded) that they want to see it solved. So the first question an experienced researcher should ask about a problem is not *Can I solve it?* but *Will readers think it should be?*

No one expects that you can do that the first time out. But your teachers do want you to practice the mental habits that prepare you for that moment. That means doing more than just accumulating and reporting facts. They want you to formulate a question that *you* think is worth answering, so that down the road, you'll know how to find a problem that *others* think is worth solving. Until you can do that, you risk the worst response a researcher can get: not *I don't agree,* but *I don't care.*

By now, all this talk about airy academic research may seem

disconnected from a world in which so many people labor so hard at getting ahead or keeping others down. But in business and government, in law and medicine, in politics and international diplomacy, no skill is valued more highly than the ability to recognize a problem, then to articulate it in a way that convinces others both to care about it and to believe it can be solved, especially by you. If you can do that in a class on medieval Tibetan rugs, you can do it in an office on Main Street, Wall Street, or on Queen's Road in Hong Kong.

Manage the Unavoidable Problem of Inexperience

We all feel anxious when we start work in a field whose basic rules we don't entirely understand, much less those tacit rules that experienced researchers follow but don't explain to others because they're taken for granted. And to our surprise, we feel a newcomer's anxiety again when we begin a new kind of project on a new topic. We three authors have felt those anxieties, not just starting out, but long after our hair had grayed. You can't avoid feeling overwhelmed and anxious at times, but there are ways to manage it:

- Know that uncertainty and anxiety are natural and inevitable. Those feelings don't signal incompetence, only inexperience.

- Get control over your topic by writing about it along the way. Don't just retype or photocopy sources: write summaries, critiques, questions, responses to your sources. Keep a journal in which you reflect on your progress. The more you write, no matter how sketchily, the more confidently you will face that intimidating first draft.

- Break the task into manageable steps and know that they are mutually supportive. Once you formulate a good question, you'll draft and revise more effectively. The more you anticipate how you will write and revise a first draft, the more effectively you will produce it.

- Count on your teachers to understand your struggles. They want you to succeed, and you can expect their help. (If they don't help, look for others who will.)

- Set realistic goals. You do something significant when you wind up your project feeling it has changed just what *you* think and that your readers think you did it well, even if they don't agree with your claims.

- Most important, recognize the struggle for what it is—a learning experience. To overcome the problems that all beginners face, do what successful researchers do, especially when discouraged: review your plan and what you've written, then press on, confident that it will turn out OK. Perhaps only "OK—considering," but probably a lot better than that.

CHAPTER FIVE

From Problems to Sources

If you are a new researcher and expect to find most of your sources in your library or on the Internet, this chapter will help you develop a plan for your research. If you are more experienced, you might skip to the next chapter; if you are very experienced, skip to part III.

If you have not yet formulated a research question, you may have to spend time reading generally on your topic to find one. But if you have a question and at least one promising answer (the philosopher C. S. Peirce called it a *hypothesis on probation*), you can start looking for data to test it.

To do that efficiently, you need a plan. If you plunge into any and all sources on your topic, you risk losing yourself in an endless trail of books and articles. To be sure, aimless browsing can be fun, even productive. Many important discoveries have begun in a chance encounter with an unexpected idea. The three of us indulge in it a lot. But if you have a deadline, you need more than luck to find good sources in time: you have to search systematically for those sources whose data will let you test your hypothesis, by supporting it or, more usefully, by challenging you to improve or abandon it.

In this chapter we discuss how to find sources and then to winnow them to a manageable number. In the next we'll discuss how to engage sources that look promising.

5.1 KNOWING HOW TO USE THREE KINDS OF SOURCES

Sources are conventionally categorized into three kinds. Their boundaries are fuzzy, but they're useful in helping you plan your search.

5.1.1 Primary Sources

These provide the "raw data" that you use first to test your working hypothesis and then as evidence to support your claim. In history, for example, primary sources include documents from the period or person you are studying, objects, maps, even clothing; in literature or philosophy, your main primary source is usually the text you are studying, and your data are the words on the page. In such fields you can rarely write a research paper without using primary sources.

5.1.2 Secondary Sources

Secondary sources are research reports that use primary data to solve research problems, written for scholarly and professional audiences. Researchers read them to keep up with their field and use what they read to frame problems of their own by disputing other researchers' conclusions or questioning their methods. You can use their data to support your argument, but only if you cannot find those data in a primary source. A secondary source becomes a primary source when you study its argument as part of a debate in a field, such as whether patriotic historians deliberately distorted Alamo stories.

5.1.3 Tertiary Sources

These are books and articles that synthesize and report on secondary sources for general readers, such as textbooks, articles in encyclopedias and mass-circulation publications like *Psychology Today*, and what standard search engines turn up first on the Web. In the early stages of research, you can use tertiary sources to get a feel for a topic. But if you use what you find in a tertiary source to support a scholarly argument, most of your readers won't trust your report—or you.

It's not that books written for general readers about brains or black holes are necessarily wrong. Many distinguished researchers write such books. But they sometimes oversimplify the research, and their work usually dates quickly. So if you start your research with a popular book, look at the journals listed in its bibliography, then go to them for more current research. (As with secondary sources, a source like an encyclopedia could be a primary source if you were studying, say, how encyclopedias deal with gender issues.)

5.2 LOCATING SOURCES THROUGH A LIBRARY

Unless you collect your own data from experiments or observation, you'll probably find data in books or articles, occasionally in photos, films, videos, or audio recordings. In that case, your first stop is not Google but your library's Web site.

If you've explored the farthest reaches of the Net, starting with a library may seem old-fashioned, but today's libraries connect you to the best online resources. So when we caution you not to rely on the Internet for your research, we don't mean that you ought not go online. The three of us work online whenever we can. But you must distinguish online resources that are extensions of libraries (and are as reliable) from random Internet sources whose reliability is always in doubt.

If your library's online resources are limited, ask your librarian whether you can access the online resources of one of your state universities. If you can't, consult the online catalog of the Library of Congress (www.loc.gov), where you'll find almost any source you could want. Most state universities allow guest access to their online catalogs (but not their databases).

If your library has few books and articles on your topic, look for a larger library nearby, but don't forget specialized ones, such as the National Rifle Association Library in Fairfax, Virginia, or the Martin Luther King Jr. Library in Atlanta. But even if a small library is all you have, it probably offers more than you think, including research guides and reference works, both general and specialized. If you use online catalogs, bibliographies, and databases thoughtfully, you can do a great deal with a small library and interlibrary loan (loans take time, so start early).

5.2.1 Planning Your Search

The first step is to *plan* your search. Start with an overview of the research on your topic. Look it up in general or specialized encyclopedias, then in reference works that summarize research in specific areas, as well as bibliographies that list research by area (see pp. 283–311). Most fields have such resources, and your library will have many of them, some online.

TALK TO LIBRARIANS. If this is your first shot at serious research, you might begin by talking to a reference librarian. They are usually ready to help when you don't know where to start. Large libraries even have specialists in particular topics. They can show you how to use the catalog and other specialized online resources. If you feel too shy or proud to ask questions in person, e-mail them.

You will save both your time and theirs if you prepare your questions, even rehearse them. You might describe your project using the three-step rubric from chapter 3:

> I am working on educational policy in the 1950s
> > to find out how school boards in the Midwest dealt with desegregation,
> > > because I want to understand regional differences in race relations.
>
> Can you help me find periodical guides that list articles on that topic?

Early on, your questions may be general, but as you narrow your topic, state your problem so that your librarian understands exactly what you need: *I want to find how school boards used court decisions on the "separate but equal" doctrine to resolve questions about how far students could be bussed.*

IF YOU DON'T KNOW, ASK

You can't learn the ropes of research if you don't know where they are, and you won't find where they are if you don't ask. On her first visit to its research library, a new graduate student at the University of Chicago couldn't find the stacks, where all the books that circulate are kept. Too embarrassed to ask, she wandered for two more days through seven floors of reading rooms, finding only reference works. Only on the third day did she get up the nerve to ask a librarian where all the books were. The librarian pointed to a door that led to acres of books. Moral of the story: The only embarrassing question is the one you *failed to* ask but should have.

TALK TO EXPERTS. You can also ask experts in a field to help you focus your topic and suggest sources. Start with your teacher, but don't expect her to have all the answers. (You might hope she doesn't; if she thinks your report will teach her something, she'll read it with greater interest.) You can also look for help from advanced students. Here, too, the quality of the help you get depends on the quality of the questions you ask. So before you ask, rehearse them.

How much help should you get? At one extreme, we know a graduate student who met his adviser every day for breakfast, reporting what he found the day before and asking for guidance for the day ahead. (It's a good thing few students want that much help.) At the other extreme are those who disappear into the bowels of the library and don't emerge until they've completed their project, sometimes years later. (We don't actually *know* anyone who has done that, but we know some who have come close.) Most researchers take the middle way, relying on regular conversations to guide their reading, which stimulate more questions and hunches to try out on others.

CONSULT GENERAL REFERENCE WORKS. If you already know a lot about your topic, you probably also know how to find sources on it. If not, start by looking at the end of an article on your topic in a general reference work such as the *Encyclopaedia Britannica*, where it may list basic sources. If you find nothing under one heading, try another. The 1993 *Books in Print* listed nothing under *gender*, a term that is now standard for researchers in women's studies, but it had many entries under *sex*.

CONSULT SPECIALIZED REFERENCE WORKS. If you are working in a particular field, look up your topic in a specialized encyclopedia or dictionary, such as the *Encyclopedia of Philosophy*, and consult the references cited there. Many libraries offer access to online bibliographical databases, many of which include abstracts that summarize journal articles. In some new or highly specialized fields, you may find bibliographical lists on Web sites maintained by individual scholars, departments, or scholarly associations. These may be less reliable than large databases, but they'll get you started.

You may also find print bibliographies covering your field. If you're lucky, you'll find an annotated bibliography that sums up current books and articles. It's an efficient way to survey what other researchers think is important. Most fields also publish a journal that annually reviews new research, which is even more useful. If you need the newest sources, the *Chronicle of Higher Education* lists new books, and many journals list "books received" (new books that publishers hope the journal will review).

Every major field has at least one guide to all these resources: lists of bibliographies, locations of important primary materials, research methods, and so on. We list many in our "Appendix: Bibliographical Resources," several of which are online.

5.2.2 Searching for Specific Sources

SEARCH YOUR LIBRARY CATALOG. Once you locate a few sources on your topic, you can expand your search in two ways: keyword searches and browsing.

Start a keyword search with the specific terms that you used to narrow your topic—for example, *Alamo, legend, Texas independence*, and so on. Once you find books under those terms, look at the Library of Congress subject headings, either on the back of their title page or on their "details" page in the online catalog. On the back of this book's title page are the terms

1. Research—Methodology. 2. Technical writing.

If you search an online catalog for those terms, you will find all the books on those subjects in that library.

You can also search most catalogs by browsing for books with similar call numbers. Once you identify one book that seems on target, find the browse link on that book's catalog entry. This list will be less focused than a keyword list, but it may also contain unexpected gems. So don't restrict yourself to books nearest your target. Invest the time to browse widely.

The problem with any online search is that it may produce an overwhelming number of titles. The University of Chicago library has more than three hundred books on Napoleon and thousands with the word *environment* in their titles. If your search turns up too many titles, cut it to those published in the last fifteen years; if that's still too many, cut to the last ten.

After you search the Library of Congress or a large university catalog, you may discover that your own library holds only a fraction of what you found, but it can borrow most of what you need. For books too new to be in a library catalog but crucial to your research, find an online bookseller. Those books might turn up on your library's new acquisitions shelf, but you'll probably have to buy them.

On the other hand, if you find nothing, your topic may be too narrow or too far off the beaten track to yield quick results. But you could also be on to an important question that nobody has thought about, at least not for a while. For example, "friendship" was once an important topic for philosophers, but it was then ignored by major encyclopedias for centuries. Recently, though, it has been revived as a topic of serious research. Chances are you'll make something of a neglected topic only through your own hard thinking. In the long run, that research might make you famous, but it won't work for a paper due in a few weeks.

CONSULT ONLINE DATABASES. If you are sure that most of your sources will be in journals (typically in the social sciences), skip the catalog and go right to your library's online journal databases. Most let you search for titles and key words in the ways we've described. (Browsing capabilities, however, are less common.) Many include abstracts, which can help you decide whether an article is worth reading carefully. Some databases even provide the full text of articles, though often for a fee. For information too current for the journals, check periodical indexes or search the online archives of a major newspaper.

PROWL THE STACKS. In many respects, doing research online is faster than on foot, but if you never go into the stacks of your library (assuming you're allowed to), you may miss crucial sources that you'll find only there. More important, you'll miss the benefits of serendipity—a chance encounter with a valuable source that occurs only when a title happens to catch your eye. (All three of us have found important sources in this way.)

If you can get into the stacks, find the shelf with books on your topic, then scan the titles on that shelf, then on the ones above, below, and on either side, especially for books with new bindings published by university presses. Then turn around and skim titles behind you; you never know. When you spot a promising title, skim its table of contents and index for key words related to your question and answer. Then skim its bibliography for titles that look relevant. You can do all that faster with a book in your hand than you can online. Be suspicious of a book with no index or bibliography. (See 5.4 for more on systematic skimming.)

You can check tables of contents for many journals online, but browsing among the shelved journals can be more productive. Once you identify promising journals online or in bibliographies, find them on the shelf. Skim the bound volumes for the last ten years (most have an annual table of contents in front). Then take a quick look at journals shelved nearby. You'll be surprised how often you find a relevant article that you would have missed online.

5.3 LOCATING SOURCES ON THE INTERNET

Not long ago, experienced researchers distrusted all data found on the Internet. That is no longer true. Researchers now log on to the Internet to access library sources, government reports and databases, primary texts from reputable online publishers, newspapers, even scholarly journals available only online. You can use—and trust—those sources as you would their print counterparts.

Beyond those traditional sources, you'll find more on the Internet than any library can—or would—provide. But the Net's strength in numbers is also its limitation, because it has no gatekeepers. It is like a publisher without editors or a library without librarians. Most people post what they are passionate about or what will make them money, with no one to check their honesty or accuracy. When a search engine points you to a site, it knows only that many others have looked at it, not whether it offers careful reporting or the ranting of an obsessed mind. Your problem is that you can't easily know that either. You would have to invest more time than you may have to determine what is reliable enough to use.

So use the Internet freely only when it's a primary source. For example, if you study how soap opera story lines respond to their fans' reactions, the fan blogs would be primary sources. But avoid the Internet for secondary or, worse, tertiary sources, unless you can show your readers that a specific Internet source is reliable. (We discuss evaluating sources in the next section.)

RESPECTING AUTHORS' RIGHTS

There are sites that provide reliable online copies of older texts no longer in copyright, but some postings of recently printed texts violate the author's copyright. Careful readers dislike seeing unauthorized copies cited because it breaks the law and the texts are often inaccurately reproduced. So unless a recent text is posted with the author's clear permission (as in a database), use its print rather than its e-version.

5.4 EVALUATING SOURCES FOR RELEVANCE AND RELIABILITY

When you start looking for sources, you'll find more than you can use, so you must quickly evaluate their usefulness; use two criteria: relevance and reliability.

5.4.1 Evaluating Sources for Relevance

If your source is a book, do this:

- Skim its index for your key words, then skim the pages on which those words occur.

- Skim the first and last paragraphs in chapters that use a lot of your key words.

- Skim prologues, introductions, summary chapters, and so on.

- Skim the last chapter, especially the first and last two or three pages.

- If the source is a collection of articles, skim the editor's introduction.

- Check the bibliography for titles relevant to your topic.

If your source is an article, do this:

- Read the abstract, if it has one.

- Skim the introduction and conclusion, or if they are not marked off by headings, skim the first six or seven paragraphs and the last four or five.

- Skim for section headings, and read the first and last paragraphs of those sections.

- Check the bibliography for titles relevant to your topic.

If your source is online, do this:

- If it looks like a printed article, follow the steps for a journal article.

- Skim sections labeled "introduction," "overview," "summary," or the like. If there are none, look for a link labeled "About the Site" or something similar.

- If the site has a link labeled "Site Map" or "Index," check it for your key words and skim the referenced pages.

- If the site has a "search" resource, type in your key words.

This kind of speedy reading can guide your own writing and revision. If you do not structure your report so your readers can skim it quickly and see the outlines of your argument, your report has a problem, an issue we discuss in chapters 12 and 14.

5.4.2 Evaluating Sources for Reliability

You can't judge a source until you read it, but there are signs of its reliability:

1. **Is the source published or posted online by a reputable press?** Most university presses are reliable, especially if you recognize the name of the university. Some commercial presses are reliable in some fields, such as Norton in literature, Ablex in sciences, or West in law. Be skeptical of a commercial book that makes sensational claims, even if its author has a PhD after his name. Be espe-

cially careful about sources on hotly contested social issues such as stem-cell research, gun control, and global warming. Many books and articles are published by individuals or organizations driven by ideology. Libraries often include them for the sake of coverage, but don't assume they are reliable.

2. Was the book or article peer-reviewed? Most reputable presses and journals ask experts to review a book or article before it is published; it is called "peer review." Many essay collections, however, are reviewed only by the named editor(s). Few commercial magazines use peer review. If a publication hasn't been peer-reviewed, be suspicious.

3. Is the author a reputable scholar? This is hard to answer if you are new to a field. Most publications cite an author's academic credentials; you can find more with a search engine. Most established scholars are reliable, but be cautious if the topic is a contested social issue such as gun control or abortion. Even reputable scholars can have axes to grind, especially if their research is financially supported by a special interest group. Go online to check out anyone an author thanks for support, including foundations that supported her work.

4. If the source is available only online, is it sponsored by a reputable organization? A Web site is only as reliable as its sponsor. You can usually trust one sponsored and maintained by a reputable organization. But if the site has not been updated recently, it may have been abandoned and is no longer endorsed by its sponsor. Some sites supported by individuals are reliable; most are not. Do a Web search for the name of the sponsor to find out more about it.

5. Is the source current? You must use up-to-date sources, but what counts as current depends on the field. In computer science, a journal article can be out-of-date in months; in the social sciences, ten years pushes the limit. Publications have a longer life in the humanities: in philosophy, primary sources are current for centuries, secondary ones for decades. In general, a source that sets out a major position or theory that other researchers accept will stay current longer than those that respond to or develop it. Assume that most textbooks are *not* current (except, of course, this one).

If you don't know how to gauge currency in your field, look at the dates of articles in the works cited of a new book or article: you can cite works as old as the older ones in that list (but perhaps not as old as the oldest). Try to find a standard edition of primary works such as novels, plays, letters, and so on (it is usually not the most recent). Be sure that you consult the most recent edition of a secondary or tertiary source (researchers often change their views, even rejecting ones they espoused in earlier editions).

6. If the source is a book, does it have a notes and a bibliography? If not, be suspicious, because you have no way to follow up on anything the source claims.

7. If the source is a Web site, does it include bibliographical data? You cannot know how to judge the reliability of a site that does not indicate who sponsors and maintains it, who wrote what's posted there, and when it was posted or last updated.

8. If the source is a Web site, does it approach its topic judiciously? Your readers are unlikely to trust a site that engages in heated advocacy, attacks those who disagree, makes wild claims, uses abusive language, or makes errors of spelling, punctuation, and grammar.

The following criteria are particularly important for advanced students:

9. If the source is a book, has it been well reviewed? Many fields have indexes to published reviews that tell you how others evaluate a source (see the "Appendix: Bibliographic Resources").

10. Has the source been frequently cited by others? You can roughly estimate how influential a source is by how often others cite it. To determine that, consult a citation index (see "Appendix: Bibliographic Resources").

These indicators do not guarantee reliability. Reviewers sometimes recommend that a reputable press publish something weakly argued or with thin data because other aspects of its argument are too important to miss—we three have each done so. So don't assume that you can read uncritically just because a report is written by a reputable researcher and published by a reputable press.

WHOM CAN YOU TRUST?

The highly respected *Journal of the American Medical Association* appointed a committee to review articles published by reputable journals for reliability. Even though those papers had been approved by experts in the field, the reviewers reported that "statistical and methodological errors were common" ("When Peer Review Produces Unsound Science," *New York Times*, June 11, 2002, p. D6). In the face of such revelations, some just dismiss what scientists publish: if the reviewers of scientific articles can't guarantee reliable data, what is a mere layperson to do? You do what we all do—the best you can: read critically, and when you report data, do so as accurately as you can. We'll return to this question in chapter 8.

Error is bad, but dishonesty is worse. One of Booth's students got a summer job with a drug company and was assigned to go through stacks of doctors' answers to questionnaires and shred certain ones until nine out of ten of those left endorsed the company's product. These bogus data were then used to "prove" that the product worked. The student quit in disgust and was, no doubt, replaced by someone less ethically careful.

5.5 FOLLOWING BIBLIOGRAPHICAL TRAILS

Most sources will give you trailheads for bibliographical searches. When you find a book that seems useful, skim its bibliography or works cited. Its index will list the authors cited most often (generally, the more citations, the more important an author is). Journal articles usually begin with a review of previous research, all cited. By following this bibliographic trail, you can navigate the most difficult research territory, because one source always leads to others, which lead to others, which lead to . . .

5.6 LOOKING BEYOND PREDICTABLE SOURCES

For a class paper, you'll probably use the sources typical in your field. But if you are doing an advanced project, an MA thesis, or a PhD dissertation, search beyond them. If, for example, your project were on the economic effects of agricultural changes in late sixteenth-century England, you might read Elizabethan plays involving country characters, look at wood prints of agricultural life, find commentary by religious figures on rural social behavior. Conversely, if you were working on visual representations of daily life in London, you might work up the economic history of the time and place. When you look beyond the standard *kinds* of references relevant to your question, you enrich not only your analysis but your range of intellectual reference and your ability to synthesize diverse kinds of data, a crucial competence of an inquiring mind. Don't ignore a work on your topic that is not mentioned in the bibliographies of your most relevant sources—you will get credit for originality if you turn up a good source that others have ignored.

WHEN THEY BEAT YOU TO THE PUNCH

Don't panic if you find a source that seems to pose and solve precisely your problem: "Transforming the Alamo Legend: History in the Service of Politics." At that moment you might think, *I'm dead. Nothing new to say.* (It happened to Williams when he was writing his doctoral dissertation and to Colomb just before his first book came out.) You may be right, but probably not. If the source does in fact settle your exact question, you have to formulate a new one. But the question your source asked is probably not as close to yours as you first feared. And you may find that you can do the source one better: if the author failed to get things entirely right, you have an unwitting ally in formulating your problem.

5.7 USING PEOPLE AS PRIMARY SOURCES

In some areas, you have to collect primary data from people, even if your research is not directly about them. They may provide useful information, if you can help them understand your interest in what they know. Don't ignore people in local business, government, or civic organizations. For example, if you were researching school desegregation in your town, you might go beyond the documents to ask the local school district whether anyone there has memories to share.

We can't explain the complexities of interviewing (there are many guides to that process), but remember that the more you plan by determining *exactly* what you want to know, the more efficiently you will get what you need. You don't need to script an interview around a set list of questions—in fact, that can be a bad idea if it freezes the interviewee. But prepare so that you don't question your source aimlessly. You can always reread a book for what you missed, but you can't keep going back to people because you didn't prepare well enough to get what you needed the first time.

☞ **QUICK TIP:** *The Ethics of Using People as Sources of Data*

In recent years we have become increasingly aware that research using people may inadvertently harm them—not just physically but by embarrassing them, violating their privacy, and so on. So every college or university now has a Human Subjects Committee that reviews all research directly or indirectly involving people, whether done by students or professional researchers. Its aim is to ensure that researchers follow the maxim that should govern research as it does medicine: *Do no harm.* Consult with that committee if you use people as sources of data—whether by interviewing, surveying, perhaps even just observing them. Jumping through these hoops may feel like bureaucratic make-work, but if you don't, you could harm those who help you and may even damage your institution.

Engaging Sources

To make your research as reliable as you expect your sources to be, you must use them fairly and accurately. In this chapter we explain how to engage your sources productively and how to take notes so that readers can trust you when you rely on or critique a source.

How you use sources depends on where you stand in your search for a problem and solution. If you still have only a topic, you may have to read a lot of sources to find a question to pursue. If you have a question, you can search sources for data to test and support your answer. You must record them so that you can accurately recover not just their data but their arguments and your responses to them. Those are skills highly valued not just in the classroom, but in every workplace.

The problem is, human nature works against us in two ways. First, most of us embrace our first answer so strongly that we read less critically than we should. We easily spot data and arguments that confirm our claim, but we just as easily overlook or distort data that qualify or even contradict it. We don't do that deliberately; it's just human nature. You have to guard against this bias, not only in your own work but in your sources, especially when they agree with you.

Second, when we read just to understand, taking notes can feel like a chore. Many new researchers take notes in a shorthand that seems understandable at the time but that betrays them later—ask Doris Kearns Goodwin, historian and TV pundit, whose reputation was scarred by accusations of plagiarism, which she attributed to careless note-taking. You have to take notes more carefully than you think you need to.

In this chapter we show you how to use secondary sources as accurately, critically, and fairly as time—and human nature—allow.

6.1 KNOWING WHAT KIND OF EVIDENCE TO LOOK FOR
Different fields use different kinds of evidence, so before you start collecting data, you must know the particular *kinds* of evidence your readers expect:

• personal beliefs and anecdotes from writers' lives, as in a first-year writing course

• direct quotations from letters, diaries, books, poems, and so on, as in most humanities courses

• verbal accounts of objects, images, and events in the form of descriptions, anecdotes, and narratives, as in history

• fine-grained records of objects and events recorded in photographs, videotapes, films, drawings, and recordings, as in anthropology

• quantitative data gathered in laboratory experiments and surveys, represented in tables, graphs, charts, as in many of the social and all of the natural sciences

Each field accepts other kinds of data, if presented properly, but each is also likely to disfavor certain kinds. Literary critics do not expect bar charts to represent an author's development; most psychologists are suspicious of self-reported anecdotes about mental processes.

6.2 RECORD COMPLETE BIBLIOGRAPHICAL DATA
Before you read one page of a source, record *all* its bibliographical data, not only to record what you read, but to credit your sources and help readers find them, should they want to check for themselves. We promise that no habit will serve you better for the rest of your career. (Different fields follow different styles for citing their sources. See 13.8. Determine the style your readers expect so that you can record your sources appropriately.)

For printed books, record

- author

- title (including subtitle)

- editor(s) and translator(s) (if any)

- edition

- volume

- place published (the first if more than one is listed)

- publisher

- date published

- page numbers of articles or chapters consulted

For journals, record

- author

- title (including subtitle) of article

- title of journal

- volume and issue number

- date

- page numbers of article

For online sources, record as much of the above as applies. Also record

- URL

- date of access

- Webmaster (if identified)

- name of database (if any)

If you access a printed text online, cite bibliographical data from the original printing as well as your source of online access.

If you photocopy a passage from a book, copy its title page and from its reverse side copy the date of publication, then record its library call number. You don't include call numbers in your list of sources, but we can tell you how frustrating it is to find in your notes the perfect quote or the essential bit of data whose source you incompletely documented, cannot find again, and so cannot use.

> DOCUMENT A POTENTIAL SOURCE WHEN YOU FIRST TOUCH IT
> Williams once had to withhold publication of research on Elizabethan social history for more than a year because he failed to document a source fully. Years earlier he had come across data (a list of renters in London in 1638) that no one else had thought to apply to a problem he thought he might one day address. But he had failed to record complete information on his source, so he could not use its data. He searched the library at the University of Chicago for hours, until one night he sat up in bed, realizing that the source was in a different library!

6.3 ENGAGING SOURCES ACTIVELY

If you can, read important sources twice. Make your first reading generous and sensitive to what sparks your interest. Reread passages that puzzle or confuse you. Don't look for disagreements right away; read in ways that help the source make sense. Otherwise, you'll be tempted to emphasize its weaknesses if it presents an argument that rivals yours. Resist that temptation, at least at first. If your source seems important or disagrees with your position, read it a second time slowly and more critically. If you can't sum up a passage in your mind, you don't understand it well enough to disagree.

Don't accept a claim just because an authority asserts it. For decades researchers cited the "fact" that the Inuit peoples of the Arctic had many terms for types of snow. But another researcher found that they have just three (or so she claims). And be wary of dueling experts. If Expert A says one thing, B will assert the opposite, and C will claim to be an expert but is not. When some students hear experts disagree, they become cynical and dismiss expert knowledge as just opinion. Don't confuse mere opinion with informed and thoughtful debate over legitimately contested issues.

If you are an advanced researcher, check the accuracy of everything important to your argument. If you ask almost anyone whose work has been used by others, he will tell you that, as often as not, it was reported inaccurately, summarized carelessly, or criticized ignorantly. Writers regularly write to the *New York Review of Books* and the "Book Review" of the *New York Times*, pointing out how reviewers distorted their ideas or made factual errors criticizing them.

CHECK—AND CHECK AGAIN
Researchers rarely misrepresent data deliberately, but carelessness and intellectual laziness do happen. Colomb heard a prominent researcher confess after her talk that she had never read the work she had just discussed. One of Booth's books was "refuted" by a critic who apparently read only the title of a section, "Novels Must Be Realistic." Failing to read beyond it, he didn't know that Booth himself was attacking the claim in the title, along with other misconceptions about fiction. One reviewer of a book by Williams misquoted him and then, thinking he was disagreeing with him, argued for the point Williams made in the first place!

6.4 USING SECONDARY SOURCES TO FIND A PROBLEM
Once you have a research problem, use it to guide your search for evidence, models, and arguments to respond to. But if you don't yet have one, you won't know which data, models, or arguments might be relevant. So read sources not randomly but deliberately to find a problem. Look for claims that seem puzzling, inaccurate, or simplistic—anything you can disagree with. You're more likely to find a research problem when you disagree with a source, but you can also find one in sources you agree with.

6.4.1 Look for Creative Agreement
If you believe what a source claims, try to extend that claim: What new cases might it cover? What new insights can it provide? Is there confirming evidence the source hasn't considered? Here are some ways to find a problem through creative agreement.

1. **Offer additional support.** You can offer new evidence to support a source's claim.

   Smith uses anecdotes to show that the Alamo story had mythic status beyond Texas, but editorials in big-city newspapers offer better evidence.

   - Source supports a claim with old evidence, but you offer new evidence.

   - Source supports a claim with weak evidence, but you offer stronger evidence.

2. **Confirm unsupported claims.** You can prove something that a source only assumes or speculates about.

   Smith recommends visualization to improve sports performance, but MRI studies of the mental activities of athletes offer evidence that shows why that is good advice.

   - Source speculates _____ might be true, but you offer evidence to show that it is.

   - Source assumes _____ is true, but you can prove it.

3. **Apply a claim more widely.** You can extend a position.

   Smith argues that medical students learn physiological processes better when they are explained with many metaphors rather than with just one. The same seems true for engineering and law students.

   - Source correctly applies _____ to one situation, but you apply it to new ones.

   - Source claims that _____ is true in a specific situation, but you show it's true in general.

6.4.2 Look for Creative Disagreement

We can't tell you what to disagree with, but we can list some ways of disagreeing that point to new research problems. (The list is not exhaustive, and some kinds overlap.)

1. **Contradictions of kind.** A source says something is one kind of thing, but it's another.

Smith says that certain religious groups are "cults" because of their strange beliefs, but those beliefs are no different in kind from standard religions.

- Source claims that _____ is a kind of _____, but it's not.

- Source claims that _____ always has _____ as one of its features or qualities, but it doesn't.

- Source claims that _____ is normal/good/significant/ useful/moral/interesting, but it's not.

You can reverse those claims and the ones that follow to state the opposite:

- Though a source says _____ is *not* a kind of _____, you can show it is.

2. **Part-whole contradictions.** You can show that a source mistakes how the parts of something are related.

Smith has argued that sports are crucial to an educated person, but in fact athletics have no place in college.

- Source claims that _____ is a part of _____, but it's not.

- Source claims that one part of _____ relates to another in a certain way, but it doesn't.

- Source claims that every _____ has _____ as one of its parts, but it doesn't.

3. **Developmental or historical contradictions.** You can show that a source mistakes the origin or development of a topic.

Smith argues that the world population will rise, but it won't.

- Source claims that _____ is changing, but it's not.

- Source claims that _____ originated in _____, but it didn't.

- Source claims that _____ develops in a certain way, but it doesn't.

4. **External cause-effect contradictions.** You can show that a source mistakes a causal relationship.

Smith claims that juveniles can be stopped from becoming criminals by "boot camps." But evidence shows that they don't.

- Source claims that _____ causes _____, but it doesn't/they are both caused by _____.

- Source claims that _____ is sufficient to cause _____, but it's not.

- Source claims that _____ causes only _____, but it also causes _____.

5. **Contradictions of perspective.** Most contradictions don't change a conceptual framework, but when you contradict a "standard" view of things, you urge others to think in a new way.

Smith assumes that advertising has only an economic function, but it also serves as a laboratory for new art forms.

- Source discusses _____ from the point of view of _____, but a new context or point of view reveals a new truth [the new or old context can be social, political, philosophical, historical, economic, ethical, gender specific, etc.].

- Source analyzes _____ using theory/value system _____, but you can analyze it from a new point of view and see it in a new way.

6.5 USING SECONDARY SOURCES TO PLAN YOUR ARGUMENT

Experienced researchers read secondary sources mainly to keep up with work in their field, but they use them in other ways as well, and so can you.

6.5.1 Reading Secondary Sources for Data to Use as Evidence

New researchers regularly read secondary sources for data to support a claim, but if you can, check the primary source. If an important quotation is available in its original form and context, it is risky and intellectually lazy not to look it up.

You don't have to agree with a source to use its data; in fact, its argument does not even have to be relevant to your question, so long as its data are. However, use statistical data only if you can judge for yourself whether they were collected and analyzed appropriately. (You serve yourself well if you take a course or two in statistics and probability, an area where most Americans are shamefully ignorant.)

Don't try to find every last jot of data relevant to your question; that's impossible. But you do need data that are sufficient and representative. Unfortunately, different fields judge that differently. For example, to have sufficient evidence for a claim about a causal correlation between baldness and IQ, a psychologist might need results from hundreds of subjects. But before accepting a claim about a new cancer drug, the FDA might demand data from thousands of subjects through scores of trials. The more at stake, the higher the threshold of reliability, and that means more data.

What counts as representative, of course, depends on the nature of the data. Anthropologists might interpret a whole culture in New Guinea on the basis of a deep acquaintance with a few individuals, but no sociologist would make a claim about American religious practices based on a single Baptist church in Oregon. If you don't know what researchers in your field judge to be sufficient and representative, ask your teacher or another expert. In particular, ask for examples of arguments that *failed* because of insufficient or unrepresentative evidence. To learn what works, you must know what doesn't.

6.5.2 Reading Secondary Sources for Claims to Use as Support

Researchers often use the results they find in secondary sources to bolster their own arguments. If you find a useful claim, you can cite it to support your own. You can use a claim as factual data, but only if it has been supported and widely accepted. But many claims show nothing more than that another researcher agrees with you—useful support, but not evidence. To use such claims as evidence, you have to report not only the conclusion of the source but its reasoning and supporting evidence as well.

6.5.3 Reading Secondary Sources for Models of Argument and Analysis

If you have never made an argument like the one you plan to, you can model it on ones you find in secondary sources. You can't use specific ideas (that would be plagiarism), but you do not plagiarize a source when you borrow its logic. Don't worry that your argument will be unoriginal. The logic of a research argument is rarely original. Readers will look for originality in your problem, claim, and evidence.

Suppose you want to argue that the Alamo legend thrived because it served the political interests of those who created it and satisfied the emotional needs of those who repeated it. You will need reasons and evidence unique to your claim, but you can raise the *kinds* of issues that readers see in similar arguments about other legends, real or fictional. If, for example, a source shows that creators of the King Arthur legend benefited from responses to it, ask how the Alamo legend benefited its creators and audience. You are not obliged to cite your model, but to gain credibility, you might note that it makes an argument similar to yours:

> As Weiman (1998) shows about the Arthurian legends, those responsible for the Alamo legend also gained the most from its depiction of Texas as an outpost civilization. . . .

6.5.4 Reading Secondary Sources to Define Your Problem

Experienced researchers usually present their problem in relation to the research that led them to it. Before they state their problem in their introduction, they describe the line of research that their work will replace, correct, refine, or extend. So as you read secondary sources, look for research questions similar to yours. You can use those earlier studies in your introduction to define a gap that your work will fill. For example, you might frame your study of Alamo legends in light of previous studies of other legends:

> Historians have been interested in ways that communities use legends to create and maintain political and social identity. For early Christian communities, it was the Grail legend (Gromke 1988); for England, it was the Arthurian legend (Weiman 1998); for . . . For the new Republic of Texas, it was the legend of the Alamo.

You can cite those sources again in the body of your report, but you don't have to. Just mentioning them in your introduction is enough to show your readers how your report is related to a wider conversation.

6.5.5 Reading Secondary Sources for Arguments to Respond To

No research report is complete until it acknowledges and responds to its readers' predictable questions and disagreements. You can find some of those competing views in secondary sources. What alternatives to your claims do they offer? What evidence do they cite that you must acknowledge? Some new researchers think they weaken their case if they mention any views opposing their own. The opposite is true. When you acknowledge the views of others, you show that you not only know those views, but have carefully considered and can confidently respond to them (for more on this, see chapter 10).

Experienced researchers also use those competing views to improve their own. You can't really understand what you think until you understand why a rational person might think differently. So as you look for sources, don't look just for those that support your claims. Be alert for sources that contradict them, because they are sources that your readers are likely to know.

6.6 RECORDING WHAT YOU FIND

Once you find a source that you think you can use, you must read it purposefully and carefully. But it does no good to understand your source when you read it if you cannot recall what you understood when you read your notes later.

6.6.1 Take Full Notes

As you hunt down data, it can feel tedious to record them accurately, but you lose what you gain from careful reading if you depend on careless notes. Some still believe that the best notes are written longhand on cards like this:

Sharman, Swearing, p. 133.   HISTORY/ECONOMICS (GENDER?)

Says swearing became economic issue in 18th c. Cites Gentleman's Magazine, July 1751 (no page reference): woman sentenced to ten days' hard labor because couldn't pay one-shilling fine for profanity.

". . . one rigid economist practically entertained the notion of adding to the national resources by preaching a crusade against the opulent class of swearers."

[*Way to think about swearing today as economic issue? Comedians more popular if they use bad language? Movies more realistic? A gender issue here? Were 18th-c. men fined as often as women?*]

GT3080/S6

- At the top left is the author, short title, and page number.

- At the top right are key words that let the researcher sort and re-sort notes into different categories and orders.

- The body of the card summarizes the source, records a direct quotation, and includes a thought about further research.

- At bottom left is the call number of the source.

This format encourages systematic note-taking, but to be honest, we three haven't used such cards in a long time. We take notes on a computer or lined pad, because a note card is usually too small a space to record our responses fully.

But we still follow these principles:

- On each sheet of notes, record the author, short title of the source, page numbers, and key words.

- Put notes on different topics on different pages.

- Perhaps most important: clearly distinguish three kinds of notes: (1) what you quote, (2) what you paraphrase and summarize, and (3) your own thoughts. On a computer, use different fonts or styles; on paper use headings or different-colored ink or paper.

We stress that you must *unambiguously* distinguish your own words from those of your sources, because it is so easy to confuse the two. (Photocopy passages longer than a few lines.) You must also distinguish your own ideas from those you paraphrase or summarize from a source.

6.6.2 Know When to Quote, Paraphrase, and Summarize

It takes too long to transcribe the exact words of every source you read, but it's a nuisance when you need to quote a passage you only summarized. So when taking notes, you must know when to quote, paraphrase, and summarize. In general, researchers in the humanities quote most often; social and natural scientists usually paraphrase and summarize. But every choice depends on how you plan to use a passage:

- Summarize when you need only the point of a passage, section, or even whole article or book. Summary is useful for context or views that are related but not specifically relevant. A summary of a source never serves as good evidence.

- Paraphrase when you can represent what a source says more clearly or pointedly than it does. Paraphrase doesn't mean changing just a word or two. You must replace most of the words and phrasing of the original with your own. A paraphrase is never as good evidence as a direct quotation.

- Record exact quotations for these purposes:
  - The quoted words are evidence that backs up your reasons. If, for example, you claimed that different regions responded to the Battle of the Alamo differently, you would quote exact words from different newspapers. You would paraphrase them if you needed only their general sentiments.
  - The words are from an authority who backs up your view.
  - The words are strikingly original or express your ideas so compellingly that the quotation can frame the rest of your discussion.
  - They state a view that you disagree with, and to be fair you want to state that view exactly.

If you don't record important words now, you can't quote them later. So copy or, better, photocopy passages more often than you think you must. *Never* abbreviate a quotation thinking you can accurately reconstruct it later. You can't. And if you misquote, you'll undermine your credibility.

6.6.3 Get the Context Right

As you use material from your sources, record not just what they say but how they use the information.

1. **When you quote, paraphrase, or summarize, be careful about context.** You cannot entirely avoid quoting out of context, because you cannot quote all of an original. So when you draft a paraphrase or summary or copy a quotation, do so within the context that matters most—that of your own grasp of the original. When you record a part of an argument, note the line of reasoning that the author was pursuing:

NOT: Bartolli (p. 123): The war was caused by Z.

NOT: Bartolli (p. 123): The war was caused by X, Y, and Z.

BUT: Bartolli: The war was caused by X, Y, and Z (p. 123). But the most important cause was Z (p. 123), for three reasons: reason 1 (pp. 124–26); reason 2 (p. 126); reason 3 (pp. 127–28).

Sometimes you will care only about the conclusion, but readers usually want to see how a conclusion emerges from the argument supporting it. So when you take notes, record not only conclusions but also the arguments that support them.

2. **When you record a claim, note its rhetorical importance in the original.** Is it a main point? A minor point? A qualification or concession? By noting these distinctions you avoid this kind of mistake:

> ORIGINAL BY JONES: "We cannot conclude that one event causes another just because the second follows the first. Nor can statistical correlation prove causation. But no one who has studied the data doubts that smoking is a causal factor in lung cancer."

> MISLEADING REPORT ABOUT JONES: Jones claims that "we cannot conclude that one event causes another just because the second follows the first. Nor can statistical correlation prove causation." No wonder responsible researchers distrust statistical evidence of health risks.

Jones did not make that point at all. He *conceded* a point that was relatively trivial compared to the point he wanted to make. Anyone who deliberately misreports in this way violates basic standards of truth. But a researcher can make such a mistake inadvertently if he notes only words and not their role in an argument.

Distinguish statements that are central to an argument from qualifications or concessions the author acknowledges but downplays. Unless you are reading "against the grain" of the writer's intention—to expose hidden tendencies, for example—do not report minor aspects of a research report as though they were major or, worse, as if they were the whole of the report.

3. **Record the scope and confidence of a claim.** These are not the same:

> Chemicals in french fries cause cancer.

> Chemicals in french fries may be a factor in cancer.

Some chemicals in french fries correlate with a higher incidence of some cancers.

4. Don't mistake a summary of another writer's views for those of an author summarizing them. Some writers do not clearly indicate when they summarize another's argument, so it is easy to quote them as saying what they set out to disprove rather than what they in fact believe.

5. Note why sources agree and disagree. Two social scientists might claim that a social problem is caused by personal factors, not by environmental forces, but one might cite evidence from genetic inheritance while the other points to religious beliefs. How and why sources agree is as important as the fact that they do. In the same way, sources might disagree, because they interpret the same evidence differently or take different approaches to the problem.

It is risky to attach yourself to what any one researcher says about an issue. It is not "research" when you uncritically summarize another's work. Even if your source is universally trusted, be careful. If you rely on at least two sources, you'll almost always find that they do not agree entirely, and that's where your own research can begin. *Which has the better argument? Which better respects the evidence?* In fact, you have a research problem right there—whom should we believe?

Remember that your report will be accurate only if you double check your notes against your sources, and after your first draft, check your quotations against your notes. If you use one source extensively, skim its relevant parts to be sure you in fact understand it. At this point, you may *believe* in your claim so strongly that you read everything in its favor. Despite our best intentions, that temptation afflicts us all. There is no cure, save for checking and rechecking. And rechecking again.

THE VALUE OF IRRELEVANT DATA

We have emphasized how important it is to have a good question to focus your search for data most relevant to its answer. Don't think, however, that you waste time reading sources that turn out to be irrelevant. In fact, when you read and record more than you use, you build up a base of knowledge crucial to the exercise of good thinking. Good thinking is a skill that you can learn, but you can exercise it only when you have a deep and wide base of facts, data, and knowledge to work on. So read sources not just to answer the question you ask today, but to help you think better about every question you'll ask for the rest of your research career. To that end, everything you read is relevant.

Manage Moments of Normal Anxiety

As you get deeper into your project, you may experience a moment when everything seems to run together into a hopeless muddle. That usually happens when you accumulate notes faster than you can sort them. The bad news is that you can't avoid all such moments; the good news is that eventually they pass. You can minimize the panic by taking every opportunity to organize and summarize what you have gathered by *writing as you go* and by returning to the central questions: *What question am I asking? What problem am I posing?* Keep rehearsing that formula, *I am working on X to learn more about Y, so that my readers can better understand Z.* You can also turn to friends, classmates, teachers—anyone who will serve as a sympathetic but critical audience. Explain how what you have learned bears on your question and helps you resolve your problem. Ask them, *Does this make sense? Am I missing anything important? What else would you like to know?* You will profit from their reactions, but even more from the mere act of explaining your ideas to nonspecialists.

PART III

Making a Claim and Supporting It

Prologue

Once you've accumulated a stack of notes, photocopies, and summaries, don't keep piling them up until they spill off your desk (or you lose track of them on your hard drive). It's time to impose some order on what you've found. The risk, however, is that you just group your data under obvious headings, arrange them into some arbitrary sequence, and start writing. Do that and you're likely to end up with a data dump that says little more than *Here are some facts about my topic.* You need a more powerful principle of organization, one based not on your data but on the solution to your problem and the logic of its support. That support takes the form of a research *argument.*

Now a research argument is not like the heated exchanges we hear every day. Those arguments usually involve a dispute: children argue over a toy; roommates over the stereo; drivers about who had the right-of-way. Such arguments can be polite or nasty, but most involve conflict, with winners and losers. To be sure, researchers sometimes wrangle over each other's reasoning and evidence and occasionally erupt into charges of carelessness, incompetence, and even fraud. But that's not the kind of argument that made them researchers in the first place.

In the next five chapters, we examine a kind of argument that is less like a prickly dispute with winners and losers and more like a lively conversation with amiable colleagues. It is a conversation in which you and your imagined readers *cooperatively* explore an issue that you both think is important to resolve, a conversation that aims not at coercing each other into agreement, but at cooperatively finding the best answer to an important but challenging question.

In that conversation, though, you do more than politely trade opinions. We are all entitled to our opinions, and no law requires us to explain or defend them. But in a research argument, we are expected to make claims not just because we believe they're true but because we think they are new and important enough to change what readers think. Then we support those claims with sound reasons and good evidence, as if our readers were asking us, quite reasonably, *Why should I believe that?*

In fact, although we more easily notice the heated disputes, we have many more of these collaborative arguments every day, each time we trade good reasons for deciding what to do—when discussing with a friend what car to buy, what movie to rent, even whether to get pizza or Chinese. As with those friendly discussions, a research argument doesn't force a claim on readers. Instead, you start where your readers do, with their predictable questions about why they should accept your claim, questions they ask not to sabotage your argument but to test it, to help both of you find and understand a truth worth sharing. Of course, when you *write* an argument, no one is there to ask you those questions in person. So you must imagine them on your readers' behalf. It's those imagined questions and your answers that make your argument seem to be, if not an actual conversation, then at least in the spirit of one.

As you become an experienced writer, you will plan your argument and your paper as a single process. But if you are writing one of your first research reports, it's useful to do that in two steps: first, assemble your argument to see if it persuades you; then revise it into a report that you think will persuade your reader. In chapter 7 we survey the elements that constitute a research argument. In chapters 8–11 we discuss each element in detail. In part 4 we discuss how to turn the plan for your argument into a plan for your paper.

GETTING TO KNOW YOU

Nothing is harder than imagining questions from someone you don't know. Experienced researchers have the advantage of knowing many of their readers personally. They talk with them about research projects, trying out ideas before writing them up. And when they don't know their readers, they try to find out. For example, some physicists wanted biologists to notice their research but were unhappy when the first manuscript they sent to a biology journal was rejected. So they attended biology conferences, read biology journals, even hung around the biology department's faculty lounge. After they figured out how biologists think, they rewrote their reports and published papers that influenced the field.

Students seldom have the time or opportunity to hang around their readers, but you can do some homework:

- Read journals that publish research like yours. Notice the kinds of questions the articles acknowledge and respond to.
- Rehearse your argument with your teacher. After you have a plan but before you draft, talk over your ideas, asking whether she thinks any seem doubtful or confusing.
- Ask someone to read your drafts and indicate where they have questions or see alternatives. Find someone as much like your intended readers as possible.

You've been told endlessly to think about your audience. To do that well, you must get to know actual readers.

CHAPTER SEVEN

Making Good Arguments: An Overview

In this chapter we discuss the nature of a research argument and the five questions whose answers constitute one.

You can't wait to plan an argument supporting the answer to your question until you have every last bit of data. In the first place, you'll never get them all. But more important, you can't know what data you need until you sketch the argument they fit into. Only after you sort your data into the elements of an argument that answers your readers' predictable questions can you see what research you still have to do. But more than that, when you plan your argument early, you grasp your material better and avoid wasted effort, especially return trips to the library.

7.1 ARGUMENT AS A CONVERSATION WITH READERS

In a research report, you make a *claim*, back it with *reasons*, support them with *evidence*, *acknowledge* and *respond* to other views, and sometimes explain your *principles* of reasoning. There's nothing arcane in any of that, because you do it in every conversation that inquires thoughtfully into an unsettled issue:

A: I hear last semester was a little rocky. How do you think this term will go? [*A poses a problem that interests her, put in the form of a question.*]

B: Better, I hope. [*B makes a claim that answers the question.*]

A: Why is that? [*A asks for a reason to believe B's claim.*]

B: I'll finally be taking courses in my major. [*B offers a reason.*]

A: Why will that make a difference? [*A doesn't see how B's reason is relevant to his claim that he will do better.*]

B: When I take courses I'm interested in, I work harder. [*B offers a general principle that relates his reason to his claim.*]

A: What courses? [*A asks for evidence to back up B's reason.*]

B: History of architecture, introduction to design. [*B offers specific instances on which he based his reason.*]

A: But what about that calculus course you have to take again? [*A offers a point that contradicts B's reason.*]

B: I know I had to drop it last time, but I found a really good tutor. [*B acknowledges A's objection and responds to it.*]

A: But won't you be taking five courses? [*A raises another reservation.*]

B: I know. It won't be easy. [*B concedes a point he cannot refute.*]

A: Will you pull up your GPA? [*A asks about the limits of B's claim.*]

B: I should. I'm hoping for a 3.0, as long as I don't have to get a part-time job. [*B limits the scope of his claim and adds a condition.*]

If you can imagine yourself in that conversation, as *either* A or B, you'll find nothing strange about assembling the argument of a research report, because every argument, research or not, is built out of the answers to five questions in that conversation, questions that you must ask yourself on your readers' behalf:

1. What is my **claim**?

2. What **reasons** support my claim?

3. What **evidence** supports my reasons?

4. Do I **acknowledge** alternatives/complications/objections, and how do I **respond**?

5. What **principle** makes my reasons *relevant* to my claim? (We call this principle a **warrant**.)

CLARIFYING SOME TERMS

So far, we've used two terms to name the sentence that sums up the results of your research. In the context of questions, we called it your *answer.* In the context of problems, we called it your *solution.* Now in the context of an argument, we'll call it your *claim.*

- A *claim* is a sentence that asserts something that may be true or false and so needs support: *The world is warming up.*
- The *main claim* of a report is the sentence (or more) that the whole report supports (some call this sentence your *thesis*). If you wrote a report to prove that the world is warming up, the sentence stating that would be your main claim.
- A *reason* is a sentence supporting a claim, main or not.

These terms can be confusing, because a reason is also a (sub)claim that can be supported by more reasons. What we call it depends on its context. For example:

TV can have harmful psychological effects on children*main claim* because when they are constantly exposed to violent images, they come to think violence is natural.*claim/reason 1 supporting main claim* Those exposed to lots of such visual entertainment tend to adopt the values of what they see.*claim/reason 2 supporting reason 1*

Reasons support main claims, but "lower" reasons can support "higher" reasons.

7.2 SUPPORTING YOUR CLAIM

At the core of every research report is the answer to your research question, the solution to your problem—your main claim. You have to back up that claim with two kinds of support: reasons and evidence.

7.2.1 Base Claims on Reasons

The first kind of support, a reason, is a statement that gives your readers cause to accept your claim. We often join a reason to a claim with *because*:

The emancipation of Russian peasants was an empty gesture*claim* because it did not improve the material quality of their daily lives.*reason*

TV violence can have harmful psychological effects on children$_{claim}$ because their constant exposure to violent images makes them think that violence is natural.$_{reason}$

You usually need more than one reason to support a contestable claim, and in a detailed argument, each reason will usually be a separate sentence.

7.2.2 Base Reasons on Evidence

The second kind of support is the evidence on which you base your reasons. Now the distinction between reasons and evidence can seem just a matter of semantics, and in some contexts the words do seem interchangeable:

You have to base your claim on good reasons.

You have to base your claim on good evidence.

But they are not synonyms, and distinguishing them is crucial in making sound arguments. Compare these two sentences:

What evidence do you base your reason on?

What reason do you base your evidence on?

That second sentence seems odd: we don't base evidence on reasons; we base reasons on evidence.

There are other differences:

• We think up reasons by the action of our mind.

• We have to search for evidence "out there" in the "hard" reality of the world, then make it available for everyone to see.

It makes no sense to ask, *Where do I go to see your reasons?* It does make sense to ask, *Where do I go to see your evidence?* For example, we can't see TV naturalizing violence for children, but we could see a child answer the question: *Do you think that fighting on TV is real?* In principle, *evidence* is what you and your readers can see, touch, taste, smell, or hear (or is accepted by everyone as a remembered fact—the sun came up yesterday morning). That oversimplifies the idea of "evidence from out there," but it illustrates the difference between evidence and reasons.

In casual conversation, we usually support a claim with just a reason:

> We should leave.$_{claim}$ It looks like rain.$_{reason}$

Few ask, *What's your evidence that it looks like rain?* But when you address serious issues, readers expect you to base each reason on its own foundation of evidence, because careful readers don't accept reasons at face value. They ask for the evidence, the data, the facts on which you base those reasons:

> TV violence can have harmful psychological effects on children$_{claim\ 1}$ because those exposed to lots of TV tend to adopt the values of what they see.$_{reason\ 1\ supporting\ claim\ 1/claim\ 2}$ Constant exposure to violent images makes them unable to distinguish fantasy from reality.$_{reason\ 2}$ $_{supporting\ reason\ 1\ and\ claim\ 2}$ Smith (1997) found that children ages 5–7 who watched more than three hours of violent television a day were 25 percent more likely to say that what they saw on television was "really happening."$_{evidence\ supporting\ reason\ 2}$

With reasons and evidence, we have the core of a research argument:

CLAIM *because of* ▸ REASON *based on* ▸ EVIDENCE

To offer a complete argument, however, you must add at least one more element and often a second: you must acknowledge other points of view and offer what we call *warrants*, which show how a reason is *relevant* to a claim.

7.3 ACKNOWLEDGING AND RESPONDING TO ANTICIPATED QUESTIONS AND OBJECTIONS

A responsible researcher supports a claim with reasons based on evidence. But unless your readers think exactly as you do (unlikely, given the fact that you have to make an argument in the first place), they may draw a different conclusion or even think of evidence you haven't. No thoughtful reader will accept your claim based solely on *your* views: you must also address theirs.

Careful readers will question *every* part of your argument, so you must anticipate as many of their questions as you can, and then acknowledge and respond to the most important ones. For example, when readers consider the claim that children exposed to violent TV adopt its values, they might wonder whether children are drawn to TV violence because they are *already* inclined to violence. If you think readers might ask that question, you would be wise to acknowledge and respond to it:

TV violence can have harmful psychological effects on children*claim 1* because those exposed to lots of it tend to adopt the values of what they see.*reason 1 supporting claim 1/claim 2* Their constant exposure to violent images makes them unable to distinguish fantasy from reality.*reason 2 supporting reason 1 and claim 2* Smith (1997) found that children ages 5–7 who watched more than three hours of violent television a day were 25 percent more likely to say that most of what they saw on television was "really happening."*evidence supporting reason 2* **Of course, some children who watch more violent entertainment might already be attracted to violence.**acknowledgment **But Jones (1999) found that children with no predisposition to violence were as attracted to violent images as those with a violent history.***response*

The challenge all researchers face, however, is not just responding to readers' questions, alternatives, and objections, but imagining them in the first place. (In chapter 10 we'll discuss the questions and objections you should expect.)

Since no research argument is complete without them, we add acknowledgment/responses to our diagram to show that they relate to all the other parts of an argument:

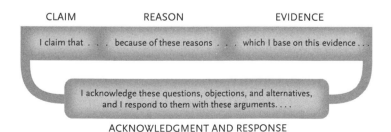

CLAIM   REASON   EVIDENCE

I claim that . . . because of these reasons . . . which I base on this evidence . . .

I acknowledge these questions, objections, and alternatives, and I respond to them with these arguments. . . .

ACKNOWLEDGMENT AND RESPONSE

7.4 WARRANTING THE RELEVANCE OF YOUR REASONS

Even when your readers agree that a reason is true, they may still object that it's not *relevant* to your claim. It's what most of us would say to this little argument:

We should leave$_{claim}$ because 2 + 2 = 4.$_{reason}$

Most of us think, *I don't get it. What's the connection?*

This is where the logic of an argument can get difficult to understand. For example, suppose you offer this less bizarre argument:

We are facing significantly higher health care costs in Europe and North America$_{claim}$ because global warming is moving the line of extended hard freezes steadily northward.$_{reason}$

Readers might accept the *truth* of that reason, but question its *relevance* to the claim, asking:

What do higher health costs have to do with hard freezes? I don't see the connection.

To answer, you must offer a *general* principle that justifies relating your *particular* reason to your *particular* claim:

When an area has fewer hard freezes, it must pay more to combat new diseases carried by subtropical insects no longer killed by those freezes.

Like all warrants, that one says that if a general circumstance exists (an area has fewer hard freezes), then we can infer a general consequence (that area will have higher costs to combat new diseases). The logic behind all warrants is that if a generalization is true, then so must be specific instances of it.

But for that logic to work, readers must agree with four things. Two are easy to understand:

1. The warrant is true: fewer hard freezes in fact mean higher medical costs.

2. The reason is true: hard freezes in fact are moving north.

The next two are more difficult:

3. The specific circumstance in the reason qualifies as a *plausible instance* of the general circumstance in the warrant.

4. The specific consequence in the claim qualifies as a *plausible instance* of the general consequence in the warrant.

We can illustrate that logic like this:

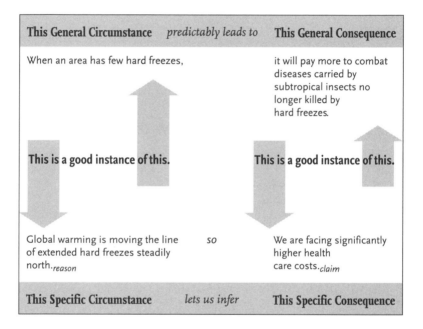

This General Circumstance	*predictably leads to*	This General Consequence

When an area has few hard freezes,

it will pay more to combat diseases carried by subtropical insects no longer killed by hard freezes.

This is a good instance of this.   This is a good instance of this.

Global warming is moving the line of extended hard freezes steadily north.*reason*   *so*   We are facing significantly higher health care costs.*claim*

This Specific Circumstance	*lets us infer*	This Specific Consequence

As we'll see, it's not easy to decide when you even need a warrant. Experienced researchers state them only when they think readers might question whether a reason is relevant to their claim. If you think they will see its relevance, you don't need a warrant. But if they might not, you must add a warrant to justify the connection, usually before you make it:

When an area has fewer hard freezes, it can expect higher medical costs to cope with diseases carried by subtropical insects that do not survive freezes.*warrant* Europe and North America must thus expect higher health care costs*main claim* because global warming is moving the line of extended hard freezes steadily north.*reason* In the last one hundred years, the line of hard freezes lasting more than two weeks has moved north at the rate of roughly . . .*evidence*

We can add warrants to our diagram to show that they connect a claim and its supporting reason:

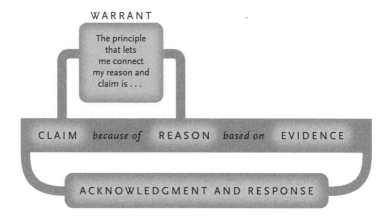

(We know this matter of warrants is not easy to grasp; we explain it again in more detail in chapter 11.)

7.5 BUILDING A COMPLEX ARGUMENT OUT OF SIMPLE ONES

Those five elements constitute the core of a "basic" argument. But arguments in research reports are more complex.

- We almost always support a claim with two or more reasons, each of which must be supported by its own evidence and perhaps justified by its own warrant.

- Since readers think of many alternatives and objections to any complex argument, careful researchers typically have to respond to more than one or two of them.

Moreover, each element of an argument may itself have to be treated as a subclaim, supported by its own argument:

- Each response to an objection may need reasons and evidence to support it.

- If your readers doubt the truth of a warrant, you may have to treat it as a subclaim and support it with its own argument, including reasons, evidence, and perhaps even its own warrant with its own acknowledgments and responses.

Only the evidence "stands alone," but even then you must explain where you got it and maybe why you think it's reliable, and that may require yet another argument.

And finally, most arguments include background, definitions, explanations of issues that readers might not understand, and so on. If, for example, you were making an argument about the relationship between inflation and money supply to readers not familiar with economic theory, you would have to explain how economists define "money." Serious arguments are complex constructions. Chapters 8–11 explain them in detail.

7.6 CREATING AN ETHOS BY THICKENING YOUR ARGUMENT

This process of "thickening" an argument is one way that writers earn the confidence of their readers. Readers judge your arguments not just by the facts you offer, but by how well you anticipate their questions and concerns. In so doing, they also judge the quality of your mind, even your implied character, traditionally called your *ethos*. Do you seem to be the sort of person who considers issues from all sides, who supports claims with evidence that readers accept, and who thoughtfully considers other points of view? Or do you seem to be someone who sees only what matters to her and dismisses or even ignores the views of others?

When you acknowledge other views and explain your principles of reasoning in warrants, you give readers good reason to work *with* you in developing and testing new ideas. In the long run, the ethos you project in individual arguments hardens into your reputation, something every researcher must care about, because your reputation is the tacit sixth element in every argument you write. It answers the unspoken question, *Can I trust you?* That answer must be *Yes.*

COGNITIVE OVERLOAD: SOME REASSURING WORDS

It's at about this point that many students new to research begin to feel overwhelmed. If so, your anxieties have less to do with your intelligence than with inexperience. One of us was explaining to teachers of legal writing how being a novice makes many first-year law students feel like incompetent writers. At the end of the talk, one woman reported that she had been a professor of anthropology whose published work was praised for the clarity of her writing. Then she switched careers and went to law school. She said that during her first six months, she wrote so incoherently that she feared she was suffering from a degenerative brain disease. Of course, she was not: she was going through a kind of temporary aphasia that afflicts most of us when we try to write about matters we do not entirely understand for an audience we understand even less. She was relieved to find that the better she understood the law, the better she wrote about it.

If you feel overwhelmed, you can take comfort in that story, as did one reader who e-mailed us this:

In *Craft of Research* you write about a woman who switched from anthropology to law and suddenly found herself unable to write clearly. After being an assistant professor of graphic design for five years, I recently switched to anthropology and suddenly found that writing anthropology papers is like pulling teeth. I thought to myself that I might have a degenerative brain disorder! I laughed out loud when I read about the anthropologist who switched to law. It made me feel a bit better.

A Common Mistake—Falling Back on What You Know

Arguments fail for many reasons, but inexperienced researchers often stumble when they rely too much on what feels familiar and fall back on kinds of argument they already know. If you learned in a first-year writing class to take a personal stand and search for evidence in your own experience, do not assume that you can do the same in fields that emphasize "objective data," such as sociology or experimental psychology. On the other hand, if as a psychology or biology major you learned to gather hard data and subject them to statistical analysis, do not assume that you can do the same in art history. This does not mean that what you learn in one class is useless in another. All fields share the elements of argument we describe here. But you have to learn what's distinctive in the way a field handles those elements and be flexible enough to adapt, trusting the skills you've learned.

You may oversimplify in a different way after you learn your field's typical problems, methods, schools of thought, and standard forms of argument. When some new researchers succeed with one kind of argument, they keep making it. They fail to see that their field, like every other, has a second kind of complexity: competing methodologies, competing solutions, competing goals and objectives—all marks of a lively field of inquiry. So when you learn to make one kind of argument, don't assume that you can apply it to every new claim. Seek out alternative methods, formulate not only multiple solutions but multiple ways of supporting them, ask whether others would approach your problem differently.

If you are new to your topic or to your field, you'll need ways to manage the complexity of new ideas and new ways of thinking. We discuss many of them in this book. But guard against the easy but risky way: uncritically imposing a familiar method on a new problem. The more you learn, the more you'll recognize that while things are not as blindingly complex as you first feared, neither are they as simple as you then hoped.

CHAPTER EIGHT

Making Claims

In this chapter we discuss how to evaluate the clarity and significance of the claim that answers your research question and serves as the main point of your report.

You need a tentative answer to your research question to focus your search for the data that will test and support its answer. As you test it, you'll likely revise it, but as you assemble your argument, you must also be sure that your claim is not just sound, but significant enough to need an argument in the first place. Ask yourself three questions:

1. What kind of claim should I make?

2. Is it specific enough?

3. Will readers think it is significant enough to need an argument supporting it?

When you can answer those three questions, you're ready to assemble your argument.

8.1 DETERMINING THE KIND OF CLAIM YOU SHOULD MAKE

The kind of problem you pose determines the kind of claim you make and the kind of argument you need to support it. As we saw in chapter 4, academic researchers usually pose not practical problems but conceptual ones, the kind whose solution asks readers not to *act* but to *understand*:

The recession of 2001–2002 was caused partly by excessive investment in IT systems that improved productivity less than expected.

Some conceptual claims seem to imply an action:

Businesses that invest in IT systems benefit only when they know how to use them to improve productivity.

But writers too often assume that readers will infer their intention better than most actually do. So if you want readers to act, be explicit about what action you want them to take:

Before investing in IT systems, a business should restructure its organization and management to use the system productively.

Be equally explicit if your claim is not practical but conceptual:

We have identified six factors IT managers should understand before making substantial investments.

You must be clear about the kind of argument you are making, because conceptual and practical claims require different kinds of arguments. If you pose a practical problem, readers will think that your claim is relevant to its solution only when they see you support *two* claims: one that explains what causes the problem and another that explains how doing what you propose will fix it.

But readers may also expect you to explain the following:

• Why your solution is feasible; how it can be implemented with reasonable time and effort.

• Why it will cost less to implement than the cost of the problem.

• Why it will not create a bigger problem than the one it solves.

• Why it is cheaper or faster than alternative solutions—a claim often difficult to support.

If readers look for but don't find those four sub-arguments, they may reject your whole argument.

So as you assemble your argument, be clear about the kind of claim you are making, whether it's conceptual or practical. Don't try to inflate the importance of a conceptual claim by tacking on a practical action, at least not early in your report. If you want to suggest a practical application of your conceptual claim, do it in your conclusion. There you can offer it as an action worth considering without having to develop a case for it (we return to this in chapter 16).

8.2 EVALUATING YOUR CLAIM

We can't tell you how to find a good claim, but we can show you how to evaluate the one you have from your readers' point of view. Most important, they expect your claim to be both specific and significant.

8.2.1 Make Your Claim Specific

Vague claims lead to vague arguments. The more specific your claim, the more it helps you plan your argument and keep your readers on track as they read it. You make a claim more specific through specific language and logic.

SPECIFIC LANGUAGE. Compare these claims:

TV inflates estimates of crime rates.

Graphic reports of violence on local TV news lead regular viewers to overestimate by as much as 150 percent both the rate of crime in their neighborhood and the personal danger to themselves and their families.

The first claim is so vague that we have little idea about what's to come. The second has more specific concepts that not only help readers understand the claim more clearly, but also give the writer a richer set of concepts to develop in what follows.

We do *not* recommend long, wordy claims for their own sake. But you benefit when you include in early versions of your claim more terms than you might ultimately use. That final claim should be only as specific as your readers need and should include only those concepts that you develop as themes in your argument.

SPECIFIC LOGIC. You can also be specific in the logic of your claim. Even with its specific language, this claim offers only a single proposition:

> Regular TV viewers overestimate both the rate of crime in their neighborhood and the personal danger to themselves and their families.

In the natural and social sciences, claims like that are common, even preferred. But in the humanities, such a claim might seem a bit thin. As you draft your working claim, try elaborating its logic in two ways:

• Introduce it with a qualifying clause beginning with *although* or *even though.*

• Conclude it with a reason clause beginning with *because.*

For example:

> **Although violent crime is actually decreasing,** regular TV viewers overestimate their neighborhood crime rate by 150 percent and therefore misjudge personal danger to themselves and their families, **because local TV evening news regularly opens with graphic reports of mayhem and murder in familiar locations, making many believe that crime happens nightly outside their front door.**

While that claim may be overblown, it foreshadows three of the five elements that you need in a full argument: (1) *Although I acknowledge X,* (2) *I claim Y,* (3) *because of reason Z.*

You can use an introductory *although* clause to acknowledge three kinds of alternative views:

• something that your readers believe but your claim challenges

> Although most people believe they are good judges of their security, regular TV viewers overestimate . . .

• a point of view that conflicts with yours

> Although many security professionals see fear as the best motiva-
> tion for safety precautions, regular TV viewers overestimate . . .

- a condition that limits the scope or confidence of your claim

> Although it is difficult to gauge their real feelings about personal
> security, regular TV viewers overestimate . . .

If readers might think of those qualifications, acknowledge them
first. You not only imply that you understand their views, but
commit yourself to responding to them in the course of your argument.

When you add a final *because* clause, you forecast some of the
reasons that support your claim:

> Although many believe that school uniforms help lower the inci-
> dence of violence in public schools,$_{qualification}$ the evidence is at best
> weak,$_{claim}$ **because researchers have not controlled for other mea-
> sures that have been instituted at the same time as uniforms**$_{reason\ 1}$
> **and because the data reported are statistically suspect.**$_{reason\ 2}$

Again, we don't suggest that your final draft should offer a claim
as bloated as these. But the richer your working claim, the more
complex your argument is likely to be.

8.2.2 Make Your Claim Significant

After the accuracy of a claim, readers look most closely at its
significance, a quality they measure by how much it asks them to
change what they think. While we can't quantify significance, we
can roughly estimate it: *If readers accept a claim, how many other
beliefs must they change?* The most significant claims ask a research community to change its deepest beliefs (and it will resist
such claims accordingly).

Some research communities consider a claim significant
enough if it asks them only to accept new data on a topic of common interest:

> I describe here six thirteenth-century Latin grammars of the
> Welsh language. Found just recently, these grammars are the only

examples of their kind. They help us better appreciate the range of grammars written in the medieval period.

(Recall those reels of newly discovered film in 2.3.3.)

Readers value research more highly when it not only offers new data but *uses* them to settle what seems puzzling, inconsistent, or otherwise problematical:

> There has been a long debate about how fluctuations in consumer confidence affect the stock market, but new statistical tools suggest little relationship.

But readers value most highly new facts when they *upset* what seemed long settled:

> It has long been an article of faith in modern physics that the speed of light is constant everywhere at all times, under all conditions, but new data suggest it might not be.

A claim like that will be contested by legions of physicists, because if it is true, they will have to change their minds about lots of things other than the speed of light.

Early in your career, you won't be expected to know what those in a field think should (or even could) be corrected. But you can still gauge the significance of your claim by asking how strongly readers might *contest* it. One way to do that is by considering the contestability of its *opposite* claim. For example, consider these two claims:

> Hamlet is not a superficial character.

> This report summarizes recent research on the disappearance of bees.

To assess how much either claim is worth contesting, change an affirmative claim into a negative one and vice versa:

> Hamlet *is* a superficial character.

> This report does *not* summarize recent research on the disappearance of bees.

If the reverse of a claim seems obviously false (like the first one) or trivial (like the second), then readers are likely to think the original claim is not worth an argument. (Of course, some great thinkers have successfully contradicted apparently self-evident claims, as Copernicus did when he asserted foolishly—or so it seemed at the time—that *the sun does* not *go around the earth.*)

If you are an advanced researcher, you measure the significance of your claim by how much it changes what your community thinks and how it does its research. Few discoveries have been as significant as Crick and Watson's structure of DNA. Not only did it make biologists think about genetics differently, but it opened up new lines of research.

But you don't have to make big claims to make a useful contribution: small findings can open up new lines of thinking. If, for example, you discovered that Abraham Lincoln read some obscure philosopher, historians would comb Lincoln's texts for traces of that influence.

If you are new to research, of course, your claim doesn't have to challenge the experts, just impress your teacher. If you can't predict whether it will, imagine your reader is someone like yourself. What did *you* think before you began your research? How much has your claim changed what *you* now think? What do *you* understand now that you didn't before? That's the best way to prepare for readers who will someday ask you the most devastating question any researcher can face: not *Why should I believe this?* but *Why should I care?*

☞ QUICK TIP: *Qualifying Claims to Enhance Your Credibility*

Some new researchers think their claims are most credible when they are stated most forcefully. But nothing damages your ethos more than arrogant certainty. As paradoxical as it seems, you make your argument stronger and more credible by modestly acknowledging its limits. You gain readers' trust when you acknowledge and respond to their views, showing that you have not only understood but considered their position (for more, see chapter 10). But you can lose that trust if you then make claims that overreach their support. Limit your claims to what your argument can actually support by qualifying their scope and certainty.

ACKNOWLEDGE LIMITING CONDITIONS
Every claim has limiting conditions:

> We conclude that the epicenter of the earthquake was fifty miles southwest of Tokyo, **assuming the instrumentation was accurately calibrated.**

> We believe that aviation manufacturing will not match its late twentieth-century levels, **unless new global conflicts increase military spending.**

But every claim is subject to countless conditions, so mention only those that readers might plausibly think of. Scientists rarely acknowledge that their claims depend on the accuracy of their instruments, because everyone expects them to ensure that they are. But economists often acknowledge limits on their claims, both because their predictions are subject to changing conditions and because readers want to know which conditions to watch for.

Consider mentioning important limiting conditions even if you feel readers would not think of them. For example, in this next example, the writer not only shows that she was careful, but gives a fuller and more accurate statement of the claim:

Today Franklin D. Roosevelt is revered as one of our most admired historical figures, but toward the end of his second term, he was quite unpopular, **at least among certain segments of American society.**_{claim} Newspapers, for example, attacked him for promoting socialism, a sign that a modern administration is in trouble. In 1938, 70 percent of Midwest newspapers accused him of wanting the government to manage the banking system. . . . Some have argued otherwise, including Nicholson (1983, 1992) and Wiggins (1973), both of whom offer anecdotal reports that Roosevelt was always in high regard,_{acknowledgment} but these reports are supported only by the memories of those who had an interest in deifying FDR._{response} **Unless it can be shown that the newspapers critical of Roosevelt were controlled by special interests,**_{limitation on claim} their attacks demonstrate significant popular dissatisfaction with Roosevelt's presidency._{restatement of claim}

USE HEDGES TO LIMIT CERTAINTY

Only rarely can we state in good conscience that we are 100 percent certain that our claims are unqualifiedly true. Careful writers qualify their certainty with words and phrases called *hedges*. For example, if anyone was entitled to be assertive, it was Crick and Watson, the discoverers of the helical structure of DNA. But when they announced their discovery, they hedged the certainty of their claims (hedges are boldfaced; the introduction is condensed):

> We **wish to suggest a** [note: not *state the*] structure for the salt of deoxyribose nucleic acid (D.N.A.). . . . A structure for nucleic acid has already been proposed by Pauling and Corey. . . . **In our opinion,** this structure is unsatisfactory for two reasons: (1) **We believe** that the material which gives the X-ray diagrams is the salt, not the free acid. . . . (2) **Some** of the van der Waals distances **appear** to be too small. (J. D. Watson and F. H. C. Crick, "Molecular Structure of Nucleic Acids.")

Without the hedges, Crick and Watson would be more concise but more aggressive. Compare that cautious passage with this more forceful version (much of the aggressive tone comes from the *lack* of qualification):

> We **announce** here **the** structure for the salt of deoxyribose nucleic acid (D.N.A.). . . . A structure for nucleic acid has already been proposed by Pauling and Corey. . . . Their structure **is** unsatisfactory for two reasons: (1) The material which gives their X-ray diagrams is the salt, not the free acid. . . . (2) Their van der Waals distances **are** too small.

Of course, if you hedge too much, you will seem timid or uncertain. But in most fields, readers distrust flatfooted certainty expressed in words like *all, no one, every, always, never,* and so on. Some teachers say they object to all hedging, but what most of them really reject are hedges that qualify every trivial claim. And some fields do tend to use fewer hedges than others. It takes a deft touch. Hedge too much and you seem mealy-mouthed; too little and you seem smug. Unfortunately, the line between them is thin. So watch how those in your field manage uncertainty, then do likewise.

CHAPTER NINE

Assembling Reasons and Evidence

In this chapter we discuss two kinds of support for a claim: reasons and evidence. We show you how to distinguish the two, how to use reasons to organize your argument, and how to evaluate the quality of your evidence.

Readers look first for the core of an argument, a claim and its support. They look particularly at its set of reasons to judge its plausibility and their order to judge its logic. If they think those reasons make consecutive sense, they will look for the evidence they rest on, the bedrock of every argument. If they don't believe the evidence, they'll reject the reasons, and with them the claim.

So as you assemble the core of your argument, you must offer readers a plausible set of reasons, in a clear, logical order, based on evidence they will accept. This chapter shows you how to do that.

9.1 USING REASONS TO PLAN YOUR ARGUMENT

When you order your reasons, you outline the logical structure of your argument. You can do that in a traditional outline, but you may find it more useful to create a chartlike outline known as a "storyboard." To start a storyboard, write your main claim and each reason (and subreason) at the top of separate cards or pages. Then below each reason (or subreason), list the evidence that supports it. If you don't have it yet, note the *kind* of evidence you'll need. Finally arrange the pages on a table or wall to make their logical relationships visible at a glance.

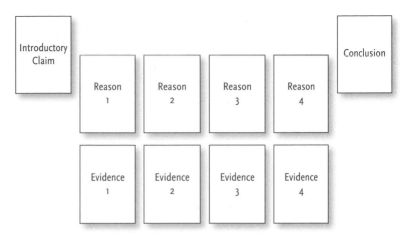

Read just the reasons across the tops of the pages to see if that order makes consecutive sense. If it doesn't, try out different orders until it does. Focus not on details, but on the major reasons; when you test different orders, move around whole reasons pages (and any connected pages). Don't worry if this chart makes your argument feel mechanical. At this point, it outlines only your argument, not your report. When you plan a first draft, you'll reconsider your reasons in light of your readers' understanding (and yours) and maybe plan a new order (for more on ordering parts, see 12.2.3).

9.2 DISTINGUISHING EVIDENCE FROM REASONS

Once you've arranged your reasons in a plausible order, be sure you have sufficient evidence to support each one. Readers will not accept a reason until they see it anchored in what *they* consider to be a bedrock of established fact.

The problem is, you don't get to decide that. Remember that to count as evidence, a statement must report a shared, public fact— what readers agree not to question, at least for the purposes of the argument. But if they do question it, what you think is hard factual evidence is for them only a reason, and you have not yet reached that bedrock of evidence on which your argument must rest.

Consider this little argument:

American higher education should review its "hands-off" policy toward off-campus drinking,*claim* because dangerous binge drinking has become a common behavior.*reason* **The injuries and death it causes have increased in frequency and intensity, not only at big "party" schools but among first-year students at small colleges.***evidence*

In that last sentence, the writer offers what she believes is a "fact" hard enough to serve as evidence to support her reason.

But a skeptical reader might ask, *That's just a generalization. What hard numbers do you have to back up "increased in frequency and intensity"? How many schools do you have solid data on? And what do you mean by "big," "party," and "small"?* Such a reader treats that statement not as an unquestioned fact but as a soft reason still in need of hard evidence. The writer would have to add something like this:

In 2001–2006, there was a 19 percent increase in episodes of binge drinking resulting in death or injury by first-year students at a representative sample of small colleges (fewer than two thousand students; see appendix 1 for a list).*evidence*

Of course a *really* skeptical reader could again ask, *What backs up those numbers?* If so, the writer would have to provide still harder data, the specific numbers for each school. If she did her own research, she could show her raw data and the questionnaires she used to gather them (which themselves might be subject to still more skeptical questioning). If she found her data in a secondary source, she could cite it and reproduce its data tables, but she might then be asked to prove that her source is reliable. Really skeptical readers just never give up.

If you can imagine readers plausibly asking, not once but many times, *How do you know that? What facts make it true?*, you have not yet reached what readers want—a bedrock of uncontested evidence. And at a time when so-called experts are quick to tell us what to do and think based on studies whose data we never see, careful readers have learned to view reports of evidence skeptically. Even when you think you have good evidence, be clear how it was collected and by whom. If it was collected by others, find and cite a source as close to the evidence as you can get.

OUR FOUNDATIONAL METAPHORS FOR EVIDENCE
When we talk about evidence, we typically use foundational metaphors: good evidence is *solid, hard, the bedrock foundation* on which we *build* arguments, something we can *see for ourselves*. Bad evidence is *flimsy, weak,* or *thin.* Language like that encourages readers to think of evidence as a reality independent of anyone's interpretation and judgment. But data are always constructed and shaped by those who collect and use them as evidence. As you build your argument, keep in mind that your evidence will *count* as evidence only if your readers accept it without question, at least for the moment.

9.3 DISTINGUISHING EVIDENCE FROM REPORTS OF IT

Now a complication that may seem to split hairs: we rarely include in any report *the evidence itself.* Even if you collect your own data, counting rabbits in a field or interviewing the unemployed, your report can only *refer to* or *represent* those rabbits and unemployed in words, numbers, tables, graphs, pictures, and so on. For example, when a prosecutor says in court, *Jones was a drug dealer, and here is the evidence to prove it,* he can hold up a bag of cocaine, even let jurors hold it in their own hands. (Of course, both he and the jurors must believe the officer who says it's the same bag he took from Jones and the chemist who says that the white stuff really is cocaine.) But when he *writes* a brief on the case, he cannot staple that bag to the page; he can only refer to or describe it.

In the same way, researchers cannot share with their readers "the evidence itself."

Emotions play a larger role in rationality than many think.*claim* In fact, without the emotional centers of the brain, we could not make rational decisions.*reason 1 supporting claim* Persons whose brains have suffered physical damage to their emotional centers cannot make the simplest decisions.*reason 2 supporting reason 1* For example, consider the case of Mr. Y, who . . .*report of evidence*

That argument doesn't offer as evidence real people with damaged brains; it can only report observations of their behavior, copies of their brain scans, tables of their reaction times, and so on. (In fact, we prefer to read reports of others than to have to test brains and read MRI scans ourselves.)

We know this distinction between evidence and reports of evidence must seem a fine one, but it emphasizes two important issues. First, data you take from a source have invariably been shaped by that source, not to misrepresent them, but to put them in a form that serves that source's ends. For example, suppose you want to show that the cult of celebrity distorts rational compensation, and you need evidence that athletes and entertainers are paid far more than top doctors, generals, and government officials. You could find government salaries in official reports. But unless you can peek at the tax returns of Oprah and Tiger Woods (and who knows how reliable they would be), you would have to depend on reports of those incomes that may or may not have been systematically collected and compiled from still more distant reports. Unless you can talk to those who counted, organized, and reported the original data, you'll be three or four removes from the evidence itself before you use it for your own purposes. (And at least one reporter in that chain of reports almost certainly miscopied some of the data.)

Second, when you in turn report that data as your own evidence, you cannot avoid manipulating them once again, at least by putting them in a new context. Even if you collected the data yourself, you tidied them up, making them seem more coherent than what you actually saw, counted, and recorded in your notes. In fact, even before you started collecting any facts at all, you had to decide what to count, how to categorize the numbers, how to order them, whether to present them in the form of a table, bar chart, or graph. Even photographs and video recordings reflect a particular point of view. In short, facts are shaped by those who collect them and again by the intentions of those who use them. This often squishy quality of reports of reports (of reports of reports) is why people who read lots of research are so demanding about the reliability of evidence. If you collect data yourself, they'll want to know how you did it. If you depend on sources, they'll expect you to use primary sources, and if you didn't, to get as close to them as you can. And they want complete citations and a bibliography so that they could, if they wanted to, look at your sources themselves. In short, they want to know that they can trust the complete chain of reports between what's "out there" and what they are reading.

We live in an age where we are all subjected to research reports and opinion surveys that are at best dubious and at worst faked, so you have to assure your readers that they can trust your data. The last link in that chain of credibility is you, so be thoughtful about whose data you use and how you use them.

TRUSTING EVIDENCE THREE HUNDRED YEARS AGO AND NOW
In the early days of experimental science, researchers conducted experiments before what they called "witnesses," reputable scientists who observed the experiments so that they could attest to the accuracy of the reported evidence. Researchers don't rely on witnesses anymore. Instead, each area of study has standardized its methodologies for collecting and reporting evidence to ensure that it is reliable (though some researchers still get away with fraud). When you observe the standard procedures in your field, you encourage readers to accept your evidence at your word, without their needing to see it themselves. So as you read secondary sources, note the kind of evidence they cite, how they cite it, then do likewise. When in sociology, do as sociologists do.

9.4 EVALUATING YOUR EVIDENCE

Once you know the kind of evidence your readers expect, you must test the reliability of yours: is it sufficient and representative, reported accurately and precisely, and taken from an authoritative source? These are not exotic criteria unique to academic research. We all apply them in our most ordinary conversations, even with children. In the following, "P" faults "C" on all those criteria:

C: I need new sneakers.*claim* Look. These are too small.*evidence*

P: Your feet haven't grown that much in a month, and they don't seem to hurt you much [*i.e., your evidence could be relevant, but I reject it because it is not accurate and because even if it were accurate, "too small" is not sufficiently precise*].

C: But they're too grungy for school.*reason* Look at this dirt and these raggedy laces.*evidence*

P: The dirt will wash off and the laces can be replaced. That's not enough to buy new sneakers [*i.e., you may be factually correct, but dirt and raggedy laces alone are not sufficient evidence that they are unfit for school*].

C: They hurt.*reason* Look at how I limp.*evidence*

P: You were walking fine a minute ago [*i.e., your evidence is not representative*].

C: Everybody thinks I should get new sneakers.*reason* Harry said so.*evidence*

P: Harry's opinion doesn't matter in this house [*i.e., Harry may have said that, but his opinions are not authoritative*].

Readers judge reports of evidence by the same criteria P uses. They want evidence to be accurate, precise, sufficient, representative, and authoritative. (Readers also expect evidence to be *relevant*, but we'll discuss that in chapter 11.) As you assemble your evidence, screen it for those criteria before you add it to your storyboard.

9.4.1 Report Evidence Accurately

Careful readers are predisposed to be skeptical, so they will seize on the most trivial mistake in your evidence as a sign of your irredeemable unreliability in everything else. Whether your paper depends on data collected in a lab, in the field, in the library, or online, record those data completely and clearly, then double-check them before, as, and after you write them up. Getting the easy things right shows respect for your readers and is the best training for dealing with the hard things. You can sometimes use even questionable evidence, *if you acknowledge its dubious quality*. In fact, if you point to evidence that seems to support your claim but then reject it as unreliable, you show yourself to be cautious, self-critical, and thus trustworthy.

9.4.2 Be Appropriately Precise
Your readers want you to state your evidence precisely. They hear warning bells in words that so hedge your claim that they cannot assess its substance:

> The Forest Service has spent **a great deal** of money to prevent forest fires, but there is still **a high probability** of **large, costly** ones.

How much money is *a great deal?* How probable is *a high probability*—30 percent? 80 percent? What counts as *large* and *costly?* Watch for words like *some, most, many, almost, often, usually, frequently, generally,* and so on. Such words can appropriately limit the breadth of a claim (see the Quick Tip in chapter 8), but they can also fudge it if the researcher didn't work hard enough to get the precise numbers.

What counts as precise, however, differs by field. A physicist measures the life of quarks in fractions of a nanosecond, so the tolerable margin of error is vanishingly small. A historian gauging when the Soviet Union was at the point of collapse would estimate it in months. A paleontologist might date a new species give or take tens of thousands of years. According to the standards of their fields, all three are appropriately precise. (Evidence can also be too precise. Only a foolhardy historian would assert that the Soviet Union reached its point of inevitable collapse at 2:13 p.m. on August 18, 1987.)

9.4.3 Provide Sufficient, Representative Evidence
Beginners typically offer too little evidence. They think they prove a claim with one quotation, one number, one personal experience

(though sometimes only one bit of evidence is sufficient to *disprove* it).

> Shakespeare must have hated women because those in *Hamlet* and *Macbeth* are evil or weak.

Readers need more than that to accept such a significant claim.

Even if you offer lots of evidence, your readers still expect it to be *representative* of the full range of variation in what's available. The women in one or two Shakespearean plays do not represent all his women, any more than Shakespeare represents all Elizabethan drama. Readers are especially wary when your evidence is a small sample from a large body of data, as in surveys. Whenever you use sampled data, not only must your data *be* representative, but you must show that it is.

Different fields define and evaluate evidence differently. If you're a beginner, you'll need time to learn the kinds of evidence that readers in your field accept and reject. The most painful way to gain that experience is to be the object of their criticism. Less painful is to seek examples of arguments that failed because their evidence was judged unreliable. Listen to lectures and class discussions for the kinds of arguments that your instructors criticize because they think the evidence is weak. Failed arguments help you understand what counts as reliable better than do successful ones.

CHAPTER TEN

Acknowledgments and Responses

No argument is complete that fails to acknowledge and respond to other points of view. This chapter shows how these acknowledgments help all researchers, beginning or advanced, convince readers that they are thoughtful and judicious.

The core of your argument is a claim backed by reasons based on evidence. You thicken that core with more reasons, perhaps supporting each reason with subreasons and their supporting evidence. But if you plan your argument only around claims, reasons, and evidence, your readers may think your argument is not only thin but, worse, ignorant or dismissive of their views. You must respond to their predictable questions and objections.

As you plan and draft your report, however, your readers won't be there to object, question you, or offer their own views. So you have to *imagine* their questions, not just the predictable ones that they ask about any argument, but those that question yours in particular. It's when you can acknowledge and respond to those imagined questions, with their suggested alternatives and ouright objections, that your report not only speaks in your voice but brings in the voices of others. That's how you establish a cooperative relationship with readers, by acknowledging their imagined presence and speaking on their behalf.

In this chapter we show you how to anticipate two kinds of questions that readers may ask about your argument:

- They may question its *intrinsic* soundness: the clarity of your claim, the relevance of your reasons, the quality of your evidence.

- They may also question its *extrinsic* soundness by asking you to consider alternatives—different ways of framing the problem, evidence you've overlooked, what others have written on your topic.

When you imagine, acknowledge, and respond to both kinds of questions, you create an argument that readers are more likely to trust.

10.1 QUESTIONING YOUR ARGUMENT AS YOUR READERS WILL

While you must acknowledge other views, don't focus on them as you assemble the core of your argument (claim, reasons, and evidence). You may freeze up if you try to imagine every possible alternative. But once you create that core, imagine colleagues questioning your argument more sharply than you hope your readers will.

For this exercise, you might suspend your conception of argument as collaborative inquiry and imagine it not quite as warfare, but as something close to a warm debate. Read your argument as someone who has a stake in a different outcome—who *wants* you to be wrong. That will be hard, because you know your argument too well and may believe in it too much.

First, question your problem:

1. Why do you think there's a problem at all? What are the costs or consequences in this situation?

2. Why have you defined the problem as you have? Is it conceptual or pragmatic? Maybe the problem involves not the issue you raise but another one.

Now question your solution:

3. What kind of solution do you propose? Does it ask me to do something or to understand something? Does it match the problem exactly? Are they both practical or both conceptual?

4. Have you stated your claim too strongly? I can think of exceptions and limitations.

5a. Why is your conceptual answer better than others? It contradicts our well-established knowledge.

5b. Why is your practical solution better than others? It will cost too much, take too much time, or create new problems.

If you imagine a question that you can't answer, decide whether you can find the answer before you go on. Don't go easy on yourself with this one: the time to fix a problem with your argument is when you find it.

Note where your argument looks weak but is not. If, for example, you anticipate that readers will think your solution has costs that it does not, you can defuse that concern by acknowledging and responding to it:

> It might seem that by recognizing genetic factors in homosexuality we challenge the role of free will in sexual orientation. But in fact . . .

Next, question your support, imagining your reader asking these questions about your evidence:

1. I want to see a different *kind* of evidence—hard numbers, not anecdotes. (Or—stories about real people, not cold numbers.)

2. Your evidence isn't accurate. The numbers don't add up.

3. It isn't precise enough. What do you mean by "many"?

4. It isn't current. There's newer research than this.

5. It isn't representative. You didn't get data on all the groups.

6. It isn't authoritative. Smith is no expert on this matter.

The toughest objection, however, is usually this one:

7. You need more evidence. One data point (quotation, number, anecdote) is not proof.

Most researchers have difficulty finding enough good evidence to make a solid case, especially those working on short deadlines.

But teachers grumble most about students who seem to think that the evidence they find first is all they need.

The problem of sufficient evidence is even worse when readers resist your solution because they have a stake in a different one. When they do, you can expect them to demand more evidence of higher quality, perhaps more than you have time to find. So if you feel your evidence is less than unassailable, you may want to admit its limitations candidly before your reader rejects your argument because you didn't acknowledge its uncertainty.

Finally, readers may also feel that your claim just doesn't follow from your reason, because that reason seems irrelevant to your claim. But that's an issue so vexed that we devote all of chapter 11 to it.

In sum: A crucial step in assembling your argument is to test your argument as your readers will, even in ways they might not. Then acknowledge and respond to at least the most important objections that you can imagine them raising. Show readers that you put your argument through your own wringer, before they put it through theirs.

10.2 IMAGINING ALTERNATIVES TO YOUR ARGUMENT

When you candidly acknowledge weak spots in your argument, you seem more credible by showing readers that you are trying to make an honest case and dealing with them fairly. But that is a defensive move, not one that actively brings their views into your argument. For that, you have to imagine those views and how they point to alternatives. That's easy when you know your readers well, but even if you don't, you can rely on some strategies to help. (At this point, return to the amiable, collaborative image of readers.)

As you read your sources, you will find examples of how others have thought, if not about your specific question, then at least about your topic (review 6.5). Note where a source takes an approach different from yours, focuses on different aspects of the problem, and so on, especially where you and your source disagree. Also note where one source takes issue with another, especially if you disagree with the second source. Even if those disagreements do not help you make your argument, they may help you see alternatives to acknowledge. If you know how you can respond to those alternatives, add them to your notes now.

Don't dismiss evidence because you think it is irrelevant or unreliable. If your readers might consider it relevant, acknowledge it but explain why you didn't use it. That's one way to compensate for not having enough evidence of your own. As you take notes, pay as much attention to disagreements and alternatives as to the data that support your claim. You'll not only understand your problem better, but you'll better anticipate weaknesses in or limits to your argument.

10.3 DECIDING WHAT TO ACKNOWLEDGE

If you can imagine just a few of the questions, alternatives, and objections your readers might have, you'll face a Goldilocks moment: acknowledge too many and you distract readers from the core of your argument; acknowledge too few and you seem indifferent to or even ignorant of their views. You need to figure out how many will feel "just right."

10.3.1 Selecting Objections to Respond To

To narrow your list of alternatives or objections, consider these priorities:

- plausible charges of weaknesses that you can rebut

- alternative lines of argument important in your field

- alternative conclusions that readers *want* to be true

- alternative evidence that readers know

- important counterexamples that you have to explain away

Look for alternatives that let you repeat a part of your argument. For example, if readers might think of exceptions to a definition that in fact are not, acknowledge them and use the response to reinforce your point:

> Some have argued that even food can be addictive, but remember we are concerned here only with substances for which addiction is the norm, not those . . .

Or if readers might think of an alternative solution close to yours, use it to reiterate the virtues of your solution:

> Most researchers argue that rules and other forms of formal writing advice degrade rather then improve performance because writing "is a non-conscious act of making meaning, not a conscious process of following rules." That is true for parts of the process: writers should not consult rules as they draft sentences. But writing involves not just drafting but many conscious processes. What we show here is what kinds of formal advice do and do not work for *conscious* aspects of writing. . . .

Finally, acknowledge alternatives that may particularly appeal to your readers, but only if you can respond without seeming to be dismissive. Better to ignore what your readers like than to disparage it.

10.3.2 Acknowledging Questions You Can't Answer

All researchers are uneasy about questions they can't answer. If you discover a flaw that you cannot fix or explain away, try to redefine your problem or rebuild your argument to avoid it. But if you cannot, you face a tough decision. You could ignore the problem, hoping readers won't notice. But that's dishonest. If they do notice, you have a bigger problem because they will doubt your competence. And if they think you tried to hide a weakness, they will question your honesty. In any case, the damage could be fatal, not only to your argument but to your own ethos and reputation.

Our advice may seem naive, but it works: Candidly acknowledge the problem and respond that

- the rest of your argument more than balances the flaw

- while the flaw is serious, more research will show a way around it

- while the flaw makes it impossible to accept your claim fully, your argument offers important insight into the question and suggests what a better answer would need

Occasionally researchers turn failure into success by turning the claim they *wanted* to support but couldn't into a hypothesis that people might *think* is reasonable but turns out not to be. Then they show why not:

> It might seem that when jurors hear the facts of a case in a form that focuses on the victim and emphasizes her suffering, they will be more likely to blame the accused. That is, after all, the standard practice of plaintiffs' lawyers. But in fact, we found no correlation between . . .

Experienced researchers and teachers understand that any one person's version of the truth is complicated, usually ambiguous, and always contestable. They will think better of your argument and of you if you acknowledge its limits, especially those that squeeze you more than you like. Concessions invite readers into the conversation by legitimizing their views, always a gesture that helps sustain a community of researchers.

10.4 FRAMING YOUR RESPONSES AS SUBORDINATE ARGUMENTS

You must, however, do more than just acknowledge your imagined readers' alternatives and objections; you must also respond to them. Even a minimal response gives a reason to limit or reject what you have acknowledged:

> Some have argued that food can be addictive,*acknowledgment of alternative claim* but we are concerned here only with substances for which addiction is the norm.*reason why alternative is irrelevant*

That initial response may be enough, but only if readers recognize the basis for it, either because it's obvious or because you've made the argument before. Otherwise, explain its basis using additional reasons and evidence:

Some have argued that food can be addictive,*acknowledgment of alternative claim* but we are concerned here only with substances for which addiction is the norm.*reason why alternative is irrelevant* Some who taste chocolate once may be unable to resist it thereafter, but their number is a fraction of those who are immediately addicted to crack cocaine after a single exposure.*subreason* Chernowitz (1998) found that just one exposure resulted . . .*report of evidence*

For more substantial responses, you need a full argument, with multiple reasons, evidence, and perhaps even warrants and additional acknowledgments and responses. (At this point, add acknowledgments and responses to the appropriate places in the working plan of your argument. In chapter 12 we'll discuss where to put them in the plan of your first draft.)

When you respond to alternatives with reasons and evidence for rejecting them, you "thicken" your argument, making it increasingly rich and complex, thereby enhancing your credibility as someone who does not oversimplify complex issues. Readers respect you and your argument when you bring their voices into your report by acknowledging their views. But this is a Goldilocks choice: not too much, not too little. Unfortunately, you can learn to make the right choices only with experience. So notice how experts do it, then do likewise.

10.5 THE VOCABULARY OF ACKNOWLEDGMENT AND RESPONSE

Some writers fail to acknowledge alternatives because they can't think of any. The strategies in this chapter will help you overcome that problem. Others can think of views to acknowledge, but fear that if they do, they weaken their argument. In fact, most readers think that such acknowledgments enhance a writer's credibility.

A third reason writers don't acknowledge objections and alternatives is the easiest to fix: they lack a vocabulary to express them. What follows is that vocabulary. To be sure (that's one of those terms), your first efforts in using these words and phrases may seem awkward (*may* is common in acknowledgments), *but* (a response typically begins with *but* or *however*) the more you use them, the more natural they will feel.

10.5.1 Acknowledging Objections and Alternatives

When you respond to an alternative or objection, you can mention and dismiss it or address it at length. We offer these expressions roughly in that order, from most dismissive to most respectful. (Brackets and slashes indicate alternative choices.)

1. You can downplay an objection or alternative by introducing it with *despite, regardless of,* or *notwithstanding*:

    [**Despite/Regardless of/Notwithstanding**] Congress's claims that it wants to cut taxes,*acknowledgment* the public believes that . . .*response*

    Use *although, while,* and *even though* in the same way:

    [**Although/While/Even though**] there are economic problems in Hong Kong,*acknowledgment* Southeast Asia remains a strong . . .*response*

2. You can signal an acknowledgment indirectly with *seem, appear, may,* and *could,* or with an adverb like *plausibly, justifiably, reasonably, surprisingly,* or even *certainly*:

    In his letters Lincoln expresses what [**seems/appears**] to be depression.*acknowledgment* But those who observed him . . .*response*

    This proposal [**may have/plausibly has**] some merit,*acknowledgment* but we . . .*response*

3. You can acknowledge alternatives by attributing them to an unnamed source or to no source at all, which gives a little weight to the objection:

    It is easy to [**think/imagine/say/claim/argue**] that taxes should . . . But there is [**another/alternative/possible**] [**explanation/line of argument/account/possibility**].

    Some evidence [**might/may/can/could/does**] [**suggest/indicate/point to/lead some to think**] that we should . . . , but . . .

4. You can attribute an alternative to a more specific source, giving it more weight:

> There are [**some/many/a few**] who [**might/may/could/would**] [**say/think/argue/claim/charge/object**] that Cuba is not . . . But in fact, . . .

Note that researchers sometimes weaken their case by prematurely downgrading those they will disagree with:

> Some **naive** researchers have claimed that . . .

> The **occasionally careless** historian H has even claimed that . . .

Save criticism for the response, and direct it at the work rather than the person.

5. You can acknowledge an alternative in your own voice, with a passive verb or with an adverb such as *admittedly, granted, to be sure,* and so on, conceding it some validity:

> I [**understand/know/realize**] that liberals believe in . . . , but . . .

> It is [**true/possible/likely/certain**] that no good evidence proves that coffee causes cancer. However, . . .

> It [**must/should/can**] be [**admitted/acknowledged/noted/ conceded**] that no good evidence proves that . . . Nevertheless, . . .

> [**Granted/Admittedly/True/To be sure/Certainly/Of course**], Adams has claimed . . . However, . . .

> We [**could/can/might/may/would**] [**say/argue/claim/think**] that spending on the arts supports pornographic . . . But . . .

10.5.2 Responding to Objections and Alternatives

Begin your response with a term that signals disagreement, such as *but, however,* or *on the other hand.* If readers do not already know the basis for that response, support it with at least one reason or even with a complete subordinate argument.

You can respond in ways that range from tactful to blunt.

1. You can regret not that the source is unclear, but that *you* don't entirely understand:

   But [**I do not quite understand how/I find it difficult to see how/It is not clear to me how**] X can claim that, when . . .

2. Or you can note that there are unsettled issues:

   But there are **other issues here** . . ./But there **remains the problem of** . . .

3. You can respond more bluntly, claiming the acknowledged position is irrelevant or unreliable:

   But as insightful as that may be, it [**ignores/is irrelevant to/does not bear on**] the issue at hand.

   But the [**evidence/reasoning**] is [**unreliable/shaky/thin**].

   But the argument is [**untenable/weak/confused/simplistic**].

   But the argument [**overlooks/ignores/misses**] key factors.

You have to decide how blunt your rejection should be; if the alternative seems obviously flawed, say so but focus on the work, not the person.

When you think a writer might not have thought through an issue carefully, you usually should say so civilly. Here are a few possibilities:

Smith's evidence is important, **but we must look at all the available evidence.**

That explains some of the problem, **but it is too complex for a single explanation.**

That principle holds in many cases, **but not in all.**

Three Predictable Disagreements

There are three kinds of alternatives that at least some readers are likely to think of.

1. **There are causes in addition to the one you claim.** If your argument is about cause and effect, remember that no effect has a single cause and no cause has a single effect. If you argue that X causes Y, every reader will think of other causes. The Soviet Union may have collapsed partly because President Reagan's military buildup forced it to spend more on arms than it could afford. But an informed reader could list many other factors, ranging from decades of poor economic performance to political corruption to self-destructive ideology. So if you focus on one cause out of many, acknowledge the others. And if you feel readers might think that some cause deserves more attention than you give it, acknowledge that view and explain why you deemphasized it.

2. **What about these counterexamples?** No matter how rich your evidence, readers are likely to think of exceptions and counterexamples that they think undermine your argument. So you must think of them first, then acknowledge the more plausible ones, especially if they are vivid. Then explain why you don't consider them as damaging as your reader might. Be particularly wary when you make claims about a phenomenon with a wide range of variation, such as the climate. Readers who do not understand statistical reasoning will focus on an aberrant case, even though it falls within a normal distribution: a cold Fourth of July in Florida does not disprove a claim about global warming, any more than a warm New England Christmas proves it.

3. **I don't define X as you do. To me, X means . . .** To accept your claim, readers must accept your definitions, because definitions are crucial warrants (see the next chapter): If you are researching nicotine addiction, your readers must understand what you mean

by that term. Does it mean just a strong craving, a craving that some people can't resist, or a craving that *no one* can? You can find definitions ranging from a few lines in a dictionary to pages in a medical reference work. But regardless of what those sources say, readers will try to redefine your terms to suit their views. Cigarette manufacturers long argued that cigarettes are not addictive because some people can quit; their critics argued that cigarettes are addictive because more people can't.

When your argument turns on the meaning of a term, define it to support your solution, then make an argument supporting your definition. (Never begin: *According to* Webster's, *"addiction" means* . . .) Be aware of plausible alternative definitions that you may need to acknowledge. If you use a technical term that also has a common meaning that your readers use (like *social class* or *theory*), acknowledge the ordinary definition and explain why you use the technical one to solve your problem. If you do not use a technical definition as expert readers expect you to, acknowledge that and explain why you use the common meaning.

CHAPTER ELEVEN

Warrants

This chapter explains when and how to use a warrant to show that a reason is relevant to the claim it is supposed to support. Issues of relevance are especially difficult for beginners in a field because we determine relevance in terms of the assumptions that those in a field take for granted and thus never state.

Consider this argument:

> Russia faces a falling standard of living,$_{,claim}$ because its birthrate is only 1.17 and men's life expectancy has dropped to about 58 years.$_{reason}$

Someone responds:

> Well, you're right about Russia's birthrate and life expectancy, but I don't see how that's relevant to your claim that its standard of living will fall. What's the connection?

How would the person making the argument answer? More important, if that argument were in writing, how would she know that she had to answer that question *before it was asked?* Such questions address the fifth and most complex element of an argument—its warrants. A warrant is a statement that connects a reason to a claim. It is an important issue, because readers may challenge not just the truth of a reason but its *relevance* as well.

In this chapter we explain how warrants work, how to test them, and when and when not to state them. But a caution: everyone struggles to understand warrants (including, from time to time, the three of us), so if at the end of this chapter you still have questions, you're not alone.

11.1 WARRANTS IN EVERYDAY REASONING

Warrants are hard to grasp, but we understand them easily enough when someone offers a proverb to justify his reasoning, because a proverb is a warrant we all know. For example, someone says:

> I hear the FBI has been questioning the mayor's staff.*reason* He must be involved in something crooked.*claim*

Someone might object, *You're right. The FBI has been questioning his staff, but why does that mean he's crooked?* To defend his reasoning, the first person might offer the proverb, *Well, where there's smoke, there's fire.* That is, when we see a sign of something wrong, we can infer that something is in fact wrong.

The logic behind that reasoning is this: if the general proverb/ warrant is true (the sign of something implies its existence), then specific instances of that situation must also be true. In the case of smoke, fire, the FBI, and the mayor, that logic looks like this:

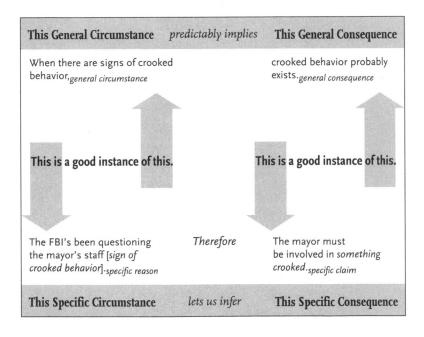

This General Circumstance	*predictably implies*	**This General Consequence**
When there are signs of crooked behavior,*general circumstance*		crooked behavior probably exists.*general consequence*
This is a good instance of this.		This is a good instance of this.
The FBI's been questioning the mayor's staff [*sign of crooked behavior*].*specific reason*	*Therefore*	The mayor must be involved in *something* crooked.*specific claim*
This Specific Circumstance	*lets us infer*	**This Specific Consequence**

We use proverbs to justify many kinds of reasoning: cause and effect (*Haste makes waste*); rules of behavior (*Look before you leap*);

principles of reasoning (*One swallow does not a summer make*). But such proverbs are not our only examples of everyday warrants. We use them everywhere: in sports (*Defense wins championships*); in cooking (*Serve oysters only in months with an "r"*); in definitions (*A prime number can be divided only by itself and one*); even in research (*When readers find an error in one bit of evidence, they distrust the rest*).

11.2 WARRANTS IN ACADEMIC ARGUMENTS

In academic arguments, warrants work like proverbs, but they are more difficult to manage, especially for those new to a field of research.

- Academic warrants aren't commonplaces that we all share; they are specific principles of reasoning that particular communities of researchers develop over centuries of thinking and writing, and they are countless.

- Advanced researchers rarely state warrants in their reports, because they assume that their readers know them, and so stating them would seem condescending.

For example, biologists argue that

a whale is more closely related to a hippopotamus than to a cow,*claim* because it shares more DNA with a hippopotamus.*reason*

No biologist would ask, *What makes DNA relevant to measuring relationship?*, so no biologist would offer colleagues a warrant justifying its relevance. If, however, a nonbiologist asked that question, a biologist would offer a warrant that other biologists take for granted:

When a species shares more DNA with one species than it does with another,*condition* we infer that it is more closely related to the first.*consequence*

(Of course, the expert would probably then have to explain that warrant.) Experts state obvious principles only when they communicate with non-experts (or when challenged). And that's why beginners in a field struggle with the *logic* of arguments written for specialists. Newcomers have to figure out what makes some reasons relevant to claims and some not, something those specialists take for granted.

There is another reason academic warrants are harder to grasp than proverbs: they are usually phrased less explicitly. Most proverbs have two distinct parts, a circumstance and its consequence: *Where there's smoke, there's fire.* But we can also compress those two parts into one short statement—*Smoke means fire*—something that we rarely do with proverbs but that specialists often do with their warrants. For example, a biologist might compress the warrant about species:

Shared DNA is the measure of the relationship between species.

In other words, some warrants don't explicitly distinguish a circumstance from its predictable consequence. But however compressed a warrant might be, we can always deconstruct it into its two parts. For purposes of clarity, we'll state warrants in their most explicit two-part form: *When X, then Y.*

11.3 UNDERSTANDING THE LOGIC OF WARRANTS

Here again is that argument about Russia's economic future:

Russia faces a falling standard of living,$_{claim}$ because its birthrate is only 1.17 and men's life expectancy has dropped to about 58 years.$_{reason}$

If someone objected that he did not see the *relevance* of the reason to the claim, the person making the argument would have to justify it with a warrant.

The warrant would consist of two parts, (1) a general circumstance that lets us draw a conclusion about (2) a general consequence.

When a nation's labor force shrinks,$_{general\ circumstance}$ its economic future is grim.$_{general\ consequence}$

But both the circumstance and consequence have to be more general than the specific reason and claim.

Visually, that logic looks like this:

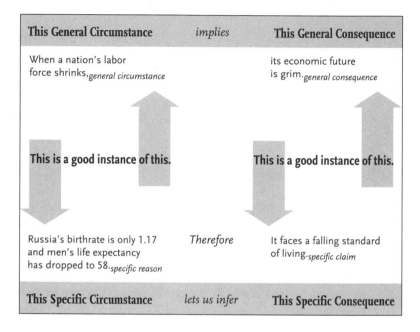

| This General Circumstance | *implies* | This General Consequence |

When a nation's labor force shrinks.*general circumstance*

its economic future is grim.*general consequence*

This is a good instance of this.

This is a good instance of this.

Russia's birthrate is only 1.17 and men's life expectancy has dropped to 58.*specific reason*

Therefore

It faces a falling standard of living.*specific claim*

| This Specific Circumstance | *lets us infer* | This Specific Consequence |

That's the same logic as in the argument about smoke, fire, and the crooked mayor. But now it gets complicated, because readers predictably question warrants in many ways.

11.4 TESTING WHETHER A WARRANT IS RELIABLE

Consider this argument:

Contrary to popular belief, gun ownership in America was probably not widespread in the first half of the nineteenth century and before,*claim* because guns were rarely mentioned in wills.*reason* A review of 4,465 wills filed in seven states from 1750 to 1850 shows that only 11 percent mention a long gun or handgun.*report of evidence*

Such a claim is likely to be resisted by those who believe that those who founded this country owned guns. So even if they accept that the reason is true—guns were in fact rarely mentioned in wills—they may still object: *I don't see how that counts as a reason to believe that few people owned a gun. It's irrelevant.*

If a writer anticipated that readers would raise that objection, she would offer a warrant to link the specific reason to the specific claim *before* she stated them:

> In the eighteenth and early nineteenth centuries, valuable objects were listed in wills, **so when someone failed to mention a valuable object in his will, he did not own one.**$_{warrant}$ Since guns were valuable but were rarely mentioned in wills before 1850,$_{reason}$ gun ownership must not have been widespread.$_{claim}$

But now she must ask herself five questions before her readers do:

1. Is that warrant basically true?

2. Is it prudently limited?

3. Is it trumped by a competing warrant?

4. Is it appropriate to this field of research?

5. Are the specific reason and claim good instances of the general warrant?

11.4.1 Is Your Warrant Basically True?

When readers think a warrant is false, no amount of good reasons and sound evidence can save the claim.

> **Nonhuman creatures are mere biological objects, lacking inner life, and so should not be objects of pity or concern.**$_{warrant}$ Apes used in medical experiments have nothing like human emotions or feelings,$_{reason}$ so we should not waste money making their conditions comfortable.$_{claim}$

Fifty years ago most psychologists believed that warrant to be true. Today almost all reject it, and it would be virtually impossible to change their minds.

So when you think readers might question the truth of your warrant, you must treat it as a claim in its own argument, supported by its own reasons and evidence:

> In the eighteenth and early nineteenth centuries, valuable objects were listed in wills, so when a will failed to mention such a valuable object, the person did not own one.*warrant/claim* Watson (1989) confirmed that to be the case.*reason* In a study of 1,356 wills filed in Cumberland County between 1750 and 1825, he found . . . *evidence*

11.4.2 Is Your Warrant Prudently Limited?

A warrant can be true but within limits. For example, that warrant about gun ownership seems to allow no exceptions:

> In the eighteenth and early nineteenth centuries, valuable objects were listed in wills.

That's stated too broadly; it might seem more plausible if it were qualified.

> In the eighteenth and early nineteenth centuries, **most** household objects **considered valuable by their owners** were **usually** listed in wills.

But once you start qualifying a warrant with words like *most* and *usually*, you have to show that its exceptions do not exclude your reason and claim: *What frequency are most and usually? Were guns always considered valuable?*

11.4.3 Can Your Warrant Be Trumped?

You may think your warrant is true and prudently limited, but is it the best warrant? Some warrants seem to contradict each other: *Out of sight, out of mind* and *Absence makes the heart grow fonder.* Which is true? Here are two more competing warrants, both arguably true:

> **When a group wants to express political views, it has a constitutional right to do so.** The teachers union believed real estate taxes

should be raised, so they had a right to picket the school board meeting.

When a group does not unanimously agree, its leaders should not express their own opinion in the name of the group. Not every member of the teachers union thought real estate taxes should be raised, so it should not have picketed the school board meeting.

How do we decide which warrant should prevail? What kind of argument would support giving one of them priority?

11.4.4 Is Your Warrant Appropriate to Your Readers' Community?

Your warrant may be true, limited, and superior, but your readers might still reject it if it is not appropriate to their particular community of research. Law students get a painful lesson in the law when they find that many warrants they take for granted have no place in legal arguments. For example, like most of us, they start law school holding this commonsense belief:

When a person is wronged, the law should correct it.

But law students have to unlearn such commonsense ideas, because legal warrants may trump them. For example:

When one ignores legal obligations, even inadvertently, one must suffer the consequences.

Therefore:

When elderly home owners forget to pay real estate taxes, others can buy their houses for back taxes and evict them.

Against their most decent instincts, law students must learn (and argue) that justice is not what they believe it to be, but what the law and the courts say it is.

11.4.5 Are Your Reason and Claim Good Instances
of the General Warrant?

Here it gets very complicated. Even if you're confident that your warrant is true, limited, superior, and appropriate, you must also be sure that your specific reason and claim are good instances of the general circumstance and consequence of your warrant, a matter that has vexed logicians for two thousand years. For example:

Ahmed: You should buy a gun, because you live alone.

Anya: Why does living alone mean I should buy a gun?

Ahmed: When you aren't safe, you should be able to protect yourself.

Anya: But living alone doesn't make me unsafe.

Anya objects not that Ahmed's reason (you live alone) is false, but that it is not *relevant* to his claim (she should buy a gun), because for her, living alone is not a valid *instance* of being unsafe. So to Anya, Ahmed's reason isn't "covered" by his warrant and is therefore not *relevant*.

Testing arguments for relevance can be hard. Here is a flawed argument about how TV violence affects children:

Few doubt that when we expose children to examples of admirable behavior, we influence them for the better. How can we then deny that when they are constantly exposed to images of sadistic violence, they are influenced for the worse?_warrant_ Violence among children 12–16 is rising faster than among any other age group._reason_ Brown (1997) has shown that . . ._evidence_ We can no longer ignore the conclusion that TV violence is a destructive influence on our children today._claim_

To diagnose what's wrong here, we break the warrant into its two parts, then align the reason and claim under them.

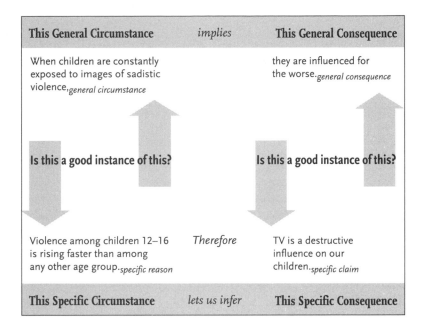

Now we can see the problem: the specific circumstance, rising violence, is not a valid *instance* of children being exposed to images of sadistic violence. So even if the reason is true, it's irrelevant to the claim.

To fix that argument, we have to revise the reason to be a good instance of the warrant:

> Few doubt that when children are exposed to examples of admirable behavior, they are influenced for the better. How then can we deny that when they are constantly exposed to images of sadistic violence, that exposure influences them for the worse?*warrant* All our data show that violence among children 12–16 is rising faster than among any other age group. This violence results from many factors, but we can no longer ignore the conclusion that because television is the major source of children's images of violence,*reason* it is a destructive influence on our children.*claim*

Now the evidence and claim seem closer to what the warrant covers or includes:

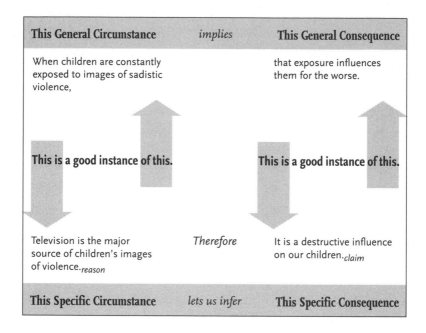

But a reader keen to derail the argument might still object:

Wait. All those images aren't "sadistic." Much of it is cartoon violence. And children aren't *constantly* exposed to it.

Now the writer would have to deal with those issues.

Warrants are difficult to grasp, but once you do, you understand why important issues are so endlessly contested; why, when you feel your case is watertight, your readers can still say, *Wait a minute. What about . . . ?* Careful readers regularly challenge reasons because they are not grounded on sound evidence, *but no less often* because they seem irrelevant to a claim. To answer the first objection, you must find better evidence. To answer the second, you must construct a warrant that makes your reasons relevant. If you can't, you must revise your argument.

11.5 KNOWING WHEN TO STATE A WARRANT

A research report depends on countless principles of reasoning, but most are so deeply embedded in our tacit knowledge that we rarely state them. There are, however, three occasions when you may have to:

- Your readers are outside your field.

When you write as an expert for readers who are not, you must be aware of reasons that only experts use, then offer a warrant to justify them.

- You use a principle of reasoning that is new or controversial in your field.

In that case, state the warrant, then justify it by referring to others who also use it. Though you are not likely to convince those set against it, you can argue that your argument may be controversial, but you're not alone in making it. Even when readers resist an unconventional principle of reasoning, you can diffuse some of their disagreement by explicitly stating *and defending* the warrant that explains it.

- You make a claim that readers will resist because they just don't want it to be true.

In this case, start with a warrant that you hope readers will accept *before* you lay out a reason and claim that you fear they will resist. They may not like the claim any better, but you will at least encourage them to see that it is not unreasonable. For example:

> Homosexuality seems to have a strong genetic component,$_{claim}$ because many of its characteristics appear in the feelings of preteens who become homosexual adults, even though they have had no contact with homosexuals.$_{reason}$

Some readers resist that claim, because they believe that we choose our sexual orientation and that any other basis for homosexuality undermines their moral views. A writer might not overcome such deep beliefs, but he might encourage his readers at least to consider a contrary claim if he first convinces them to accept a warrant connecting a true reason to that claim:

When children manifest behavior arising not from teaching or modeling but spontaneously, such behavior is probably genetically based.$_{warrant}$ [Reasons and evidence follow.] We must therefore consider whether homosexuality has a genetic component,$_{claim}$ because many of its characteristics appear in the feelings of preteens who become homosexual adults, even though they have had no contact with homosexuals.$_{reason}$

When readers think that both a warrant and reason are true, and that the specific reason and claim are good examples of the warrant, they are logically obliged at least to consider the claim. If they don't, no rational argument is likely to change their minds.

> WHAT YOU DON'T SAY SAYS WHO YOU ARE
> You treat readers courteously when you state and support warrants to explain principles of reasoning that they may not recognize. But you make an equally strong (though less friendly) gesture when you keep silent about warrants you should state for readers not in the know. One way or the other, warrants significantly affect how readers perceive the ethos you project through your arguments.

11.6 CHALLENGING OTHERS' WARRANTS

As hard as it is to convince readers to accept new warrants, it is even harder to argue them out of ones they hold. When you challenge one of their warrants, first imagine how they would *defend* it. For example, an economist might argue:

The population of Zackland must be controlled,$_{claim}$ because it is outstripping its resources and heading for demographic disaster.$_{reason}$

If challenged to defend the relevance of the reason to the claim, an economist could offer a warrant and back it with economic facts:

When a population outgrows its resources, only a reduction in population will save a country from demographic collapse.$_{claim/}$

warrant For example, countries A, B, and C exceeded their resources and tried to prevent collapse by every means other than population control, but they failed.*reason/evidence*

But a religious person might challenge that argument with a different warrant, one grounded not on economic facts but on moral principles:

> It is immoral to discourage couples from having children.*claim*
> When people are advised to defy God's revealed law, that advice is sinful.*warrant*

A third person might reject population control with a third warrant:

> When we put our minds to the problem of limited resources, a can-do spirit will solve it.*warrant*

That warrant is based not on data or religious belief but on cultural values.

Since warrants can be based on different *kinds* of supporting arguments, you have to challenge them in different ways.

11.6.1 Challenging Warrants Based on Experience

We base some warrants on our experience or on reports by others.

> When people habitually lie, we don't trust them.

> When insecticides leach into the ecosystem, eggshells of wild birds become so weak that fewer chicks hatch and the bird population falls.

To challenge those warrants, you have two choices, both difficult: (1) challenge the reliability of the experience; (2) find counterexamples that cannot be dismissed as special cases. To challenge the experience, you have to tackle readers head-on, rarely an easy argument to make. Choose the second strategy when you have good counterexamples. You can then argue for exceptions without directly contradicting the experience or reasoning of your readers.

11.6.2 Challenging Warrants Based on Authority

We believe some people because of their expertise, position, or charisma.

> When authority X says Y, Y must be so.

Challenging authority is difficult. The easiest—and friendliest— way is to argue that, on the matter in question, the authority does not have all the evidence or reaches beyond its expertise. The most aggressive way is to argue that the source is in fact not an authority at all.

11.6.3 Challenging Warrants Based on Systems of Knowledge

These warrants are backed by systems of definitions, principles, or theories:

> FROM MATHEMATICS: When we add two odd numbers, we get an even one.

> FROM BIOLOGY: When an organism reproduces, its individual offspring differ.

> FROM LAW: When we drive without a license, we commit a misdemeanor.

When you challenge these warrants, "facts" are largely irrelevant. You must either challenge the system, always difficult, or show that the case does not fall under the warrant.

11.6.4 Challenging General Cultural Warrants

These warrants are backed not by individual experience but by the common experience of an entire culture. To members of that culture, they seem unassailable "common sense."

> Out of sight, out of mind.

> An insult justifies retaliation.

> Handling toads causes warts.

Warrants like these may change over time, but slowly. You can challenge them, but readers will resist, because you seem to challenge their heritage.

11.6.5 Challenging Methodological Warrants

Think of these as "meta-warrants," general patterns of thought with no content until applied to specific cases. We use them to explain abstract reasoning (they are the source of many proverbs):

> GENERALIZATION: When every known case of X has quality Y, then all X's probably have quality Y. (*See one, see them all.*)

> ANALOGY: When X is like Y in most respects, then X will be like Y in other respects. (*Like father, like son.*)

> SIGN: When Y regularly occurs before, during, or after X, Y is a sign of X. (*Cold hands, warm heart.*)

Philosophers have questioned these warrants, but in matters of practical argumentation, we challenge only their application or point out limiting conditions: *Yes, we can analogize X to Y, but not if . . .*

11.6.6 Challenging Warrants Based on Articles of Faith

Some warrants are beyond challenge: Jefferson invoked one when he wrote, *We hold these truths to be self-evident, that all men are created equal. . . .* Others include:

> When a claim is experienced as revealed truth, it must be true.

> When a claim is based on divine teaching, it must be true.

Such warrants are backed not by the evidence of our senses but by the certainty of those who espouse them. It is pointless to challenge them, because they are statements of faith, impervious to argument or evidence. If you encounter them as you gather your data, ignore them or treat them not as a subject for research but as an inquiry into the meaning of life.

ONE MORE USE OF WARRANTS

If you listen carefully to how politicians answer questions they would rather avoid, you can hear another use of warrants, this one devious:

> REPORTER: Senator, do you support measures to cut greenhouse gases?
> SENATOR: I support all sound ideas aimed at correcting serious problems.

Note first that the senator doesn't answer yes or no—he offers a generalization that we can represent as a warrant:

> When ideas are sound and aimed at correcting serious problems, I support them.

That answer might encourage us to infer that he does support the measures:

> This is a sound idea aimed at correcting a problem,$_{reason}$ so he must support it.$_{claim}$

But what we *infer* is not what the senator *says*. He can always later say that the measures are not sound. Answering a question with a warrant can seem to imply *yes* (or *no*) while avoiding the question.

You must distinguish two fundamentally different kinds of arguments, because readers evaluate them differently:

- One kind of argument backs up a claim with reasons based on evidence.

- The other infers a claim from a reason and warrant.

Researchers trust the first kind of argument more than they do the second.

This argument presents a claim based on a reason based on evidence:

> Needle-exchange programs contribute to increased drug use,$_{claim}$ because when addicts think they can avoid the risk of disease, they feel it is safe to use more drugs.$_{reason}$ A study of those who participated in one such program reported that 34 percent of the participants increased their use of drugs from 1.7 to 2.1 times a week because they reported feeling protected from needle-transmitted diseases.$_{evidence}$

If we think the evidence is sound, sufficient, and relevant to the reason, and the reason seems plausibly to support the claim, the claim will seem plausible, though by no means forever beyond challenge, because we might find new and better evidence.

This next argument makes the same claim based on the same reason. But the claim is supported not by evidence but by the logic of a warrant.

> Needle-exchange programs contribute to increased drug use,$_{claim}$ because when addicts think that they can avoid the risk of disease, they feel it is safe to use more drugs.$_{reason}$ Whenever the costs of risky behavior are reduced, people engage in it more often.$_{warrant}$

That claim "must" be true if the warrant and reason are true and the reason and claim are valid instances of the warrant. But lacking massive evidence to back up the unlimited certainty of that warrant, that argument is shaky.

All arguments ultimately rely on warrants. But readers of *research* reports tend to distrust a claim that's based only on an unqualified and unlimited warrant, because such arguments are usually more ideological than factual. Researchers want to see claims based on sound reasons based on hard evidence, not derived from articles of faith. If it helps, add a warrant to nail down your claim, but always back up your reasons with good evidence.

PART IV

Planning, Drafting, and Revising

Prologue

No formula can tell you when to start drafting. Booth began writing before he had a full plan, but then as his ideas became clearer, he faced the nasty job of having to discard good but irrelevant pages. Colomb is an inveterate outliner, producing as many as a dozen plans and two or three "advance summaries" before he begins. Williams tries out as many versions as do Booth and Colomb, but in his head; he writes as he goes but starts a serious draft only when he has a sense of the whole. You have to find your own way to start a first draft, but you can prepare for that moment if you keep writing summaries, analyses, and critiques from the start.

You're ready to plan a draft when you know the following:

- You know who your readers are, what they know, and why they should care about your problem.

- You know the kind of ethos or character you want to project.

- You can sketch your question and its answer in two or three sentences.

- You can sketch the reasons and evidence supporting your claim.

- You know the questions, alternatives, and objections that your readers are likely to raise, and you can respond to them.

- You know when your readers may not see the relevance of a reason to a claim and can state the warrant that connects them.

Even when they have a plan and are ready to draft, though, experienced writers know that they won't march straight through to a finished product. They know they'll go down blind alleys, but also make new discoveries, maybe even rethink their whole project. They also know that a lot of their early drafting will not make it into their final draft, and so they start early enough to leave time for revision.

Part IV will lead you through the process of creating your final report. In chapter 12 we walk through planning your paper, then in chapter 13 drafting it. In chapter 14 we discuss the demanding task of revising its organization. In chapter 15 we discuss how to present complex data in visual form, and in chapter 16 how to write an introduction that motivates readers to read carefully. Finally, in chapter 17 we deal with problems of writing in a clear and direct style.

SORTING OUT TERMS:
WORKING HYPOTHESIS, ANSWER, SOLUTION, CLAIM, POINT

In part II we used the terms *answer, working hypothesis,* and *solution* to name the sentence that resolved the central issue of your research. In part III we used the term *main claim* to refer to the answer, hypothesis, or solution that constitutes the key assertion that the rest of your argument supports. Here in part IV we use *point* to name the sentence that states the main claim in a written report (some use the term *thesis*). *Working hypothesis, answer, solution, claim,* and *point*—all those terms refer to the same sentence. We use different terms because each defines the role of that sentence from a different angle.

Outlining and
Storyboarding

As an aid to planning, outlines can be useful but also a nuisance. The three of us remember when teachers forced us to worry more over the form of our outlines than the substance of our papers: no subhead "A" without a "B," and so on. (Of course, we usually outlined our papers after we wrote them, then pretended we did it the other way around.) We still use outlines but rarely formal ones. For one book, Booth had a file of twenty-one outlines that guided his writing through seven years. For his first book, Colomb used almost as many, but with every new outline, he made it a point to discard the old one. Williams outlined his book on the history of the English language on the back of an envelope. In fact, different kinds of outlines are useful at different stages in the process: the key is to distinguish *topic-based* and *point-based* outlines and to know when each is useful.

A topic-based outline consists of just nouns or phrases. It works for short papers, so long as you already know the point you want to make in each section.

I. Introduction: Laptops in Classrooms
II. Uses
   A. Labs
   B. Classroom
III. Revision Studies
   A. Study A
   B. Study B
IV. Conclusions

But for a longer paper, you may find points, explicit or implied, more useful:

I. Introduction: Value of classroom computers uncertain.
II. Different uses have different effects.
  A. All uses increase flexibility.
  B. Networked computer labs allow student interaction.
  C. Classroom computers rarely enhance learning.
  D. In-class laptops often a distraction (Facebook, e-mail, surfing).
III. Studies show benefits to revision are limited.
  A. Study A: writers more wordy.
  B. Study B: writers need hard copy to revise effectively.
IV. Conclusion: Too soon to tell how much classroom laptops improve learning.
  A. Too few reliable empirical studies.
  B. Too little history, too many programs in transition.
  C. Some schools adding programs; some dropping programs.

A point outline helps you see whether your argument hangs together better than does a topic outline. You might not be able to create a point outline until you have a draft, but the sooner you make one to test your argument, the better. The downside of an outline is that it can lock you into a final form before you've done your best thinking.

To avoid that problem, many researchers, including those outside the academic world, plan their reports on a *storyboard* (see the figure in 9.1). A storyboard is like an outline, except that each main point is on a separate page left blank for adding data and ideas later. As opposed to fixed lines in an outline, you can physically move storyboard pages around without having to print out a new plan every time you try a new organization. You can spread its pages across a wall, group related pages, and put minor sections below major ones to create a "picture" of your project that shows at a glance the design of the whole and your progress through it.

CHAPTER TWELVE

Planning

Once you've assembled your argument, you might be ready to draft it.
But experienced writers know that time spent planning a first draft more
than pays off when they start writing it. A plan helps you reorganize the
elements of your argument from a form that may seem coherent to you
into one that will be both coherent and persuasive to your readers.

Some fields stipulate the plan of a research report. In the experimental sciences, for example, readers expect reports to follow a plan something like this:

> Introduction – Methods and Materials – Results – Discussion – Conclusion

If your field requires you to follow a conventional plan, ask your instructor for a model or find one in a secondary source. In most fields, however, you have to create a plan of your own, but that plan must still help readers find what they are looking for.

12.1 AVOID THREE COMMON BUT FLAWED PLANS

Not all plans are equally good.

1. **Do not organize your report as a narrative of your thinking.** Few readers care what you found first, then dead ends you hit, then problems you overcame. They become especially annoyed when they have to slog through the history of your project to get to a main point you've saved for the end.

To test your draft for this problem, highlight sentences that refer not to the results of your research but to how you did it or to what you were thinking. You see signs of this in language like

The first issue was . . . ; Then I compared . . . ; Finally I conclude. If you highlight more than a few such sentences, you may not be supporting a claim but rather telling the story of how you found it. If so, reorganize your report around the core elements of your argument—your claim and the reasons supporting it.

2. Do not assemble your report as a patchwork of your sources. Readers want *your* analysis, not a summary of your sources. New researchers go wrong when they patch together quotations, summaries of sources, especially downloads from the Web. The worst form of this is called "quilting," stitched-together passages from a dozen sources in a design that reflects little of your own thinking. It invites the charge *This is all summary, no analysis.* Quilting is a particular risk if you do most of your research online. Experienced readers recognize such patchworks, so you're unlikely to slip one past your teacher, and you risk a charge of plagiarism.

Advanced researchers rarely offer patchwork summaries, but they can follow sources too closely in another way: they map their report onto the organization of a major source rather than create a new one that serves their argument better. If the key terms that run through your report are the same as those in one or more sources, consider whether you are making your own argument or mimicking theirs.

3. Do not map your report directly on to the language of your assignment. If you echo the language of your assignment in your first paragraph, your teacher may think that you've contributed no ideas of your own, as in this example:

ASSIGNMENT: Different theories of perception give different weight to cognitive mediation in processing sensory input. Some claim that input reaches the brain unmediated; others that receptive organs are subject to cognitive influence. Compare two theories of visual, aural, or tactile perception that take different positions on this matter.

STUDENT'S OPENING PARAGRAPH: Different theorists of visual perception give different weight to the role of cognitive mediation in processing sensory input. In this paper I will compare two theories of visual perception, one of which . . .

If your assignment lists a series of issues to cover, avoid addressing them in the order given. If, for example, you were asked to "compare and contrast Freud and Jung on the imagination and unconscious," you do not have to organize your report into two parts, the first on Freud, the second on Jung, a kind of organization that too often results in a pair of unrelated summaries. Try breaking the topics into their conceptual parts, such as elements of the unconscious and the imagination, their definitions, and so on; then order those parts in a way useful to your readers.

12.2 PLANNING YOUR REPORT
12.2.1 Sketch a Working Introduction

Writers are often advised to write their introduction last. A few writers can wait until they've written their last words before they write their first ones, but most of us need a working introduction to start us on the right track. Expect to write your introduction twice, a sketchy one for yourself right now, then later a final one for your readers. That final introduction will usually have four parts (see chapter 16), so you might as well sketch your working introduction to anticipate them.

1. **At the top of the first page of your storyboard, sketch a *brief* summary of *only* the key points in *only* those sources most relevant to your argument.** A long account of marginally relevant references is more annoying than impressive. Summarize only the sources that you intend to correct, modify, or expand on. Then order those sources in a way that is useful to your readers: chronologically, by quality, significance, point of view, and so on. Under *no* circumstances follow the order in which you happened to read them or record them in your notes. If you're sure what will go into this summary, just list the sources in a useful order.

2. **After your summary of sources, rephrase your question as a statement about a flaw or gap that you see in them:**

Why is the Alamo story so important in our national mythology?

→ Few of these historians, however, have explained why the Alamo story has become so important in our national mythology.

3. Sketch an answer to *So what if we don't find out?* You may be only guessing but try to find *some* answer.

If we understood how such stories become national legends, we would better understand our national values, perhaps even what makes us distinct.

If you can't think of any answer to *So what?*, skip it; we'll return to it in chapter 14.

4. State the answer to your question as your point, or promise an answer in a launching point. You have two choices here:

• State the point of your paper at the end of your introduction to frame what follows and again near the beginning of your conclusion.

• State it only in your conclusion, as a climax to your reasoning.

This is a crucial choice, because it creates your social contract with your readers. If you state your main point toward the end of your introduction, you put your readers in charge: *Reader, you control how to read this report. You know my problem and its solution, my point. You can decide how—even whether—to read on. No surprises.* On the other hand, if you wait until your conclusion to state your main claim, you create a more controlling relationship: *Reader, you must follow me though every twist and turn until we reach the end, where I will finally reveal my point.* Most readers prefer to see your main point at the end of your introduction, because that lets them read what follows faster, understand its relevance better, and remember it all longer. Stating your claim early also helps keep *you* on track.

Some new researchers fear that if they reveal their main point too early, readers will be "bored" and stop reading. Others worry about repeating themselves. Both fears are baseless. If you ask an interesting question, readers will want to see how well you can answer it.

If you decide to announce your claim only in your conclusion, you still need a sentence at the end of your introduction that launches your reader into the body of your report. That sentence should include terms that name the key concepts that will run through your report (see 6.6.1, 8.2.1, 12.2.2). You'll be better prepared to write that launching sentence after you draft your final introduction. So for purposes of planning, put your main claim at the bottom of your storyboard's introduction page; you can move it later.

Some writers add a "road map" at the end their introduction:

In part 1, I discuss the issue of . . . Part 2 addresses . . . Part 3 examines . . .

Road maps are common in the social sciences, but many in the humanities find them clumsy. You can add a road map to your storyboard to guide your drafting, then cut it from your final draft. If you keep it, make it short.

Here is how the first page of your storyboard might now look:

Research reports A, B, and C suggest that firstborn middle-class native Caucasian males earn more, stay employed longer, and report more job satisfaction._context_ [Summary of key sources follows.]

But those reports tell us nothing about recent immigrants from Southeast Asia._question rephrased as gap in research_

Until we see how these patterns occur in other cultures, we can't know whether the influence of birth order is cross-cultural._consequences of question_

The predicted influence seems to cut across groups, though it partly depends on how long a family has been in the United States and their economic level before they arrived._your tentative main point_

Sketchy as it is, this introduction is enough to start you on track. In your last draft, you'll revise it to state your problem more completely (see chapter 16).

12.2.2 Identify Key Concepts That Will Run Through Your Whole Report
For a report to seem coherent, readers must see a few key concepts running through all its parts. You might find them among the terms you used to categorize your notes, but they must include key words from the sentences stating your problem and main point. On the introduction page, circle four or five words that express those concepts. Ignore words that name your general topic; focus on those relevant to your specific question:

> employment, job satisfaction, recent SE Asian immigrants, cross-cultural, length of residence, prior economic level

If you find few key terms, your topic and point may be too general (review 8.2.1). List those key terms at the top of each storyboard page, and keep them in mind as you draft.

12.2.3 Plan the Body of Your Report
1. Sketch background and define terms. After the introduction page of your storyboard, add a page on which you outline necessary background. You may have to define terms, spell out your problem or review research in more detail, set limits on your project, locate your problem in a larger historical or social context, and so on. Keep it short.

2. Create a page for each major section of your report. At the top of each of these pages, write the point that the rest of that section supports, develops, or explains. Usually, this will be a reason supporting your main claim.

3. Find a suitable order. When you assembled your argument, you ordered its parts in a way that may have been clear to you. But when you plan a draft, you must order them in a way that meets the needs of your readers. When you're not sure what that order should be, consider these options. The first two are based on your topic:

- **Part-by-part.** If you can break your topic into its parts, you can deal with each in turn, but you must still order those parts in a way that helps readers understand them—by their functional relationships, hierarchy, and so on.

- **Chronological.** This is the simplest: earlier to later or cause to effect.

These next six are based on your readers' knowledge and understanding.

- **Short to long, simple to complex.** Most readers prefer to deal with simple issues before they work through more complex ones.

- **More familiar to less familiar.** Most readers prefer to read about more familiar issues before they read about new ones.

- **Less contestable to more contestable.** Most readers move more easily from what they agree with to what they don't.

- **More important to less important (or vice versa).** Readers prefer to read more important reasons first (but those reasons may have more impact if they come last).

- **Earlier understanding to prepare for later understanding.** Readers may have to understand some events, principles, definitions, and so on before they understand something else.

- **General analysis followed by specific applications.** Readers may have to understand the outlines of your overall position before they can follow how you apply it to specific texts, events, situations, and so on.

Often, these principles cooperate: what readers agree with and easily understand might also be short and familiar. But these principles may also conflict: readers might reject most quickly reasons that are most important. Whatever your order, it must reflect *your readers'* needs, not the order that the material seems to impose on itself (as in an obvious compare-contrast organization), least of all the order in which those reasons occurred to you.

Finally, make the principle of order you choose clear by sketching at the top of each page words that show it: *First* . . . , *second* . . . ; *Later* . . . , *Finally* . . . ; *More important* . . . ; *A more complex issue is* . . . ; *As a result* . . . Don't worry if these terms feel awkward. At this point, they're for your benefit, not your readers'. You can revise or even delete them from your final draft.

FINDING A WORKABLE ORDER FOR THIS BOOK
You may have to try out several orders to find the right one. We did. What you are reading is organized differently from both the first and second editions, either because readers told us that some parts didn't "flow" or because we just had a better idea. Among other changes, we moved the chapter on the most difficult topic, warrants, to the end of part III, so that if readers got discouraged in that chapter, they would at least have covered the other parts of argument first. We've also moved parts around from one chapter to another. But changing that order was nothing new: we had already tried out more than a dozen orders for the first edition—and still didn't get it quite right.

12.2.4 Plan Each Section and Subsection

1. Highlight the key terms in each section and subsection. Just as your whole report needs an introduction, so does each of its sections. Earlier we told you to state the point of each section at the top of its storyboard page. Now, just as you picked out key terms to run through your whole report, circle the ones that uniquely distinguish this section from all the others; they should be in the sentence that states the point of that section. If you cannot find terms to distinguish a section, look closely at how it contributes to the whole. It may offer little or nothing.

2. Indicate where to put evidence, acknowledgments, warrants, and summaries. Add these parts to the storyboard page for each section. They may, in turn, need to be supported by their own arguments.

- **Evidence.** Most sections consist of evidence supporting a reason. If you have different kinds of evidence supporting the same reason, group and order them in a way that makes sense to readers. Note where you may have to explain your evidence—where it came from, why it's reliable, exactly how it supports a reason.

- **Acknowledgments and responses.** Imagine what readers might object to, then outline a response. Responses may be sub-arguments with a claim, reasons, evidence, and even another response to an imagined response to your response.

- **Warrants.** Generally speaking, if you need a warrant, state it before you offer its claim and supporting reason. This following argument, for example, needs a warrant if it's intended for non-experts in Elizabethan social history:

> Since most students at Oxford University in 1580 signed documents with only their first and last names,$_{reason}$ most of them must have been commoners.$_{claim}$

That argument is clearer to everyone (even experts) when introduced by a warrant:

> In late sixteenth-century England, when someone was not a gentleman but a commoner, he did not add "Mr." or "Esq." to his signature.$_{warrant}$ Most students at Oxford University in 1580 signed documents with only their first and last names,$_{reason}$ so most of them must have been commoners.$_{claim}$

If you think readers might question your warrant, make an argument supporting it.

If your report is long and "fact-heavy" with dates, names, events, or numbers, you might end each major section by briefly summarizing the progress of your argument. What have you established in that section? How does your argument shape up so far? If in your final draft those summaries seem clumsy, cut them.

12.2.5 Sketch a Working Conclusion

State your point again at the top of a conclusion page of your story-board. After it, if you can, sketch its significance (another answer to *So what?*).

In doing all this, you may discover that you can't use all the notes you collected. That doesn't mean you wasted time. Research is like gold mining: dig up a lot, pick out a little, toss the rest. Ernest Hemingway said that you know you're writing well when you discard stuff you know is good—but not as good as what you keep.

START DRAFTING AS SOON AS YOU CAN

Deadlines come too soon: we long for another month, a week, just one more day. (The three of us fought deadlines for every edition of this book.) In fact, some researchers seem never able to finish, thinking they have to keep working until their report, dissertation, or book is perfect. That perfect report has never been written and never will be. All you can do is to make yours as good as you can in the time available. When you've done that, you can say to yourself: *Reader, after my best efforts, here's what I believe—not the whole or final truth, but a truth important to me and I hope to you. I have tested and supported that truth as fully as time and my abilities allow, so that you might find my argument strong enough to consider, perhaps to accept, maybe even to change what you believe.*

CHAPTER THIRTEEN
Drafting Your Report

Some writers think that once they have an outline or a storyboard, they can just grind out sentences. Experienced writers know better. They know that drafting can be an act of discovery that planning can never replace, because it is then that we often experience one of research's most exciting moments: we discover ideas that we didn't have until we expressed them. But like other steps in the process, even surprises happen better with a plan.

13.1 DRAFT IN A WAY THAT FEELS COMFORTABLE

Many experienced writers begin to write long before they fill up their storyboard. They create a rough plan, use early drafts to explore what they think, then create a final plan based on what they discover. They know that much of that early writing will not survive, so they start early. Exploratory drafting can help you discover ideas you never imagined, but it works only if you have a distant deadline. If you are new to your topic or have a short deadline, draft when you have a clearer plan.

Once they have a plan, many writers draft quickly: they let the words flow, omitting quotations and data that they can plug in later, skipping ahead when they get stuck. If they don't remember a detail, they insert a "[?]" and keep writing until they run out of gas, then go back to look it up. But quick drafters need time to revise, so if you draft quickly, start early.

Other writers can work only slowly and carefully: they have to get every sentence right before they start the next one. To do that, they need a meticulous plan. So if you draft slowly, create a detailed outline or storyboard.

Most writers work best when they draft quickly, revise carefully, and toss what's irrelevant. But draft in any way that works for you.

13.2 USE KEY WORDS TO KEEP YOURSELF ON TRACK

One problem with drafting is staying on track. A storyboard helps, but you might also keep your key concepts in front of you and, from time to time, check how often you use them, especially those that distinguish each section. But don't let your storyboard or key terms stifle fresh thinking. If you find yourself wandering, follow the trail until you see where it takes you. You may be on the track of an interesting idea.

Even if reports in your field don't use headings and subheadings, we suggest that you do when you draft. Create each heading out of the words that are unique to the section or subsection it heads:

Sam Houston as a Hero in Newspapers Outside of Texas

These headings also show the structure of your report at a glance (numbered headings are common in some social sciences, rare in the humanities). If your field doesn't use heads, delete them from your final draft.

13.3 QUOTE, PARAPHRASE, AND SUMMARIZE APPROPRIATELY

You must build your report out of your own words that reflect your own thinking. But you'll support much of that thinking with quotations, paraphrases, and summaries. As we've said, different fields use them differently: researchers in the humanities quote more than do social and natural scientists, who typically paraphrase and summarize. But you must decide each case for itself, depending on how you use the information. Here again are some principles:

- Summarize when details are irrelevant or a source isn't important enough to warrant much space.

- Paraphrase when you can state what a source says more clearly or concisely or when your argument depends on the details in a source but not on its specific words.

- Quote for these purposes:
  —The words themselves are evidence that backs up your reasons.
  —The words are from an authority who backs up your claims.
  —The words are strikingly original or express your key concepts so compellingly that the quotation can frame an extended discussion.
  —A passage states a view that you disagree with, and to be fair you want to state it exactly.

For every summary, paraphrase, or quotation you use, cite its bibliographic data in the appropriate style (see 13.8 and the Quick Tip). Under no circumstances stitch together downloads from the Web with a few sentences of your own. Teachers grind their teeth reading such reports, dismayed by their lack of original thinking. Readers of advanced projects reject such patchworks out of hand.

13.4 INTEGRATING DIRECT QUOTATIONS INTO YOUR TEXT

Signal direct quotations in one of two ways:

- For four or fewer quoted lines, run them into your text, surrounded by quotation marks.

- For five or more lines, set them off as an indented block.

You can insert run-in and block quotations in your text in three ways.

- Drop in the quotation with a few identifying words (*Author says*, *According to Author*, *As Author puts it*, etc.).

  Diamond says, "The histories of the Fertile Crescent and China . . . hold a salutary lesson for the modern world: circumstances change, and past primacy is no guarantee of future primacy" (417).

- Introduce the quotation with a sentence that interprets or characterizes it.

Diamond suggests what we can learn from the past: "The histories of the Fertile Crescent and China . . . hold a salutary lesson for
the modern world . . ." (417).

- Weave the grammar of the quotation into the grammar of your
own sentence.

Diamond suggests what political leaders can learn from history,
that the "lesson for the modern world" in the history of the Fertile
Crescent and China is that "circumstances change, and past primacy is no guarantee of future primacy" (417).

You can modify a quotation, so long as you don't change its meaning
and you signal deletions with three dots (called *ellipses*) and changes
with square brackets. This sentence quotes the original intact:

Posner focuses on religion not for its spirituality, but for its social
functions: "A notable feature of American society is religious pluralism, and we should consider how this relates to the efficacy of
governance by social norms in view of the historical importance of
religion as both a source and enforcer of such norms" (299).

This version modifies the quotation to fit the grammar of the writer's sentence:

In discussing religious pluralism, Posner says that "a notable
feature of American society is [our] religious pluralism" and notes
how social norms affect "the efficacy of governance . . . in view of
the historical importance of religion as both a source and enforcer
of such norms" (299).

13.5 SHOW READERS HOW EVIDENCE IS RELEVANT

By this point you may be so sure that your evidence supports your
reasons that you'll think readers can't miss its relevance. But evidence never speaks for itself, especially not long quotations or
complex sets of numbers. You must speak for such evidence by
introducing it with a sentence stating what you want your readers to get out of it. For example, this passage bases a claim about
Hamlet on the evidence of the following quotation:

When Hamlet comes upon his stepfather, Claudius, at prayer, he demonstrates cool rationality.*claim*

> *I, his sole son, do this same villain send to heaven[?]*
> *Now might I do it [kill him] pat, now he is praying:*
> *And now I'll do't; and so he goes to heaven;*
> *And so am I reveng'd.* . . . *[Hamlet pauses to think]*
> *[But this] villain kills my father; and for that,*
> *I, his sole son, do this same villain send to heaven[?]*
> *Why, this is hire and salary, not revenge.* (3.3) *report of evidence*

It is not clear how that quotation supports the claim, because nothing in it specifically refers to Hamlet's rationality. In contrast, compare this:

When Hamlet comes upon his stepfather, Claudius, at prayer, he demonstrates cool rationality.*claim* **He impulsively wants to kill Claudius but pauses to reflect: If he kills Claudius while praying, he will send his soul to heaven, but Hamlet wants him damned to hell, so he coolly decides to kill him later:***reason*

> *I, his sole son, do this same villain send to heaven[?]*
> *Now might I do it [kill him] pat,* . . . *report of evidence*

Now we see the connection. (Do the same with tables and figures; see 15.3.1.)

Lacking a reason that explains the evidence, readers may not see what it *means*. So introduce complex evidence with a sentence explaining it.

13.6 GUARD AGAINST INADVERTENT PLAGIARISM

It will be as you draft that you risk the worst mistake a researcher can make: you lead readers to think that you're trying to pass off as your own the work of another writer. Do that and you risk an accusation of plagiarism, a charge that, if sustained, could mean a failing grade or even expulsion. Students know they cheat when they put their name on a paper purchased on the Internet or copied from a fraternity or sorority file. Most also know they cheat when they pass off as their own page after page copied from a source or downloaded from the Web. For those cases, there's nothing to say beyond *Don't*.

But many students don't realize when they risk being charged with plagiarism because they are careless or misinformed. You run that risk when do any of the following:

- You quote, paraphrase, or summarize a source but fail to cite it.

- You use ideas or methods from a source but fail to cite it.

- You use the exact words of a source and you do cite it, but you fail to put those words in quotation marks or in a block quotation.

- You paraphrase a source and cite it, but you use words so similar to those of the source that anyone can see that as you paraphrased, you followed the source word by word.

13.6.1 Cite the Source of Every Quotation, Paraphrase, or Summary

You must cite your source every time you use its words, even if you only paraphrase or summarize them. If the quotations, paraphrases, or summaries come from different pages of your sources, cite each one individually. If a paraphrase or summary extends over several paragraphs, cite it only once at the end. (See the Quick Tip at the end of this chapter for guidance on citing sources in your text.)

The most common problem is not that students don't know that they should cite a source, but that they lose track of which words are theirs and which are borrowed. That's why we urged you in chapter 6 to distinguish in your notes between quotations, paraphrases, and summaries of sources and your own analyses, thoughts, and commentary. Always include the citation as soon as you add a quotation because you may not remember to do so later. Be especially careful to cite a paraphrase or summary as you draft it; otherwise, you may not even remember that it originated with a source.

13.6.2 Signal Every Quotation, Even When You Cite Its Source

Even if you cite the source, readers must know exactly which words arc not yours, even if they are *as few as a single line*. It gets complicated, however, when you copy less than a line. Read this:

> Because technology begets more technology, the importance of an invention's diffusion potentially exceeds the importance of the original invention. Technology's history exemplifies what is termed an autocatalytic process: that is, one that speeds up at a rate that increases with time, because the process catalyzes itself (Diamond 1998, 301).

If you were writing about Jared Diamond's ideas, you would probably have to use some of his words, such as *the importance of an invention*. But you wouldn't put that phrase in quotation marks, because it shows no originality of thought or expression.

Two of his phrases, however, are so striking that they do require quotation marks: *technology begets more technology* and *autocatalytic process*. For example:

> The power of technology goes beyond individual inventions because "technology begets more technology." It is, as Diamond puts it, an "autocatalytic process" (301).

Once you cite those words, you can use them again without quotation marks or citation:

> As one invention begets another one and that one still another, the process becomes a self-sustaining catalysis that spreads across national boundaries.

This is a gray area: words that seem striking to some are not to others. If you put quotation marks around too many ordinary phrases, readers might think you're naive, but if you fail to use them when readers think you should, they may suspect you of plagiarism. Since it's better to seem naive than dishonest, especially early in your career, use quotation marks freely. (You must, however, follow the standard practices of your field. Lawyers, for example, often use the exact language of a statute or judicial opinion with no quotation marks.)

13.6.3 Don't Paraphrase Too Closely

You paraphrase appropriately when you represent an idea in your own words more clearly or pointedly than the source does. But readers will think that you plagiarize if they can match your words and phrasing with those of your source.

For example, these next sentences plagiarize the two sentences you just read:

> Booth, Colomb, and Williams claim that appropriate paraphrase uses one's own words to represent an idea to make a passage clearer or more pointed. Readers can accuse a student of plagiarism, however, if his paraphrase is so similar to its source that someone can match words and phrases in the sentence and those in that source.

This next paraphrase borders on plagiarism:

> Appropriate paraphrasing rewrites a passage into one's own words to make it clearer or more pointed. Readers think plagiarism occurs when a source is paraphrased so closely that they see parallels between their words and phrases. (Booth, Colomb, and Williams 2008)

This paraphrase does not plagiarize:

> According to Booth, Colomb, and Williams (2008), paraphrase is the use of your own words to represent the ideas of another more clearly. It becomes plagiarism when readers see a word-for-word similarity between a paraphrase and a source.

To avoid seeming to plagiarize, read the passage, look away, think about it for a moment; *then still looking away*, paraphrase it in your own words. Then check whether you can run your finger along your sentence and find synonyms for the same ideas in the same order in your source. If you can, try again.

13.6.4 Usually Cite a Source for Ideas Not Your Own

Most of our ideas are based on sources somewhere in history. But readers don't expect you to cite a source for the idea that the world is round. They do, however, expect you to cite a source for an idea when (1) the idea is associated with a specific person *and* (2) it's new enough *not* to be part of a field's common knowledge. For example, psychologists claim that we think and feel in different parts of our brains. But no reader would expect you to cite a source for that idea, because it's so familiar that no one would think you are implying it is yours. On the other hand, some psychologists argue that emotions are crucial to rational decision making. That idea is so new and tied to particular researchers that you'd have to cite them.

13.6.5 Don't Plead Ignorance, Misunderstanding, or Innocent Intentions

Some students sincerely believe that they don't have to cite material downloaded from the Web because it's free and publicly available. They are wrong. Other students defend themselves by claiming they didn't *intend* to mislead. Well, we read words, not minds. Here is how to think about this issue: If the person you borrowed from read your report, would she recognize your words or ideas as her own, including paraphrases, summaries, or even general ideas or methods? If so, you must cite that source and enclose any of her exact words in quotation marks or set them off in a block quotation. No exceptions, no excuses.

13.7 THE SOCIAL IMPORTANCE OF CITING SOURCES

13.7.1 Citations Benefit You

Citations protect you from a charge of plagiarism, but beyond that narrow self-interest, correct citations contribute to your ethos. First, readers don't trust sources they can't find. If they can't find yours because you failed to document them adequately, they won't trust your evidence; and if they don't trust your evidence, they won't trust your report or you. Second, many experienced researchers think that if a writer can't get the little things right, he can't be trusted on the big ones. Getting the details of citations right distinguishes reliable, experienced researchers from careless beginners. Finally, teachers assign research papers to help you learn how to integrate the research of others into your own thinking. Proper citations show that you have learned one important part of that process.

13.7.2 Citations Help Your Readers

Readers use citations before, while, and after they read your report. Before, many experienced readers will preview your report by skimming your list of sources to see whose work you read and whose you didn't. As they read, readers use citations to decide how much they can trust the reliability, currency, and completeness of your evidence. Finally, just as you depended on sources to start your bibliographical trail, so will some readers depend on your list to start theirs.

13.7.3 Citations Honor Your Sources

Finally, citations honor your sources. Few academic researchers get rich writing on topics such as "Ohio education, 1825–1850." Their reward isn't money; it's the reputation they earn for doing good work and the pleasure they take in knowing that colleagues respect it enough to cite it—even in disagreement. Your sources may never know you cited them, but that doesn't matter. When you cite sources, you honor them by acknowledging your intellectual debts.

In short, when you cite sources fully and accurately, you sustain and enrich the sense of community that gives written research both its scholarly and social value.

WHY THE FUSS OVER HONEST MISTAKES?
Some students wonder why teachers are so unforgiving of honest slip-ups. *What's the harm?*

First, it harms your credibility. One failure to acknowledge a source can lead readers to doubt your honesty, a career-ending judgment for an advanced student. But it matters even to a beginner. Your teacher is preparing you to write not for her but for others who will have only your words to judge your ethos. She needs to see that you know not only how to use sources thoughtfully but how to acknowledge them carefully and completely.

Other students think plagiarism is a victimless offense. It is not. Recently, two young scholars were praised when they used in a new way methods and ideas published twenty years earlier. They mentioned their source in passing but failed to acknowledge their specific debt fully. In doing so, they not only claimed undeserved credit but deprived the older scholar of credit he deserved. Worse, by omitting the bibliographical trail that led to his work, they kept readers from rediscovering it. The credit he lost cost him not only reputation but also perhaps grants, promotions, and ultimately higher pay.

13.8 FOUR COMMON CITATION STYLES

It would be easier if we all cited sources in the same style, but we don't. For academic research, there are two basic patterns, each with two common versions. The many differences among the styles can seem picky and irrelevant, but they matter to readers. So be sure to find out which style you should use and consult the proper guide for your style. (You can also find reliable online guides.)

Many researchers use computerized citation systems that automatically format citations in the style they choose. Some teachers encourage that practice. Others feel that students should not rely on such assistance, but rather memorize the details. If you don't know where your teacher stands on the issue, ask.

13.8.1 Two Basic Patterns: Author-Title and Author-Date

All citation forms begin with the name of the author, editor, or whoever else is responsible for the source. We distinguish styles by what follows the author. If the title follows the author, the style is called *author-title*.

Anes, Lee J. *A Story of Ohio: Its Early Days.* Boston: Hobson Press, 1988.

This pattern is common in the humanities.

If the date follows the author, the style is called *author-date.*

Anes, Lee. 1988. *A story of Ohio: Its early days.* Boston: Hobson Press.

This pattern is used in the natural sciences and most of the social sciences, because in those rapidly changing fields, readers want to know quickly how old a source is. They can spot dates more easily when they come at the beginning of a citation.

13.8.2 Two Author-Title Styles

There are two versions of author-title style, each based on a well-known style manual.

• One is called **Chicago style:** *The Chicago Manual of Style,* 15th ed. (Chicago: University of Chicago Press, 2003). It is sometimes called *Turabian* style, based on a widely used condensed manual: Kate L. Turabian, *A Manual for Writers of Research Papers, Theses, and Dissertations,* 7th ed. (Chicago: University of Chicago Press, 2007).

• The second is called **MLA style:** Joseph Gibaldi, *MLA Handbook for Writers of Research Papers,* 6th ed. (New York: Modern Language Association, 2003).

These styles differ only in minor details, but those details matter, so be sure to consult the proper style guide.

13.8.3 Two Author-Date Styles

The two versions of author-date style are also based on style manuals.

• One is called **Chicago style**, found in *The Chicago Manual of Style.* It is also sometimes called Turabian style.

• The second is called **APA style:** *Publication Manual of the American Psychological Association,* 5th ed. (Washington, DC: American Psychological Association, 2001).

These styles differ only in minor details, but those details matter, so be sure to consult the proper style guide and follow its prescriptions down to the last comma, space, and capital letter.

13.9 WORK THROUGH PROCRASTINATION AND WRITER'S BLOCK

If you can't start writing or you struggle to draft even a few words, you may have writer's block. Some cases arise from anxieties about school and its pressures; if that might be you, see a counselor. But most cases have causes you can address:

• You feel so intimidated by the task that you don't know where to begin. If so, divide the process into small tasks; then focus on one step at a time.

• You have set no goals or goals that are too high. If so, create a routine that sets goals you can meet, then use devices such as a progress chart or regular meetings with a writing partner.

• You feel you must make every sentence or paragraph perfect before you move to the next one. You can avoid some obsession with perfection if you write informally along the way, telling yourself you are writing only to help you think on paper. In any event, know that every researcher compromises on perfection to get the job done.

If you have problems like these, go to the student learning center. Advisers there have worked with every kind of procrastinator and blocked writer and can give you advice tailored to your problem.

On the other hand, some cases of writer's block may really be opportunities to let your ideas simmer in your subconscious while they combine and recombine into something new and surprising. If you're stuck but have time (another reason to start early), let your unconscious work on the problem while you do something else for a day or two. Then return to the task to see if you can get back on track.

☞ **QUICK TIP:** *Indicating Citations in Your Text*

You must indicate in your text every place where you use a source. The four most common citation styles (see 13.8) use parenthetical citations that direct readers to specific pages in the source, with enough information to find the corresponding entry in a list of sources.

> Some have claimed that Castro would reform Cuban politics (Smith, 1999, 233).

If you use Chicago author-title style, you may instead use a raised number that directs readers to a correspondingly numbered note at the bottom of the page or at the end of the report.

> Some have claimed that Castro would reform Cuban politics.[5]
>
> ---
> 5. George Smith, *Travels in Cuba* (Boston: Hasbro Press, 1999), 233.

PARENTHETICAL CITATIONS

A parenthetical citation includes only the information a reader needs to find the source in your list of sources at the end of your report. What you include depends first on whether you use author-title or author-date citation style. For example, here are the author-title forms for citing a single-author work if you do not mention the author in your sentences and you have only one work by that author in your list of sources:

Chicago Author-Title (Author, page[s])

> Only one writer provides data on this matter (Kay, 220).

MLA (Author page[s])

> Only one writer provides data on this matter (Kay 220).

If in your list of sources, you list more than one publication for an author, you must add a short title so that readers will know which publication you are citing:

Chicago Author-Title (Author, *Short Title*, page[s])

> Only one writer provides data on this matter (Kay, *A Life*, 220).

MLA (Author, *Short Title*, page[s])

> Only one writer provides data on this matter (Kay, *A Life*, 220).

In author-date style, you must add the date to every citation:

Chicago Author-Date (Author date, page[s])

> Only one writer provides data on this matter (Kay 2006, 220).

APA (Author, date, p. xxx)

> Only one writer provides data on this matter (Kay, 2006, p. 220).

If you have mentioned the author, drop the name from the citation:

Chicago Author-Title: Kay is the only writer who provides data on this matter (220).
MLA: Kay is the only writer who provides data on this matter (220).
Chicago Author-Date: Kay is the only writer who provides data on this matter (2006, 220).
APA: Kay is the only writer who provides data on this matter (2006, p. 220).

There are additional rules for citations if a work has more than one author, if you cite more than one work by the same author, and so on. For these, consult the appropriate guide.

NOTES

In Chicago author-title style, you can also use notes to direct readers to sources. Notes include the same information as a bibliography entry, but the form differs in three ways: notes list names not last name, first name, but first name last name; individual elements of a note are separated by commas rather than periods; and publication data are in parentheses.

NOTE FORM: 5. George Smith, *Travels in Cuba* (Boston: Hasbro Press, 1999), 233.

BIBLIOGRAPHY FORM: Smith, George. *Travels in Cuba*. Boston: Hasbro Press, 1999.

For details, consult the Turabian guide or *The Chicago Manual of Style*.

Researchers have increasingly used parenthetical citations rather than notes, because notes duplicate the information listed in a bibliography. If in doubt, ask your teacher.

CHAPTER FOURTEEN

Revising Your Organization and Argument

This chapter presents a plan for revising that will help you anticipate where your drafts might be clearer to you than to your readers. At first, this plan may seem too detailed and mechanical. But if you follow it one step at a time, you can analyze your draft more reliably than by just rereading it.

Some new researchers think that once they've churned out a draft, they're done. The best writers know better. They write a first draft not to show readers, but to discover what case they can actually make for their point and whether it stands up to their own scrutiny. Then they revise and revise until they think their readers will think so too. Revising for readers is hard, though, because we all know our own work too well to read it as others will. You must first know what readers look for, then determine whether your draft helps them find it. To do that, you have to analyze your draft objectively; otherwise, you'll just read into it what you want your readers to get out of it.

Some writers resist *any* revising for readers, fearing that if they accommodate their readers, they compromise their integrity. They think that the truth of their discovery should speak for itself and, if readers have a hard time understanding it, well, they just have to work harder. But revising for readers doesn't mean pandering to them. In fact, you only improve your ideas when you imagine drawing readers into an amiable conversation in which they engage your beliefs as you engage theirs.

In this chapter we show you how to diagnose and revise your organization and argument so that readers get out of it what you think you put into it.

14.1 THINKING LIKE A READER

Readers do not read word by word, sentence by sentence, as if they were adding up beads on a string. They want to begin with a sense of the whole, its structure, and, most important, why they should read your report in the first place. Then they use that sense of the whole and its aims to interpret its parts. It thus makes sense to start revising your overall organization, then its parts, then the clarity of your sentences, and, last, matters of spelling and punctuation. In reality, of course, no one revises so neatly. All of us revise as we go, correcting spelling as we rearrange our argument, clarifying evidence as we revise a paragraph. But when you have a draft and systematically revise top-down, from global structure to words, you are more likely to read as your readers will than if you start at the bottom, with words and sentences, and work up.

14.2 REVISING THE FRAME OF YOUR REPORT

Readers must recognize three things instantly and unambiguously:

- where your introduction stops

- where your conclusion begins

- what sentence in one or both states your main point

To ensure that, do this:

1. Put an extra space after your introduction and before your conclusion. If your field approves, put headings at those joints so that readers can't miss them.

2. State your main point at or close to the end of your introduction. Then compare that point with the one in your conclusion. They should at least not contradict each other. Nor should they be identical; make the one in your conclusion more specific and contestable.

3. If the point sentence in your introduction is not your main point but a launching point (see 12.2.1, 16.4.2), don't use it

merely to announce your topic. Revise to make it more specific: add the key concepts that run through your report as themes.

For example, consider this introductory paragraph (much abbreviated). What does it imply about the point of the report?

> In the eleventh century, the Roman Catholic Church initiated several Crusades to recapture the Holy Land. In a letter to King Henry IV in the year 1074, Gregory VII urged a Crusade but failed to carry it out. In 1095 his successor, Pope Urban II, gave a speech at the Council of Clermont in which he also called for a Crusade, and in the next year, in 1096, he initiated the First Crusade. In this paper I will discuss the reasons for the Crusades.

The closest thing to a point sentence appears to be that vague last one. But it merely announces the Crusades as a topic.

Here are the first few sentences from the first paragraph of the conclusion (again, much abbreviated). What is its point?

> As these documents show, popes Urban II and Gregory VII did urge the Crusades to restore the Holy Land to Christian rule. But their efforts were also shrewd political moves to unify the Roman and Greek churches and to prevent the breakup of the empire from internal forces threatening to tear it apart. In so doing, they . . .

The point sentence in the conclusion seems to be the second one ("But their efforts . . . apart"). That point is specific, substantive, and plausibly contestable. We could add a shortened version of that point to the end of the introduction, or we could write a new sentence for the introduction that, while not revealing the full point, would at least introduce the key concepts of the paper more clearly:

> In a series of documents, the popes proposed their Crusades to restore Jerusalem to Christendom, but their words suggest other issues involving **political concerns** about European and Christian **unity** in the face of **internal forces** that were **dividing** them.

14.3 REVISING YOUR ARGUMENT

Once you determine that the outer frame of your paper will work for readers, analyze its argument. We know this seems to repeat earlier steps, but once drafted, your argument may look different from the way it did in your storyboard or outline.

14.3.1 Identify the Substance of Your Argument

Does the structure of your argument match the structure of your report?

1. Is each reason the point of a section of its own? If not, the organizing points of your paper may conflict with the structure of your argument.

2. In each section, identify everything that counts as evidence, all the summaries, paraphrases, quotations, facts, figures, graphs, tables—whatever you report from a primary or secondary source. If what you identify as evidence and its explanation are less than a third or so of a section, you may not have enough evidence to support your reasons. If you have lots of evidence but few or no reasons, you may really have a data dump.

14.3.2 Evaluate the Quality of Your Argument

What might cause your readers to reject your argument?

1. Is your evidence sufficient, reliable, and clearly connected to your claims? If you are close to a final draft, it may be too late to find more or better evidence. But you can check other matters:

   • Check your data and quotations against your notes.

   • Make sure your readers see how quotations and data relate to your claim.

   • Be sure you haven't skipped intermediate subreasons between a major reason and its supporting evidence.

2. Have you appropriately qualified your argument? Can you drop in a few appropriate hedges like *probably, most, often, may*, and so on?

3. Does your report read less like a contest between competitors and more like a conversation with colleagues who have minds of their own, asking hard but friendly questions? If you haven't acknowledged alternative views or objections, go back through your argument, imagining a reader asking, *Why do you believe that? Are you really making that strong a point? Could you explain how this evidence relates to your point? But what about . . . ?* (Review 10.1–2.)

4. The hardest question: What warrants have you not expressed but should? There is no easy test for this. Once you identify each section and subsection of your argument, write in the margin its most important unstated warrant. Then ask whether readers will accept it. If not, you have to state and support it.

14.4 REVISING THE ORGANIZATION OF YOUR REPORT

Once you are confident in the outer frame of your report and the substance of its argument, make sure that readers will find the whole report coherent. To ensure that they do, check the following:

1. Do key terms run through your whole report?

- Circle key terms in the main point in your introduction and conclusion.

- Circle those same terms in the body of your report.

- Underline other words related to concepts named by those circled terms.

Here again is that concluding paragraph about the Crusades, with its key words circled:

> As these documents show, popes Urban II and Gregory VII did urge the Crusades to restore the Holy Land to Christian rule.

But their efforts were also (shrewd political moves) to (unify) the Roman and Greek churches and to (prevent the breakup) of the empire from (internal forces) threatening to (tear it apart.)

If readers don't see at least one of those key terms in most paragraphs, they may think your report wanders.

If you find a passage that lacks key terms, you might shoehorn a few in. If that's difficult, you may have gotten off track and need to rewrite or even discard that passage.

2. Is the beginning of each section and subsection clearly signaled? Could you quickly and confidently insert headings to mark where your major sections begin? If you can't, your readers probably won't recognize your organization. If you don't use headings, add an extra space at the major joints.

3. Does each major section begin with words that signal how that section relates to the one before it? Readers must not only recognize where sections begin and end, but understand why they are ordered as they are. Have you signaled the logic of your order with phrases such as *More important . . . , The other side of this issue is . . . , Some have objected that . . . , One complication is . . .* , or even just *First, Second, . . .?*

4. Is it clear how each section relates to the whole? For each section ask: *What question does this section answer?* If it doesn't answer one of the five questions whose answers constitute an argument (7.1), does it create a context, explain a background concept or issue, or help readers in some other way? If you can't explain how a section relates to your point, consider cutting it.

5. Is the point of each section stated in a brief introduction or (less helpfully) at its end? If you have a choice, state the point of a section at the end of its introduction. Never bury it in the middle. If a section is longer than four or five pages, you might summarize it at the end, restating its point and summarizing your argument, especially if it's fact-heavy with names, dates, or numbers.

6. Do terms that unify each section run through it? Each section needs its own key terms to unify and uniquely distinguish it from the others. To test that, create a heading that uniquely distinguishes that section from all the others. Repeat step 1 for each section: find the point sentence and circle in it the key terms for that section (do not circle terms you circled in the main point of the whole paper). Check whether those terms run through that section. If you find no terms that differ from those running through the whole, then your readers may not see what new ideas that section contributes. If you find that some of the terms also run through another section, the two sections may only repeat each another. If so, consider combining them.

14.5 CHECK YOUR PARAGRAPHS

Just as each section should be relevant to your main point, so should every paragraph be relevant to the point of its section. And just as sections do, each paragraph should have a sentence or more introducing it, with the key concepts that the rest of the paragraph develops. If those opening sentences don't state its point, then the last one must. Order your sentences by some principle and make them relevant to the point of the paragraph (for principles of order, see 12.2.3).

Avoid very long paragraphs (for most fields, more than a page) or long strings of short ones (fewer than five lines). Use two- or three-sentence paragraphs only for lists, transitions, introductions and conclusions to sections, or for statements that you want to emphasize. (We use short paragraphs so that you can more easily skim, rarely a consideration in report writing.)

14.6 LET YOUR DRAFT COOL, THEN PARAPHRASE IT

If you start your project early, you'll have time to let your revised draft cool. What seems good one day often looks different the next. When you return to it, don't read straight through; skim its top-level parts: its introduction, the first paragraph of each major section, and its conclusion. Then based only on what you've read, paraphrase it for someone who hasn't read it. Does the paraphrase hang together? Does it accurately sum up your argument? Even better, ask someone else to skim your report and summarize it: how well that test reader summarizes your argument will predict how well your final readers will understand it. Finally, always revise in light of a teacher's or adviser's advice. If you don't, not only will you pass up an opportunity to improve your report; you will offend whoever took time to read it and make suggestions, only to see them ignored. You need not follow every suggestion, but you should consider each one carefully.

MISTAKES ARE INEVITABLE

For both beginners and experts, mistakes are part of the game. All three of us have discovered them in our published work (and desperately hoped no one else would). Mistakes are most likely when you copy a long quotation. When Booth was in graduate school, his bibliography class was told to copy a poem *exactly* as written. Not one student in the class of twenty did so perfectly. His professor said he had assigned that task to hundreds of students, and perfect copies had been made by just three. But even when you make an especially foolish mistake, don't think you are the only one who ever has. Booth would still wince over the graduate paper he turned in on Shakespeare's *McBeth* (it's *Macbeth*, of course); and Williams would like to forget the report he was supposed to give but never did, because he could find nothing on his assigned topic, that great Norwegian playwright Henry Gibson (the playwright was Henrik Ibsen). In fact, until our last proofreading of the first edition of this book, the story about Booth on page xiv had him standing before heaven's "Golden Gate."

In many fields, reports begin with an abstract, a paragraph that tells readers what they will find in the report. It should be shorter than an introduction but do three things that an introduction does:

- state the research problem

- announce key themes

- state the main point or a launching point that anticipates the main point

Abstracts differ in different fields, but most follow one of three patterns. To determine which suits your field, ask your teacher or look in a standard journal.

1. Context + Problem + Main Point
This kind of abstract is an abbreviated introduction. It begins with a sentence or two to establish the context of previous research, continues with a sentence or two to state the problem, and concludes with the main result of the research.

> Computer folklore has held that character-based user interfaces promote more serious work than do graphical user interfaces (GUI), a belief that seemed to be confirmed by Hailo (1990).*context* But Hailo's study was biased by the same folklore that it purported to confirm.*problem* In this study, no significant differences were found in the performance of students working with a character-based interface (MS-DOS) or with a graphical interface (Macintosh OS).*main point*

2. Context + Problem + Launching Point
This pattern is the same as the previous one, except that the abstract states not the specific results, only their general nature (see 12.2.1).

> Computer folklore has held that character-based user interfaces promote more serious work than do graphical user interfaces

(GUI), a belief that seemed to be confirmed by Hailo (1990).*context* But Hailo's study was biased by the same folklore that it purported to confirm.*problem* This study tested the performance of thirty-eight business communication students using either a character-based or a graphical interface.*launching point*

3. Summary

A summary also states the context and the problem; but before reporting the result, it summarizes the rest of the report, focusing either on the evidence supporting the result or on the procedures and methods used to achieve it:

> Computer folklore has held that character-based user interfaces promote more serious work than do graphical user interfaces (GUI), a belief that seemed to be confirmed by Hailo (1990).*context* But Hailo's study was biased by the same folklore that it purported to confirm.*problem* In this study, thirty-eight students in a technical communication class were randomly assigned to one of two computer labs, one with character-based interfaces (MS-DOS), the other with graphical interfaces (Macintosh OS). Documents produced were evaluated on three criteria: content, format, and mechanics.*summary* The two groups did not differ on any of the three criteria.*main point*

In years to come, some researcher may search for exactly your research report, using a search engine that looks for key words in titles and abstracts. So imagine searching for your own report. What words should a researcher look for? Put them in your title and the first sentence of your abstract.

CHAPTER FIFTEEN

Communicating Evidence Visually

Most readers grasp quantitative evidence more easily in tables, charts, and graphs than they do in words. But some visual forms suit particular data and messages better than others. In this chapter, we show you how to choose the graphic form that best helps readers both grasp your data and understand how they support your argument.

A note on terminology: We use the term *graphics* for all visual representations of data. Traditionally, graphics are divided into *tables* and *figures*. A table is a grid with columns and rows. Figures are all other graphic forms, including graphs, charts, photographs, drawings, and diagrams. Figures that present quantitative data are divided into *charts* and *graphs*. Charts typically consist of bars, circles, points, or other shapes; graphs consist of continuous lines.

15.1 CHOOSING VISUAL OR VERBAL REPRESENTATIONS

When the data are few and simple, readers can grasp them as easily in a sentence as in a table:

In 1996, on average, men earned $32,144 a year, women $23,710, a difference of $8,434.

TABLE 15.1. Male-female salaries ($), 1996

Men	32,144
Women	23,710
Difference	8,434

But if you present more than a few numbers, readers will struggle to keep them straight:

Between 1970 and 2000, the structure of families changed in two ways. In 1970, 85 percent of families had two parents, but in 1980 that number declined to 77 percent, then to 73 percent in 1990, and to 68 percent in 2000. The number of one-parent families rose, particularly families headed by a mother. In 1970, 11 percent of families were headed by a single mother. In 1980 that number rose to 18 percent, in 1990 to 22 percent, and to 23 percent in 2000. There were some marginal changes among single fathers (headed 1 percent of the families in 1970, 2 percent in 1980, 3 percent in 1990, and 4 percent in 2000). Families headed by no adult remained stable at 3–4 percent.

15.2 CHOOSING THE MOST EFFECTIVE GRAPHIC

When you graphically present data as complex as in that paragraph, the most common choices are tables, bar charts, and line graphs, each of which has a distinctive rhetorical effect.

A table seems precise and objective. It emphasizes discrete numbers and requires readers to infer relationships or trends on their own (unless you state them in an introductory sentence).

TABLE 15.2. Changes in U.S. family structure, 1970–2000

| Family type | Percentage of total families | | | |
	1970	1980	1990	2000
2 Parents	85	77	73	68
Mother	11	18	22	23
Father	1	2	3	4
No adult	3	4	3	4

Charts and line graphs present a visual image that communicates values less precisely than do the exact numbers of a table but with more impact. But charts and graphs also differ. A bar chart emphasizes contrasts among discrete items:

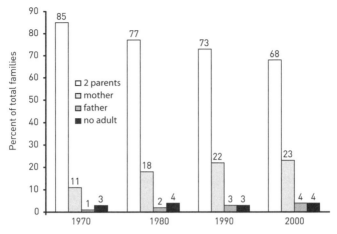

Figure 15.1. Changes in U.S. family structure, 1970–2000

A line graph suggests continuous change over time:

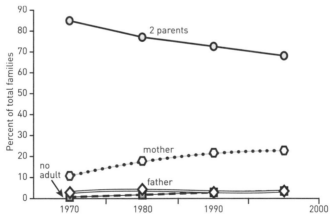

Figure 15.2. Changes in U.S. family structure, 1970–2000

Choose the form that achieves the effect you want, not the one that comes to mind first.

How many choices you should consider depends on your experience. If you're new to quantitative research, limit your choices to basic tables, bar charts, and line graphs. Your computer software offers more choices, but ignore those that you aren't familiar with. If you're doing advanced research, readers will expect you to draw from a larger range of graphics favored in your field. In that case, consult table 15.7, which describes the rhetorical uses of other common forms. You may have to consider even more creative ways of representing data if you are writing a dissertation or article in a field that routinely displays complex relationships in large data sets. (See the bibliography for additional resources.)

What follows is a guide to the basics of tables, charts, and graphs.

15.3 DESIGNING TABLES, CHARTS, AND GRAPHS

Computer programs create graphics so dazzling that many writers let their software determine their design. That's a mistake. Readers don't care how fancy a graphic looks if it doesn't communicate your point clearly. Here are some principles for designing effective graphics. To follow them, you may have to change default settings in your graphics software.

15.3.1 Frame Each Graphic to Help Readers Understand It

A graphic representing complex numbers rarely speaks for itself. You must frame it to show readers what to see in it and how to understand its relevance to your argument:

1. Label every graphic in a way that describes its data. For a table, the label is called a *title* and is set flush left above the table; for a figure, the label is called a *legend* and is set flush left below the figure. Keep titles and legends short but descriptive enough to distinguish every graphic from every other one.

   • Avoid making the title or legend a general topic.

   N O T: Heads of households

   B U T: Changes in one- and two-parent heads of households, 1970–2000

   • Do not give background information or characterize what the data imply.

N O T: Weaker effects of counseling on depressed children before professionalization of staff, 1995–2004

B U T: Effect of counseling on depressed children, 1995–2004

• Be sure labels distinguish graphics presenting similar data.

N O T: Risk factors for high blood pressure

B U T: Risk factors for high blood pressure among men in Cairo, Illinois

Risk factors for high blood pressure among men in St. Louis, Missouri

2. Insert into the table or figure information that helps readers see how the data support your point. For example, if numbers in table show a trend and the size of the trend matters, indicate the change in a final column. If a line on a graph changes in response to an influence not mentioned on the graph, add text to the image to explain it.

Although reading and math scores declined by almost 100 points following redistricting, that trend reversed when supplemental math and reading programs were introduced.

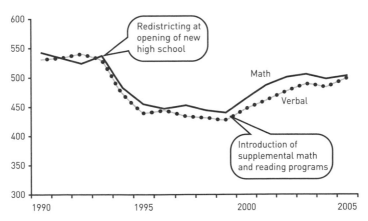

Figure 15.3. SAT scores for Mid-City High, 1990–2005

3. Introduce the table or figure with a sentence that explains how to interpret it. Then highlight what it is in the table or figure that you want readers to focus on, particularly any number or relationship mentioned in that introductory sentence. For example, we have to study table 15.3 to understand how it supports the sentence before it:

Most predictions about increased gasoline consumption have proved wrong.

TABLE 15.3. Gasoline consumption

	1970	1980	1990	2000
Annual miles (000)	9.5	10.3	10.5	11.7
Annual consumption (gal.)	760	760	520	533

We need a sentence to explain how the numbers support or explain the claim, a more informative title, and visual help that highlights what we should see in the table:

Gasoline consumption has not grown as predicted. Though Americans drove 23 percent more miles in 2000 than in 1970, they used 32 percent less fuel.

TABLE 15.4. Per capita mileage and gasoline consumption, 1970–2000

	1970	1980	1990	2000
Annual miles (000)	9.5	10.3	10.5	11.7
(% change vs. 1970)		8.4%	10.5%	23.1%
Annual consumption (gal.)	760	760	520	533
(% change vs. 1970)		0%	(31.5%)	(31.6%)

The added sentence tells us how to interpret the key data in table 15.4, and the highlight tells us where to find them.

15.3.2 Keep All Graphics as Simple as Their Content Allows
Some guides encourage you to cram as much data as you can into a graphic. But readers want to see only the data relevant to your point, free of distractions. For all graphics:

1. Include only relevant data. If you include data only for the record, label it accordingly and put it in an appendix.

2. Keep the visual impact simple.

   - Box a graphic only if you group two or more figures.

   - Do not color or shade the background.

   FOR TABLES
   - Never use both horizontal and vertical dark lines to divide columns and rows. Use light gray lines only if the table is complex or you want to direct your reader's eyes in one direction to compare data.

   - For tables with many rows, lightly shade every fifth row.

   FOR CHARTS AND GRAPHS
   - Use background grid lines only if the graphic is complex or readers need to see precise numbers. Make them light gray.

   - Color or shade lines or bars only to show a contrast. Use color only if the text will be printed in color and not photocopied later. (Black-and-white photocopies make many colors look alike.)

   - Never use iconic bars (for example, images of cars to represent automobile production) or add a third dimension merely for effect. Both look amateurish and can distort how readers judge values.

   - Plot data on three dimensions only when your readers are familiar with such graphs and you cannot display the data in any other way.

3. Use clear labels.

   - Label all rows and columns in tables and both axes in charts and graphs.

   - Use tick marks and labels to indicate intervals on the vertical axis of a graph.

- If possible, label lines, bar segments, and the like on the image rather than in a legend set to the side. Use a legend only if labels would make the image too complex to read.

- When specific numbers matter, add them to bars or segments in charts or to dots on lines in graphs.

15.4 SPECIFIC GUIDELINES FOR TABLES, BAR CHARTS, AND LINE GRAPHS

15.4.1 Tables

Tables with lots of data can seem dense, so organize them to help readers.

- Order the rows and columns by a principle that lets readers quickly find what you want them to see. Do not automatically choose alphabetic order.

- Round numbers to a relevant value. If differences of less than 1,000 don't matter, then 2,123,499 is irrelevantly precise.

- Sum totals at the bottom of a column or at the end of a row, not at the top or left.

Compare tables 15.5 and 15.6.

TABLE 15.5. Unemployment in major industrial nations, 1990–2000

	1990	2001	Change
Australia	6.7	6.5	(.2)
Canada	7.7	5.9	(1.8)
France	9.1	8.8	(.3)
Germany	5.0	8.1	3.1
Italy	7.0	9.9	2.9
Japan	2.1	4.8	2.7
Sweden	1.8	5.1	3.3
UK	6.9	5.1	(1.8)
USA	5.6	4.2	(1.6)

Table 15.5 looks cluttered and its items aren't helpfully organized. In contrast, table 15.6 is clearer because it has an informative title, less visual clutter, and items organized to let us see the pattern more easily:

TABLE 15.6. Changes in unemployment rates of industrial nations, 1990–2000

	1990	2001	Change
English-speaking vs. non-English-speaking nations			
Canada	7.7	5.9	(1.8)
UK	6.9	5.1	(1.8)
USA	5.6	4.2	(1.6)
Australia	6.7	6.5	(0.2)
France	9.1	8.8	(.3)
Japan	2.1	4.8	2.7
Italy	7.0	9.9	2.9
Germany	5.0	8.1	3.1
Sweden	1.8	5.1	3.3

15.4.2 Bar Charts

Bar charts communicate as much by visual impact as by specific numbers. But bars arranged in no pattern imply no point. If possible, group and arrange bars to create an image that matches your message. For example, look at figure 15.4 in the context of the explanatory sentence before it. The items are listed alphabetically, an order that doesn't help readers see the point.

Most of the world's deserts are concentrated in North Africa and the Middle East.

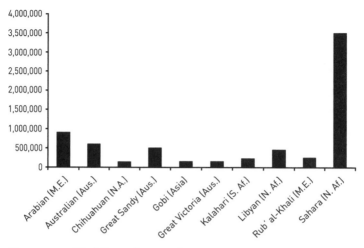

Figure 15.4. World's ten largest deserts

In contrast, figure 15.5 supports the claim with a coherent image.

Most of the world's deserts are concentrated in North Africa and the Middle East.

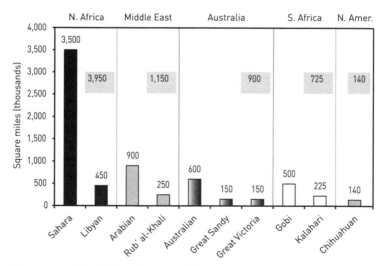

Figure 15.5. World distribution of large deserts

In standard bar charts, each bar represents 100 percent of a whole. But sometimes readers need to see specific numbers for parts of the whole. You can do that in two ways:

- Divide the bars into proportional parts, creating a "stacked" bar.

- Give each part of the whole its own bar, then group the parts into clusters

Use stacked bars only when you want readers to compare whole values for different bars rather than their divided segments, because readers can't easily compare the proportions of segments by eye alone. If you do use stacked bars, do this:

- Arrange segments in a logical order. If possible, put the largest segment at the bottom in the darkest shade.

- Label segments with specific numbers and to assist comparisons, connect corresponding segments with gray lines

Compare figures 15.6 and 15.7:

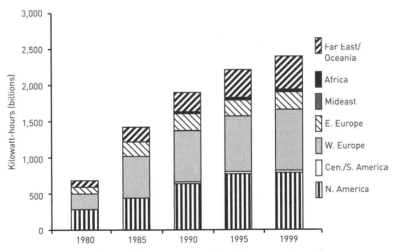

Figure 15.6. World generation of nuclear energy, 1980–1999

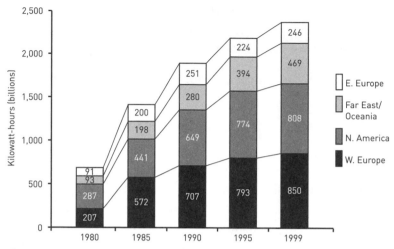

Figure 15.7. Largest generators of nuclear energy, 1980–1999

If you group bars because segments are as important as the wholes, do this:

* Arrange groups in a logical order; if possible put bars of similar size next to one another (order bars in the same way through all the groups).

* Label groups with the number for the whole, either above each group or below the labels on the bottom.

Most data that fit a bar chart fit in a pie chart. But while pie charts are popular in magazines, tabloids, and annual reports, they are harder to read than bar charts and invite misinterpretation. Readers must mentally compare proportions of segments whose size is hard to judge in the first place. Most researchers consider them amateurish. Use bar charts instead.

15.4.3 Line Graphs

Because a line graph emphasizes trends, readers must see a clear image to interpret it correctly. Do the following:

- Choose the variable that makes the line go in the direction, up or down, that supports your point. If the good news is a reduction (down) in high school dropouts, you can more effectively represent the same data as a rising line indicating increase in retention (up). If you want to emphasize bad news, find a way to represent your data as a falling line.

- Plot more than six lines on one graph only if you cannot make your point in any other way.

- If you have fewer than ten or so data points, indicate them with dots. If only a few are relevant, insert numbers to show their exact value.

- Do not depend on different shades of gray to distinguish lines, as in figure 15.8.

Compare figure 15.8 and figure 15.9:

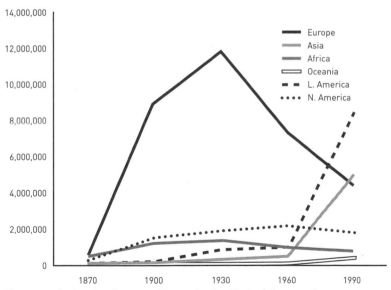

Figure 15.8. Foreign-born residents in the United States, 1870–1990

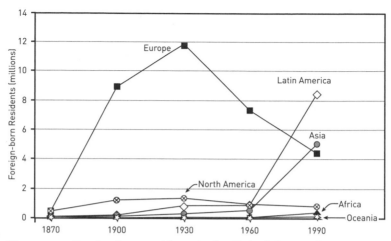

Figure 15.9. Foreign-born residents in the United States, 1870–1990

Figure 15.8 is harder to read because the shades of gray do not distinguish the lines well against the background and because our eyes have to flick back and forth to connect the lines to the legend. Figure 15.9 makes those connections clearer.

These different ways of showing the same data can be confusing. To cut through that confusion, test different ways of representing the same data. Construct alternative graphics; then ask someone unfamiliar with the data to judge them for impact and clarity. Be sure to introduce the figures with a sentence that states the claim you want the figure to support.

15.5 COMMUNICATING DATA ETHICALLY

Your graphic must be not only clear and accurate, but honest. Do not distort the image of the data to make your point. For example, the two line graphs below display identical data, yet imply different messages:

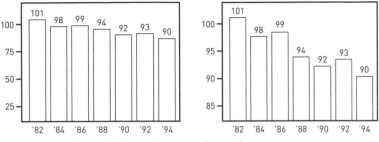

Figure 15.10. Capitol City pollution index, 1982–1994

The 0–100 scale in the figure on the left creates a fairly flat slope, which makes the drop in pollution seem small. The vertical scale in the figure on the right, however, begins not at 0 but at 80. When a scale is so truncated, it creates a sharper slope that exaggerates small contrasts.

Graphs can also mislead by implying false correlations. Someone might claim that unemployment goes down as union membership goes down and offer figure 15.11 as evidence. And indeed, in that graph, union membership and the unemployment rate do seem to move together so closely that a reader might infer one causes the other:

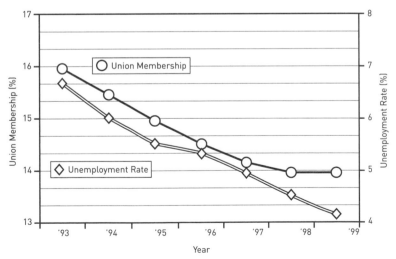

Figure 15.11. Union membership and unemployment rate, 1993–1999

But the scale for the left axis (union membership) differs from the scale for the right axis (the unemployment rate), making it seem that the two trends could be causally related. They may be, but that distorted image doesn't prove it.

Graphs can also mislead when the image encourages readers to misjudge values. The two charts in figure 15.12 represent exactly the same data but seem to communicate different messages:

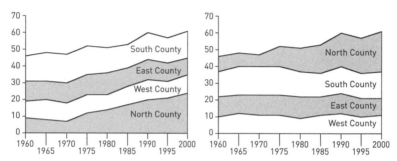

Figure 15.12. Representation of suburban counties in state university undergraduates (percent of total)

The charts in figure 15.12 are both stacked area charts. Despite their visual differences, they represent the same data. Area charts such as these represent changes in values not by the *angles* of the lines, but by the areas *between* them. In both charts, the bands for south, east, and west are roughly the same width throughout, indicating little change in the values they represent. The band for the north, however, widens sharply, representing a sharp increase in the numbers it represents. In the chart on the left, readers could easily misjudge the top three bands, because they are on top of the rising north band, making those bands seem to rise as well. In the chart on the right, on the other hand, those three bands do not rise because they are on the bottom. Now only the band for the north rises.

Here are four guidelines for avoiding visual misrepresentation:

- Do not manipulate a scale to magnify or reduce a contrast.

- Do not use a figure whose image distorts values.

- Do not make a table or figure unnecessarily complex or misleadingly simple.

- If the table or figure supports a point, state it.

Table 15.7 Common graphic forms and their uses

	Data	Rhetorical Uses
Bar Chart		
	Compares the value of one variable across a series of items called cases (e.g., average salaries for service workers*variable* in six companies*cases*).	Creates strong visual contrasts among individual cases, emphasizing individual comparisons. For specific values, add numbers to bars. Can show ranks or trends. Vertical bars (called *columns*) are most common, but can be horizontal if cases are numerous or have complex labels. See section 15.4.3.
Bar Chart, Grouped or Split		
	Compares the value of one variable, divided into subsets, across a series of cases (e.g. average salaries*variable* for men and women service workers*subsets* in six companies*cases*).	Contrasts subsets within and across individual cases; not useful for comparing total values for cases. For specific values, add numbers to bars. Grouped bars show ranking or trends poorly; useful for time series only if trends are unimportant. See section 15.4.3.
Bar Chart, Stacked		
	Compares the value of one variable, divided into two or more subsets, across a series of cases (e.g. harassment complaints*variable* segmented by region*subsets* in six industries*cases*).	Best for comparing totals across cases and subsets *within* cases; difficult to compare subsets across cases (use grouped bars). For specific values, add numbers to bars and segments. Useful for time series. Can show ranks or trends for total values only. See section 15.4.3.
Histogram		
	Compares two variables, with one segmented into ranges that function like the cases in a bar graph (e.g., service workers*continuous variable* whose salary is $0–5,000, $5,000–10,000, $10,000–15,000, etc.*segmented variable*).	Best for comparing segments within continuous data sets. Shows trends, but emphasizes segments (e.g., a sudden spike at $5,000–10,000 representing part-time workers). For specific values, add numbers to bars.
Image Chart		
	Shows value of one or more variable for cases displayed on a map, diagram, or other image (e.g., states*cases* colored red or blue to show voting patterns*variable*).	Shows the distribution of the data in relation to preexisting categories; de-emphasizes specific values. Best when the image is familiar, as in a map or diagram of a process.
Pie Chart		
	Shows the proportion of a single variable for a series of cases (e.g., the budget share*variable* of U.S. cabinet departments*cases*).	Best for comparing one segment to the whole. Useful only with few segments or segments that are very different in size; otherwise comparisons among segments are difficult. For specific values, add numbers to segments. Common in popular venues, frowned on by professionals. See 15.4.3.

Table 15.7 (*continued*)

	Data	Rhetorical Uses
Line Graph		
	Compares continuous variables for one or more cases (e.g., temperature$_{variable}$ and viscosity$_{variable}$ in two fluids$_{cases}$).	Best for showing trends; deemphasizes specific values. Useful for time series. To show specific values, add numbers to data points. To show the significance of a trend, segment the grid (e.g., below or above average performance). See 15.4.3.
Area Chart		
	Compares two continuous variables for one or more cases (e.g., reading test scores$_{variable}$ over time$_{variable}$ in a school district$_{case}$).	Shows trends; deemphasizes specific values. Can be used for time series. To show specific values, add numbers to data points. Areas below the lines add no information, but will lead some readers to misjudge values. Confusing with multiple lines/areas.
Area Chart, Stacked		
	Compares two continuous variables for two or more cases (e.g., profit$_{variable}$ over time$_{variable}$ for several products$_{cases}$).	Shows the trend for the total of all cases, plus how much each case contributes to that total. Likely to mislead readers on the value or the trend for any individual case, as explained in section 15.5.
Scatterplot		
	Compares two variables at multiple data points for a single case (e.g., housing sales$_{variable}$ and distance from downtown$_{variable}$ in one city$_{case}$) or at one data point for multiple cases (e.g., brand loyalty$_{variable}$ and repair frequency$_{variable}$ for ten manufacturers$_{cases}$).	Best for showing the distribution of data, especially when there is no clear trend or when the focus is on outlying data points. If only a few data points are plotted, it allows a focus on individual values.
Bubble Chart		
	Compares three variables at multiple data points for a single case (e.g., housing sales,$_{variable}$ distance from downtown,$_{variable}$ and prices$_{variable}$ in one city$_{case}$) or at one data point for multiple cases (e.g. image advertising,$_{variable}$ repair frequency,$_{variable}$ and brand loyalty$_{variable}$ for ten manufacturers$_{cases}$).	Emphasizes the relationship between the third variable (bubbles) and the first two; most useful when the question is whether the third variable is a product of the others. Readers easily misjudge relative values shown by bubbles; adding numbers mitigates that problem.

CHAPTER SIXTEEN

Introductions and Conclusions

A good introduction encourages readers to read your report with interest and prepares them to understand it better. A good conclusion leaves them with a clear statement of your point and renewed appreciation of its significance. In this chapter we show you how to write both. The time you spend revising your introduction and conclusion may be the most important revision you do.

Once you think you have a draft that works, you're ready to write your final introduction and conclusion. Some writers think that means following the standard advice: *Grab their attention with something snappy or cute.* That's not useless advice, but those who read research reports want more than cute and snappy. What seizes their attention is a problem they think needs a solution, and what holds it is a promise that you've found it. As we've said, you can always work with readers who say, *I don't agree.* What you can't survive are those who shrug and say, *I don't care.*

16.1 THE COMMON STRUCTURE OF INTRODUCTIONS

As we've emphasized, different research communities do things in different ways, but nowhere do those differences seem greater than in their introductions. These three condensed examples are from the fields of cultural criticism, computer design, and legal history. But while they look different on the surface, their underlying structures are identical.

> (1) Why can't a machine be more like a man? In almost every episode of *Star Trek: The Next Generation*, the android Data wonders what makes a person a person. In the original *Star Trek*, similar questions were raised by the half-Vulcan Mr. Spock, whose status

as a person was undermined by his machinelike logic and lack of emotion. In fact, Data and Spock are only the most recent "quasi-persons" who have explored the nature of humanity. The same question has been raised by and about creatures ranging from Frankenstein to Terminator II. But the real question is why these characters who struggle to be persons are always white and male. As cultural interpreters, do they tacitly reinforce destructive stereotypes of what it means to be "normal"? The model person seems in fact to be defined by Western criteria that exclude most of the people in the world.

(2) As part of its program of Continuous Quality Improvement ("CQI"), Motodyne Computers plans to redesign the user interface for its UnidyneTM online help system. The specifications for its interface call for self-explanatory icons that let users identify their function without verbal labels. Motodyne has three years' experience with its current icon set, but it has no data showing which icons are self-explanatory. Lacking such data, we cannot determine which icons to redesign. This report provides data for eleven icons, showing that five of them are not self-explanatory.

(3) In today's society, would Major John André, a British spy in civilian clothes captured behind American lines in 1780, be hanged? Though considered a noble patriot, he suffered the punishment mandated by military law. Over time our traditions have changed, but the punishment for spying has not. It is the only offense that mandates death. Recently, however, the Supreme Court has rejected mandatory death sentences in civilian cases, creating an ambiguity in their application to military cases. If Supreme Court decisions apply to the military, will Congress have to revise the Uniform Code of Military Justice? This article concludes that it will.

The topics and problems posed in those three introductions differ as much as their intended readers, but behind them is a shared pattern that readers look for in all introductions, regardless of field. That common structure consists of three elements:

- contextualizing background

- statement of the problem

- response to the problem

Not every introduction has all three elements, but most do. Here is that pattern of *Context + Problem + Response* in each of those introductions:

(1) CONTEXT: Why can't a machine be more like a man? . . . The same question has been raised by and about creatures ranging from Frankenstein to Terminator II.
PROBLEM: But the real question is . . . do they tacitly reinforce destructive stereotypes of what it means to be "normal"?
RESPONSE: The model person seems in fact to be defined by Western criteria that exclude most of the people in the world.

(2) CONTEXT: As part of its program of Continuous Quality Improvement ("CQI"), Motodyne Computers plans to redesign the user interface. . . . Motodyne has three years' experience with its current icon set . . .
PROBLEM: but it has no data showing which icons are self-explanatory. Lacking such data, we cannot determine which icons to redesign.
RESPONSE: This report provides data for eleven icons, showing that five of them are not self-explanatory.

(3) CONTEXT: In today's society, would Major John André . . . be hanged [for spying]? . . . It is the only offense that mandates death.
PROBLEM: Recently, however, the Supreme Court has rejected mandatory death sentences in civilian cases, creating an ambiguity in their application to military cases. . . . Will Congress have to revise the Uniform Code of Military Justice?
RESPONSE: This article concludes that it will.

Each of those elements plays it own role not only in motivating readers to read your report, but in helping them understand it.

16.2   STEP 1: ESTABLISH COMMON GROUND

We call the opening context *common ground* because it establishes a shared understanding between reader and writer about the larger issue the writer will address. But it does more, illustrated by the opening of a fairy tale:

> One sunny morning Little Red Riding Hood was skipping through the forest on her way to Grandmother's house.*stable context [imagine butterflies dancing around her head to flutes and violins]*

Like the opening to most fairy tales, this one establishes an unproblematic, even happy context, just so that it can be disrupted with a problem:

> . . . when suddenly Hungry Wolf jumped out from behind a tree*disrupting condition [imagine trombones and tubas]* frightening her [and, if they've lost themselves in the story, little children as well].*cost*

The rest of the story elaborates that problem and then resolves it.

Unlikely though it may seem, introductions to most research reports follow the same strategy. They open with a stable context of a common ground—some apparently unproblematic account of research already known. The writer then disrupts it with a problem, saying in effect: *Reader, you may think you know something, **but** your knowledge is flawed or incomplete.*

> (3) STABLE COMMON GROUND: In today's society, would Major John André, a British spy . . . be hanged? . . . [Spying] is the only offense that mandates death.

> DISRUPTING PROBLEM: Recently, **however**, the Supreme Court has rejected mandatory death sentences. . . .

Not every research report opens with common ground. This one opens directly with a problem:

Recently the chemical processes that thin the ozone layer have been found to be less well understood than once thought. We may have labeled hydrofluorocarbons as the chief cause incorrectly.

Some readers might find that problem disturbing enough to motivate their reading, but we can heighten its rhetorical punch by introducing it with the seemingly unproblematic context of prior research, *specifically so that we can disrupt it*:

As we have investigated environmental threats, our understanding of chemical processes in acid rain and the buildup of carbon dioxide has improved, allowing us to understand better their effects on the biosphere.*common ground* [*Sounds good.*] **But recently the processes that thin the ozone layer have been found to be less well understood than once thought.***destabilizing condition* We may have labeled hydrofluorocarbons as the chief cause incorrectly.*consequence*

Readers now have not one reason to see their self-interest in the problem, but two: not just the problem itself, but also their incomplete understanding of the whole matter.

Common ground can describe a misunderstanding:

The Crusades are widely believed to have been motivated by religious zeal to restore the Holy Land to Christendom.*common ground* **In fact**, the motives were at least partly, if not largely, political.

It can survey flawed research:

Few sociological concepts have fallen out of favor as fast as Catholicism's alleged protective influence against suicide. Once one of sociology's basic beliefs, it has been called into question by a series of studies in both Europe and North America. . . .*common ground* **However**, certain studies still find an effect of religion . . .

Or it can point to a misunderstanding about the problem itself:

American education has focused on teaching children to think critically, to ask questions and test answers.*common ground* **But** the field of critical thinking has been taken over by fads and special interests.

Some inexperienced researchers skimp on common ground, opening their report as if they were picking up a class conversation where it left off. Their introductions are so sketchy that only others in the course would understand them:

> In view of Hofstadter's failure to respect the differences among math, music, and art, it is not surprising that the response to *The Embodied Mind* would be stormy. It is less clear what caused the controversy. I will argue that any account of the human mind must be interdisciplinary. . . .

When you draft your introduction, imagine you are writing to someone who has read some of the same sources as you and is generally interested in the same issues, but does not know what specifically happened in your class.

Others make the opposite mistake, thinking they should list every source they read that remotely touches their topic. Survey only those sources whose findings you will *directly* modify. Add more *only* if you need to locate the problem in a wider context.

16.3 STEP 2: STATE YOUR PROBLEM

Once you establish common ground, disrupt it with a problem. As we've said, the statement of a research problem has two parts:

* a *condition* of incomplete knowledge or understanding, and

* the *consequences* of that condition, a more significant gap in understanding

You can state the condition directly:

> . . . but Motodyne has no data showing which icons are self-explanatory.

Or you can imply it in an indirect question:

> The real question is why these characters are always white and male.

You make this condition of ignorance or flawed understanding part of a *full* research problem *only* when you imagine someone asking *So what?* and then spell out as an answer the *consequence* of that flawed understanding. You can state that consequence as a direct cost:

> Lacking such data, we cannot determine which icons to re-design.*cost*

Or you can transform the cost into a benefit:

> With such data, we could determine which icons to redesign.*benefit*

Those are not merely stylistic differences. Some research suggests that readers are more motivated by a real cost than by a potential benefit.

That's the straightforward version of stating a problem; there are variations.

16.3.1 **When Should You State the Condition of a Problem Explicitly?** Occasionally, you tackle a problem so familiar that its name implies both its condition and consequence to those in the field: *the role of DNA in personality; Shakespeare's knowledge of foreign languages.* Here again is that (condensed) introduction to perhaps the most significant report in molecular biology, Crick and Watson's account of the double-helix structure of DNA:

> We wish to suggest a structure for the salt of deoxyribose nucleic acid (D.N.A.). This structure has novel features which are of considerable biological interest. A structure for nucleic acid has already been proposed by Pauling and Corey. They kindly made their manuscript available to us in advance of publication. Their model consists of three intertwined chains, with the phosphates near the fibre axis, and the bases on the outside. In our opinion, this structure is unsatisfactory. . . .

It was enough for them merely to "suggest" a structure for DNA, because they knew everyone wanted to know what it was. (Note, though, that they do raise a problem by mentioning Pauling and Corey's *incorrect* model.)

In the natural sciences and most social sciences, researchers usually address questions familiar to readers. In that case, you might think you do not need to spell out your problem. But readers won't know the *particular* flaw in their knowledge that your research will correct unless you tell them.

In the humanities and some social sciences, researchers more often pose questions that they alone have found or even invented, questions that readers find new and often surprising. In that case, you must explicitly describe the gap in knowledge or flawed understanding that you intend to resolve.

16.3.2 Should You Spell Out Consequences and Benefits?

To convince readers that they should take your problem seriously, you must state the cost *they* will pay if it is not resolved or the benefits *they* gain if it is. Sometimes you can describe tangible costs that your research helps your readers avoid (see 4.1):

> Last year the River City Supervisors agreed that River City should add the Bayside development to its tax base. Their plan, however, was based on little economic analysis. If the Board votes to annex Bayside without understanding what it will cost the city, **the Board risks worsening River City's already shaky fiscal situation.** When the burden of bringing sewer and water service up to city code are included in the analysis, the annexation will cost more than the Board assumes.

This is the kind of problem that motivates *applied* research. The area of ignorance (no economic analysis) has tangible consequences (higher costs).

In pure research, you formulate the same kind of problem when you explain the consequence not in money, but as misunderstanding or, alternatively, as the possible benefit of better understanding:

> Since 1972 American cities have annexed upscale neighborhoods to prop up tax bases, often bringing disappointing economic benefits. But those results could have been predicted had they done basic economic analysis. The annexation movement is a case

study of how political decisions at the local level fail to use expert information. What is puzzling is why cities do not seek out that expertise. **If we can discover why cities fail to rely on basic economic analyses, we might better understand why their decision making fails so often in other areas as well.** This paper analyzes the decision-making process of three cities that annexed surrounding areas without consideration of economic consequences.

16.3.3 Testing Conditions and Consequences

In chapter 4 we suggested a way to test how clearly you articulate the consequences of not solving a problem: after the sentences that best state your readers' condition of ignorance or misunderstanding, ask *So what?*

> Motodyne has no data showing which icons are self-explanatory. [*So what?*] Without such data, it cannot determine which icons to redesign.

> Stories about the Alamo in Mexican and U.S. versions differ in obvious ways, but U.S. versions from different eras also differ. [*So what?*] Well . . .

Answering *So what?* can be exasperating, even dismaying. If you fall in love with stories about the Battle of the Alamo, you can pursue them to your heart's content, without having to answer to anyone but yourself: *I just like reading about them.* But for others to appreciate your research, you have to "sell" them on its significance. Otherwise, why should they spend time on your report?

You have to convince readers that if they go on not knowing, say, how Hollywood turned the Alamo story into myth, they will fail to understand something more important about our national identity. To be sure, some readers will ask again, *So what? I don't care about our national identity.* To which you can think only, *Wrong audience.* Successful researchers know how to find and solve interesting problems, but a skill no less important is knowing how to find (or create) an audience interested in the problems they solve.

If you're sure your readers know the consequences of your

problem, you might decide not to spell them out. Crick and Watson did not specify either the consequences or benefits of knowing the structure of DNA, because every biologist knew that to understand genetics, they first had to understand the structure of DNA. Had Crick and Watson spelled out those consequences, they might have seemed both redundant and condescending.

If you are tackling your first research project, no reasonable teacher will expect you to state the consequences of your problem in detail, because you probably don't yet know why other researchers think it is significant. But you take a big step in that direction when you can state *your own* incomplete knowledge or flawed understanding in a way that shows *you* are committed to improving it. You take an even bigger step when you can show that by better understanding one thing, you better understand something much more important, *even if only to you.*

16.4 STEP 3: STATE YOUR RESPONSE

Once you disrupt your readers' stable context with a problem, they expect you to resolve it with your main point. You can state that point in one of two ways.

16.4.1 State the Gist of Your Solution

You can state your main point/solution explicitly toward the end of your introduction:

As we have investigated environmental threats, our understanding of chemical processes in acid rain and the buildup of carbon dioxide has improved, allowing us to understand better their effects on the biosphere.*common ground* [*Sounds good.*] But recently the chemical processes that thin the ozone layer have been found to be less well understood than once thought.*condition* [*So what?*] We may have labeled hydrofluorocarbons as the chief cause incorrectly.*consequence* **We have found that the bonding of carbon** . . .*gist of solution/main point*

16.4.2 Promise a Solution

Alternatively, you can delay your main point by stating toward the end of your introduction only where your paper is headed, implying that you will present that point in your conclusion. This approach provides a launching point and creates a point-last paper:

> As we have investigated environmental threats, our understanding . . . has improved. . . . But recently the chemical processes . . . have been found to be less well understood. . . . [*So what?*] We may have labeled hydrofluorocarbons as the chief cause incorrectly. [*Well, what* have *you found?*] **In this report we describe a hitherto unexpected chemical bonding between** . . . *promise of point to come*

This introduction launches us into the paper, not with its main point but with a promise of one to come.

The weakest launching point is one that merely announces a vague topic:

> This study investigates processes leading to ozone depletion.

If you have reason to save your point for the end of your paper, your launching point must do more than just announce a general topic. It should suggest the conceptual outlines of your solution or announce a plan (or both).

> There are many designs for hydroelectric turbine intakes and diversion screens, but on-site evaluation is not cost-effective. A more viable alternative is computer modeling. **To evaluate hydroelectric diversion screens, this study will evaluate three computer models—Quattro, AVOC, and Turbo-plex—to determine which is most cost-effective in reliability, speed, and ease of use.**

This kind of plan is common in social sciences, but less frequent in the humanities, where many consider it a bit ham-handed.

16.5 SETTING THE RIGHT PACE FOR YOUR INTRODUCTION

A final decision is how quickly to raise your problem. That depends on how much your readers know. In this next example, the writer devotes one sentence to announcing a consensus among well-informed engineers; then, in the second, he briskly disrupts it:

> Fluid-film forces in squeeze-film dampers (SFDs) are usually obtained from the Reynolds equation of classical lubrication theory. **However, the increasing size of rotating machinery requires the inclusion of fluid inertia effects in the design of SFDs. Without them . . .**

(We have no idea what any of that means, but the structure of *Common Ground + Problem* is clear.)

This next writer also addresses technical concepts but patiently lays them out for readers who have little technical knowledge:

> A method of protecting migrating fish at hydroelectric power developments is diversion by screening turbine intakes . . . [*another 110 words explaining screens*]. Since the efficiency of screens is determined by the interaction of fish behavior and hydraulic flow, screen design can be evaluated by determining its hydraulic performance . . . [*40 more words explaining hydraulics*]. **This study provides a better understanding of the hydraulic features of this technique, which may guide future designs.**

When you open quickly, you imply an audience of peers; when you open slowly, you imply readers who know less than you. If your readers are knowledgeable and you open slowly, they may think *you* know too little. But if they know little and you open quickly, they may think you are inconsiderate of their needs. It's a Goldilocks problem.

You may feel overwhelmed with so many choices here, but they all follow what is in fact a simple "grammar." A full introduction consists of just three elements:

Context + Problem + Response

You don't need all three in every report:

• If the problem is well known, omit the common ground.

• If the consequences of the problem are well known, omit them.

- If you want readers to follow your thinking before they know your answer, offer a launching point at the end of your introduction and state your main point in your conclusion,

All this may seem formulaic, but it's what readers expect. And when you master a rhetorical pattern like this, you have more than a formula for writing. You also have a tool for thinking. By forcing yourself to work through a full statement of your common ground and problem, you have to think hard about what your readers know, what they don't, and, in particular, what they should know and why.

16.6 WRITING YOUR CONCLUSION

Not every research report has a section called *Conclusion*, but all have a paragraph or two that serve as one. You may be happy to know that you can write your conclusion using the same elements in your introduction, in reverse order.

16.6.1 Start with Your Main Point

State your main point near the beginning of your conclusion. If you already stated it in your introduction, repeat it here but more fully; do not simply repeat it word-for-word.

16.6.2 Add a New Significance or Application

After your point, say why it's significant, preferably with a new answer to *So what?* For example, the writer of this conclusion introduces an additional consequence of the Supreme Court's decision on military death sentences: If Congress changes the law, the military will have to change its culture.

> In light of recent Supreme Court decisions rejecting mandatory capital punishment, the mandatory death penalty for treason is apparently unconstitutional and must therefore be revised by Congress. **More significantly, though, if the Uniform Code of Military Justice is changed, it will challenge the fundamental value of military culture that ultimate betrayal requires the ultimate**

penalty. Congress will then have to deal with the military's sense
of what is just.

The writer could have included that in his introduction, as another consequence of the new Supreme Court decision, but he
may have felt that it was too volatile to raise that early.

As you write your conclusion, take care not to broaden a
significance so much that it seems to be your main point. You can
be clear about its role by introducing it almost "by the way," as an
additional *possible* implication of your solution.

16.6.3 Call for More Research

Just as your opening context surveys research already done, your
conclusion can call for research still to do:

> These differences between novice and expert diagnosticians define
> their maturation and development. But while we know how nov-
> ices and experts think differently, **we do not understand which
> elements in the social experience of novices contribute to that
> development and how. We need longitudinal studies on how men-
> toring and coaching affect outcomes and whether active explana-
> tion and critique help novices become skilled diagnosticians more
> quickly.**

When you state what remains to do, you keep the conversation
alive. So before you write your last words, imagine someone fascinated by your work who wants to follow up on it: What more would
you like to know? What research would you suggest they do? After
all, that may have been how you found your own problem.

16.7 FINDING YOUR FIRST FEW WORDS

Many writers find the first sentence or two especially difficult to
write, and so they fall into clichés.

- Don't start with a dictionary entry: "*Webster's* defines *ethics*
  as . . ." If a word is important enough to define, a dictionary
  definition won't serve.

- Don't start grandly: "The most profound philosophers have for centuries wrestled with the important question of . . ." If your subject is grand, it will speak its own importance.

- Don't repeat the language of your assignment. If you are struggling to start, prime your pump by paraphrasing it, but when you revise, rewrite it.

Here are three standard choices for your first sentence or two.

16.7.1 Open with a Striking Fact Relevant to Your Problem

Those who think that tax cuts for the rich stimulate the economy should contemplate the fact that the top 1 percent of Americans earn one-third of America's total income.

16.7.2 Open with a Striking Quotation

Do this only if its words anticipate key terms in the rest of your introduction:

"From the sheer sensuous beauty of a genuine Jan van Eyck there emanates a **strange fascination** not unlike that which we experience when permitting ourselves to be **hypnotized** by **precious stones**." Edwin Panofsky suggests here something **strangely magical** in Jan van Eyck's works. His images hold a **jewel-like** fascination. . . .

16.7.3 Open with a Relevant Anecdote

Do this only if its language anticipates your topic and vividly illustrates your problem. The following paper addressed the economics of school segregation:

This year Tawnya Jones begins junior high in Doughton, Georgia. Though her classmates are mostly African American like herself, her school system is considered racially integrated, at least legally. But except for a few poor whites and Hispanic students, Tawnya's school still resembles the segregated and economically depressed one that her mother entered in 1962. . . .

16.8 FINDING YOUR LAST FEW WORDS

You can bring your report to a graceful, even literary close with an echo of your opening fact, anecdote, or quotation. For example, this next introduction begins with a quotation, an epigraph that highlights the themes of religion and modernity. The writer echoes those themes with a parallel quotation in the last words of her conclusion:

> **Flannery O'Connor and the Spiritual Foundations of Racism: Suffering as Southern Redemption in the Modern World**_{title}
>
> *"I write the way I do because . . . I am a Catholic peculiarly possessed of the **modern consciousness**."*_{epigraph}
>
> Although Flannery O'Connor's stories give us insights into **modern** southern culture, some have said her attitude toward race was the product of "an imperfectly developed **sensibility**" and that "large social issues as such were never the subject of her writing." But that criticism ignores . . ._{·introduction}

Here is the conclusion:

> Those who claim that O'Connor ignored racism fail to see that she understood racism as a **modern** crisis of faith, as a failure to recognize the healing knowledge of suffering, insights that put her among a few southern writers who saw the **modern** world as **spiritually** bankrupt. Seen in this light, a rereading of her private correspondence might reveal . . . **As she said in one letter (May 4, 1955), "What I had in mind to suggest [was] . . . the redemptive quality of the Negro's suffering for us all. . . . I meant [a character in the story to suggest] in an almost physical way . . . the mystery of existence."**_{conclusion}

This echoing device may seem a bit literary, but it is not uncommon.

The first thing readers read—and the last thing you should write—is your title. Beginning writers just attach a few words to suggest the topic of a report. That's a mistake: a title is useful when it helps readers understand *specifically* what is to come. Compare these three titles:

The Crusades

Political Motives and the Crusades

The Crusades as a Force in European Unity:
Preventing Internal Political and Theological Division
through External Distraction

Put into your title the key words in your main point, the ones you circled when you checked for the continuity of conceptual themes (6.6.1, 8.2.1, 12.3.2, 13.2, 14.4). When readers see those concepts turn up again in your main point and again through the body of your paper, they will feel that your text has met their expectations. (Two-line titles give you more room for key terms. End the first line with a colon that introduces a more specific second line.)

CHAPTER SEVENTEEN

Revising Style:
Telling Your Story Clearly

So far we have focused on the argument and organization of your report.
In this chapter we show you how to revise your sentences so that readers
will think they are clear and direct.

Readers will accept your claim only if they understand your argument, but they won't understand your argument if they can't understand your sentences. Once you revise your report so that readers will judge its argument to be sound and well organized, find time to make a last pass to make your sentences as easy to read as the complexity of your ideas allows. But again, you face a familiar problem: you can't know which sentences need revising just by reading them. Since you already know what you want them to mean, you will read into them what you want your readers to get out of them. To ensure that your sentences will be as clear to your readers as they are to you, you need a way to identify difficult sentences even when they seem fine to you.

17.1 JUDGING STYLE

If you had to read a report written in the style of one of the following examples, which would you choose?

> 1a. Too precise a specification of information-processing requirements incurs a risk of a decision-maker's over- or underestimation, resulting in the inefficient use of costly resources. Too little precision in specifying needed processing capacity gives no indication with respect to the procurement of needed resources.

1b. A person who makes decisions sometimes specifies what he needs to process information. He may do so too precisely. He may over- or underestimate the resources that he needs. When he does that, he may use costly resources inefficiently. He may also fail to be precise enough. He may not indicate which resources others should procure.

1c. When a decision-maker specifies too precisely the resources he needs to process information, he may over- or underestimate them and thereby use costly resources inefficiently. But if he is not precise enough, he may not indicate which resources to procure.

Few readers choose (1a): it sounds like a machine speaking to a machine (it appeared in a respectable journal). Some choose (1b), but it sounds simpleminded, like an adult speaking slowly to a child. Most choose (1c). It sounds like one colleague speaking to another. One of the worst problems in academic writing today is that too many researchers sound like (1a).

A few researchers prefer (1a), claiming that heavy thinking demands heavy writing, that when they try to make complicated ideas clear, they sacrifice nuances and complexity of thought for too-easy understanding. If readers don't understand, too bad; they should work harder.

Perhaps. Everyone who reads philosophers like Immanuel Kant or Friedrich Hegel struggles with their complex prose style, at least at first. But what they have to say proves to be worth the effort. The problem is, few of us think as well as Kant or Hegel. For most of us most of the time, our dense writing indicates not the irreducible difficulty of a work of genius, but the sloppy thinking of a writer indifferent to his readers. And even when complex thinking does require a complex style (less often than we think), every sentence profits from a second look (and truth be told, Kant and Hegel would have benefited from a good editor).

Some writers do go too far in avoiding a complex style, using simplistic sentences like those in (1b) above. But we assume that most of you do not have that problem, and that you need little help with spelling and grammar. (If you think you do, talk to a writing tutor.) We address here the problem of a style that is too "academic," which is to say, more difficult than it has to be. Convoluted and indirect prose is not what good writers aim for, but what thoughtless ones get away with.

This problem especially afflicts those just starting advanced work because they are hit by double trouble. First, when any of us writes about new and complex ideas that challenge our understanding, we write less clearly than we ordinarily can. This problem afflicts even the most experienced researchers. But new researchers compound that problem when they think that a complex style bespeaks academic success and they imitate the tangled prose they read. That we can avoid.

17.2 THE FIRST TWO PRINCIPLES OF CLEAR WRITING

17.2.1 Distinguishing Impressions from Their Causes

If we asked you to explain how you chose between (1a) and (1c) above, you would probably describe (1a) with words like *unclear, wordy,* and *dense;* (1c) with words like *clear, concise,* and *direct.* But those words refer not to those sentences on the page, but to how you *felt* as you read them. If you said that (1a) was *dense,* you were really saying that *you* had a hard time getting through it; if you said (1c) was *clear,* you were saying that *you* found it easy to understand.

There's nothing wrong with using impressionistic words to describe your feelings, but they don't help you *fix* unclear sentences like (1a), because they don't explain *what it is on the page that makes you feel as you do.* For that, you need a way to think about sentences that connects an impression like *confusing* to what it is *in the sentence, on the page* that confuses you. More important, you have to know how to revise your own sentences when they are clear to you but won't be to your readers.

There are a few principles that distinguish the felt complexity of (1a) from the mature clarity of (1c). These principles focus on only two parts of a sentence: the first six or seven words and the last four or five. Get those words straight, and the rest of the sentence will (usually) take care of itself. To use these principles, though, you must understand five grammatical terms: *simple subject, whole subject, verb, noun,* and *clause.* (If you haven't used those terms for a while, review them before you read on.)

This is important: don't try to apply these principles as you write new sentences but to revising those you've already written. If you follow the advice here *as you draft,* you may tie yourself in knots. Save your concern for revising sentences until you have sentences to revise.

17.2.2 Subjects and Characters

The first principle may remind you of something you learned in grammar school. At the heart of every sentence are its subject and verb. In grammar school you probably learned that subjects are the "doers" or agents of an action. But that's not always true, because subjects can be things other than doers, even actions. Compare these two sentences (the whole subject in each clause is underlined):

2a. Locke frequently repeated himself because he did not trust the power of words to name things accurately.

2b. The reason for Locke's frequent repetition lies in his distrust of the accuracy of the naming power of words.

The two subjects in (2a) —*Locke* and *he*—fit that grammar-school definition: they are doers. But the subject of (2b)—*The reason for Locke's frequent repetition*—does not, because *reason* doesn't really *do* anything here. The real doer is still Locke.

To get beyond sixth-grade definitions, we have to think not only about the grammar of a sentence—its subjects and verbs—but also about the *stories* they tell—about doers and their actions. Here is a story about rain forests and the biosphere:

3a. If rain forests are stripped to serve short-term economic interests, the earth's biosphere may be damaged.

3b. The stripping of rain forests in the service of short-term economic interests could result in damage to the earth's biosphere.

In the clearer version, (3a), look at the whole subjects of each clause:

3a. If rain forests_{subject} are stripped_{verb} . . . the earth's biosphere_{subject} may be damaged._{verb}

Those subjects name the main characters in that story in a few short, concrete words: *rain forests* and *the earth's biosphere*. Compare (3b):

3b. The stripping of rain forests in the service of short-term economic interests_{subject} could result_{verb} in damage to the earth's biosphere.

In (3b) the simple subject (*stripping*) names not a concrete character but rather an action; it is only part of the long abstract phrase that is the whole subject: *the stripping of rain forests in the service of short-term economic interests*.

Now we can see why grammar-school definitions may be bad language theory but good advice about writing. The first principle of clear writing is this:

Readers will judge your sentences to be clear and readable to the degree that you make their subjects name the main characters in your story. When you do this, your subjects will be short, specific, and concrete.

17.2.3 Verbs, Nouns, and Actions

There is a second difference between clear and unclear prose: it is in the way writers express the crucial *actions* in their stories—as verbs or as nouns. For example, look again at the pairs of sentences (2) and (3) below. (Words naming actions are boldfaced; actions that are verbs are underlined; actions that are nouns are double-underlined.)

2a. Locke frequently **repeated** himself because he did not **trust** the power of words to **name** things accurately.

2b. The reason for Locke's frequent **repetition** lies in his **distrust** of the accuracy of the **naming** power of words.

3a. If rain forests are **stripped** to **serve** short-term economic interests, the earth's biosphere may be **damaged**.

3b. The **stripping** of rain forests in the **service** of short-term economic interests could result in **damage** to the earth's biosphere.

Sentences (2a) and (3a) are clearer than (2b) and (3b) because their subjects are characters, but also because their actions are expressed not as nouns but as verbs:

(2A) VERB	VS.	(2B) NOUN	(3A) VERB	VS.	(3B) NOUN
repeat	vs.	repetition	strip	vs.	stripping
trust	vs.	distrust	serve	vs.	service
name	vs.	naming	damage	vs.	damage

(We'll discuss the passive verbs *are stripped* and *be damaged* in 17.4.)

When you express actions not with verbs but with abstract nouns, you also clutter a sentence with articles and prepositions. Look at all the articles and prepositions (boldfaced) in (4b) that (4a) doesn't need:

4a. Now that we$_{subject}$ have standardized$_{verb}$ an index to measure thought disorders, we$_{subject}$ can quantify$_{verb}$ how patients$_{subject}$ respond$_{verb}$ to different treatments.

4b. Our standardization **of** an index **for the** measurement **of** thought disorders$_{subject}$ has made$_{verb}$ possible **the** quantification **of** response **as a** function **of** treatment differences.

Sentence (4b) adds one *a*, *as*, and *for*; two *thes*, and four *ofs*, all because four verbs were turned into nouns: *standardize* → *standardization, measure* → *measurement, quantify* → *quantification, respond* → *response*.

There is a technical term for turning a verb (or adjective) into a noun: we *nominalize* it. (This term defines itself: when we nominalize the verb *nominalize*, we create the nominalization *nominalization*.) Most nominalizations end with suffixes such as *-tion, -ness, -ment, -ence, -ity.*

Verb	→ Nominalization	Adjective	→ Nominalization
decide	decision	precise	precision
fail	failure	frequent	frequency
resist	resistance	intelligent	intelligence

But some are spelled like the verb: *change* → *change; delay* → *delay; report* → *report.*

When you turn adjectives and verbs into nouns, you can tangle up your sentences in two more ways:

- You have to add verbs that are less specific than the verbs you could have used. In (4b), instead of the specific verbs *standardize, measure, quantify,* and *respond,* we have the single vague verb *made.*

- You are likely to make the characters in your story modifiers of nouns or objects of prepositions or to drop them from a sentence altogether: in (4b), the character *we* becomes *our,* and thereafter the rest of the characters are missing in action.

So here are two principles of a clear style:

- Express crucial actions in verbs.

- Make your central characters the subjects of those verbs; keep those subjects short, concrete, and specific.

17.2.4 Diagnosis and Revision
Given how readers judge sentences, we can offer ways to diagnose and revise yours.
   To diagnose:

1. Underline the first six or seven words of every clause, whether main or subordinate.

2. Perform two tests:

- Are the underlined subjects concrete characters, not abstractions?

- Do the underlined verbs name specific actions, not general ones like *have, make, do, be*, and so on?

3. If the sentence fails either test, you should probably revise.

To revise:

1. Find the characters you want to tell a story about. If you can't, invent them.

2. Find what those characters are doing. If their actions are in nouns, change them into verbs.

3. Create clauses with your main characters as subjects and their actions as verbs.

You will probably have to recast your sentence in some version of *If X, then Y; X, because Y; Although X, Y; When X, then Y*; and so on.

That's the simple version of revising dense prose into something clearer. Here is a more nuanced one.

17.2.5 Who or What Can Be a Character?

You may have wondered that we called *rain forests* and *the earth's biosphere* "characters," because we usually think of characters as flesh-and-blood people. But for our purposes, a character is anything we can make the subject of a lot of verbs in a sequence of sentences. That means we can also tell stories whose characters are things like *rain forests* and even abstractions like *thought disorders*. In your kind of research, you may have to tell a story about *demographic changes, social mobility, isotherms,* or *gene pools*.

Sometimes you have a choice: a paper in economics might tell a story about real or virtual people, such as *consumers* and the *Federal Reserve Board*, or about abstractions associated with them, such as *savings* and *monetary policy*. Note, however, that you can still make those abstract characters part of a story with action verbs:

5a. When <u>consumers</u> **save** more, <u>the Federal Reserve</u> **changes** its monetary policy to influence how <u>banks</u> **lend** money.

5b. When <u>consumer</u> **savings rise**, <u>Federal Reserve monetary policy</u> **adapts** to **influence** bank **lending** practices.

A passage might be about real people or about abstractions associated with them: *banks* vs. *lending practices, savers* vs. *micro-economics,* or *analysts* vs. *predictions.* All things being equal, though, readers prefer characters to be at least concrete things or, better, flesh-and-blood people.

Experts, however, like to tell stories about abstractions (bold-faced; subjects are underlined).

6. <u>Standardized indices to measure **thought disorders**</u> help us quantify how <u>patients</u> respond to different **treatments**. <u>These **measurements**</u> indicate that <u>**treatments** requiring long-term **hospitalization**</u> do not reduce the number of psychotic episodes among schizophrenic patients.

The abstract nominalizations in the second sentence—*measurements, treatments, hospitalization*—refer to concepts as familiar to its intended readers as *doctors* and *patients.* Given those readers, the writer would not need to revise them.

In a way, that example undercuts our advice about avoiding nouns made out of verbs, because now instead of revising every abstract noun into a verb, you have to choose which ones to change and which ones to leave as nouns. For example, the abstract nouns in the second sentence of (6) are the same as those in (7a):

7a. The **hospitalization** of patients without appropriate **treatment** results in the unreliable **measurement** of outcomes.

But we would improve that sentence if we revised those abstract nouns into verbs:

7b. We cannot **measure** outcomes reliably when patients **are hospitalized** but not **treated** appropriately.

So what we offer here is no iron rule of writing, but rather a principle of diagnosis and revision that you must apply judiciously. In general, though, readers prefer sentences whose subjects are short, specific, and concrete. And that usually means flesh-and-blood characters.

17.2.6 Avoiding Excessive Abstraction

You create the worst problems for readers when you make abstract nouns your main character and subjects of your sentences, then sprinkle more abstractions around them. Here is a passage about two abstract characters, *immediate intention* and *prospective intention*. Those characters are obscure enough, but the passage can be clear for its intended readers, so long as it is not thickened with more abstractions (subjects are underlined; verbs and key adjectives are boldfaced):

> 8a. My argument **is** this: The cognitive component of intention **is** quite **complex**. Intention is temporally divisible into two kinds: prospective intention and immediate intention. Prospective intention **represents** a subject's current situation, how he has **acted** similarly in the past, and how he will **act** in the future. That is, the cognitive component of prospective intention **lets** him **plan** ahead. Immediate intention, on the other hand, **monitors** and **guides** his body as he **moves** it. Taken together, these cognitive mechanisms **are** too **complex** to be **explained** by folk psychology.

Note how the story becomes less clear when the key abstraction *intention* is surrounded by other abstract nouns (subjects are underlined; the additional abstractions are boldfaced):

> 8b. The **argument** is this: The cognitive component of intention exhibits a high degree of **complexity**. Intention is temporally divisible into two: prospective intention and immediate intention. The **cognitive function** of prospective intention is the **representation** of a subject's current situation, his similar past **actions**, and his course of future **actions**. That is, the cognitive component of

prospective intention is a **plan**. The **cognitive function** of immediate intention is the **monitoring** and **guidance** of ongoing bodily movement. Taken together, these cognitive mechanisms exhibit significant **complexity**. There is, however, limited **capacity** for accounting for this **complexity** found in the folk psychological notion of **belief**, which therefore misses most of the cognitive component of intention.

The point: Don't change every abstract noun into a verb. If your best central character is an abstraction, avoid others you don't need. As always, the trick is knowing which ones you need and which you don't (usually fewer than you think). Knowing one from the other is a skill that comes only from practice—and criticism.

17.2.7 Creating Main Characters

Having qualified our principle once, we complicate it again. If your sentences are readable, your characters will be the subjects of verbs that express the crucial actions those characters are involved in. But most stories have several characters, any one of whom you can turn into a main character by making it the subject of sentences. Take the sentence about rain forests:

> 9. If rain forests are stripped to serve short-term economic interests, the earth's biosphere may be damaged.

That sentence tells a story that implies other characters but does not specify them: Who is stripping the forests? More important, does it matter? This story could focus on them, but who are they?

> 9a. If developers strip rain forests to serve short-term economic interests, they may damage the earth's biosphere.

> 9b. If loggers strip rain forests to serve short-term economic interests, they may damage the earth's biosphere.

> 9c. If Brazil strips its rain forests to serve short-term economic interests, it may damage the earth's biosphere.

Which is best? It depends on whom you want *your readers to think* the story is about. As you revise sentences, put characters in subjects and actions in verbs, when you can. But be sure that the character is your *central* character, if only for that sentence.

17.3 A THIRD PRINCIPLE: OLD BEFORE NEW

There is a third principle of reading and revising even more important than the first two. Fortunately, all three principles are related. Compare the (a) and (b) versions in the following. Which seems clearer? Why? (Hint: Look at the beginnings of sentences, this time not just for characters as subjects, but whether those subjects express information that is familiar or information that is new and therefore unexpected.)

> 10a. Because the naming power of words was distrusted by Locke, he repeated himself often. Seventeenth-century theories of language, especially Wilkins's scheme for a universal language involving the creation of countless symbols for countless meanings, had centered on this naming power. A new era in the study of language that focused on the ambiguous relationship between sense and reference begins with Locke's distrust.

> 10b. Locke often repeated himself because he distrusted the naming power of words. This naming power had been central to seventeenth-century theories of language, especially Wilkins's scheme for a universal language involving the creation of countless symbols for countless meanings. Locke's distrust begins a new era in the study of language, one that focused on the ambiguous relationship between sense and reference.

Most readers prefer (10b), saying not just that (10a) is *too complex* or *inflated,* but that it's also *disjointed;* it doesn't *flow*—impressionistic words that again describe not what we see on the page but how we *feel* about it.

We can explain what causes those impressions if we again apply the "first six or seven words" test. In the disjointed (a) version, the sentences after the first one begin with information that a reader could not predict:

the naming power of words

Seventeenth-century theories of language

A new era in the study of language

In contrast, the sentences after the first one in (10b) begin with information that readers would find familiar:

Locke

This naming power [repeated from the previous sentence]

Locke's distrust [a useful abstract noun because it repeats something from the previous sentence]

In (10a) each sentence begins unpredictably, so we can't easily see the "topic" of the whole passage. In (10b) each sentence after the first opens with words referring to ideas that readers recall from the previous sentence.

Readers follow a story most easily if they can begin each sentence with a character or idea that is familiar to them, either because it was already mentioned or because it comes from the context. From this principle of reading, we can infer principles of diagnosis and revision:

To diagnose:

1. Underline the first six or seven words of every sentence.

2. Have you underlined words that your readers will find familiar and easy to understand (usually words used before)?

3. If not, revise.

To revise:

1. Make the first six or seven words refer to familiar information, usually something you have mentioned before (typically your main characters).

2. Put at the ends of sentences information that your readers will find unpredictable or complex and therefore harder to understand.

This old-new principle happily cooperates with the ones about characters and subjects, because older information usually names a character (after you introduce it, usually at the *end* of a prior sentence). But should you ever have to choose between beginning a sentence with a character or with old information, *always choose the principle of old before new.*

17.4 CHOOSING BETWEEN ACTIVE AND PASSIVE

You may have noted that some of the clearer sentences had passive verbs. This seems to contradict familiar advice from English teachers to avoid them. Followed mindlessly, that advice will make your sentences *less* clear. Rather than worry about active and passive, ask a simpler question: Do your sentences begin with familiar information, preferably a main character? If you put familiar characters in your subjects, you will use the active and passive properly.

For example, which of these two passages "flows" more easily?

11a. The quality of our air and even the climate of the world depend on healthy rain forests in Asia, Africa, and South America. But the increasing demand for more land for agricultural use and for wood products for construction worldwide now threatens these forests with destruction.

11b. The quality of our air and even the climate of the world depend on healthy rain forests in Asia, Africa, and South America. But these rain forests are now threatened with destruction by the increasing demand for more land for agricultural use and for wood products used in construction worldwide.

Most readers think (11b) flows more easily. Why? Note that the beginning of the second sentence in (11b) picks up on the character introduced at the end of the first sentence:

11b. . . . rain forests in Asia, Africa, and South America. But these rain forests . . .

The second sentence of (11a), on the other hand, opens with information completely unconnected to the first sentence:

11a. . . . rain forests in Asia, Africa, and South America. But the increasing demand for more land . . .

In other words, the passive allowed us to move the older, more familiar information from the end of its sentence to its beginning, where it belongs. And that's the main function of the passive: to build sentences that begin with older information. If we don't use the passive when we should, our sentences won't flow as well as they could.

In English classes, students are told that they should use only active verbs, but they hear the opposite in engineering, the natural sciences, and some social sciences. There teachers demand the passive, thinking that it makes writing more objective. Most of that advice is equally misleading. Compare the passive (12a) with the active (12b):

12a. Eye movements **were measured** at tenth-of-second intervals.

12b. We **measured** eye movements at tenth-of-second intervals.

These sentences offer equally objective information, but their *stories* differ: one is about eye movements, the other about a person measuring them, who happens also to be the author. The first is supposed to be more "objective" because it ignores the person and focuses on the movements. But just avoiding *I* or *we* doesn't make writing more "objective." It simply changes the story.

In fact, the issue of the passive is still more complicated. When a scientist uses the passive to describe a *process*, she implies that the process can be repeated by anyone. In this case, the passive is the right choice, because anyone who wanted to repeat the research would have to measure eye movements.

On the other hand, consider this pair of sentences:

13a. It <u>can be concluded</u> that the fluctuations result from the Burnes effect.

13b. <u>We</u> **conclude** that the fluctuations result from the Burnes effect.

The active verb in (13b), *conclude*, and its first-person subject, *we*, are not only common in the sciences, but appropriate. The difference? It has to do with the kind of action the verb names. The active (and therefore first person) is appropriate when authors refer to actions that only the *writer/researcher* can perform—not only rhetorical actions, such as *suggest, conclude, argue,* or *show*, but also those for which they get credit as scientists, such as *design* experiments, *solve* problems, or *prove* results. Everyone can *measure*, but only author/researchers are entitled to *claim* what their research means.

Scientists typically use the first person and active verbs at the beginning of journal articles, where they describe how *they* discovered their problem and at the end where they describe how *they* solved it. In between, when they describe processes that anyone can perform, they regularly use the passive.

17.5 A FINAL PRINCIPLE: COMPLEXITY LAST

We have focused on how clauses begin. Now we look at how they end. You can anticipate the principle for ending sentences: if familiar information goes first, the newest, most complex information goes last. This principle is particularly important in three contexts:

• when you introduce a new technical term

• when you present a unit of information that is long and complex

• when you introduce a concept that you intend to develop in what follows

17.5.1 Introducing Technical Terms

When you introduce technical terms new to your readers, construct your sentences so that those terms appear in the last few words. Compare these two:

14a. An understanding of the role of calcium blockers in the control of cardiac irregularity depends on understanding of the calcium activation of muscle groups. The regulatory proteins actin, myosin, tropomyosin, and troponin affect the action of muscle fibers in the sarcomere, the basic unit of muscle contraction.

14b. Muscles contract when their cells are activated by calcium. When heart muscles contract irregularly, we can control them with drugs called calcium blockers. Calcium blockers limit the action of muscle fibers in the basic unit of muscle contraction, known as the sarcomere. It consists of four proteins that regulate contraction: they are actin, myosin, tropomyosin, and troponin.

In (14a) all the technical-sounding terms appear early in the sentences; in (14b) the technical terms appear at the end of the sentences.

17.5.2 Introducing Complex Information

Put complex bundles of ideas that require long phrases or clauses at the end of a sentence, never at the beginning. Compare (11a) and (11b) again:

11a. The quality of our air and even the climate of the world depend on healthy rain forests in Asia, Africa, and South America. But the increasing demand for more land for agricultural use and for wood products for construction worldwide now threatens these forests with destruction.

11b. The quality of our air and even the climate of the world depend on healthy rain forests in Asia, Africa, and South America. But these rain forests are now threatened with destruction by the increasing demand for more land for agricultural use and for wood products used in construction worldwide.

In (11a) the second sentence begins with a long, complex unit of information, a subject that runs on for more than a line. In contrast, the subject of the second sentence in (11b), *these rain forests*, is short, simple, and easy to read, again because the passive verb (*are now threatened*) lets us flip the short and familiar information to the beginning and the long and complex part to the end.

In short, don't begin your sentences with complexity; save it for the end. Unfortunately that's not easy to do, because you may be so familiar with your ideas that you can't distinguish what is *for your readers* old and simple from what's new and complex.

17.5.3 Introducing What Follows

When you start a paragraph, put at the end of its first or second sentence the key terms that appear in the rest of the paragraph. Which of these two sentences would best introduce the rest of the paragraph that follows?

> 15a. The political situation changed, because disputes over succession to the throne plagued seven of the eight reigns of the Romanov line after Peter the Great.

> 15b. The political situation changed, because after Peter the Great seven of the eight reigns of the Romanov line were plagued by turmoil over disputed succession to the throne.

> The problems began in 1722, when Peter the Great passed a law of succession that terminated the principle of heredity and required the sovereign to appoint a successor. But because many tsars, including Peter, died before they named successors, those who aspired to rule had no authority by appointment, and so their succession was often disputed by lower-level aristocrats. There was turmoil even when successors were appointed.

Most readers feel that (15b) is more closely connected to the rest of the passage. The last few words of (15a) seem unimportant in relation to what follows (in another context, of course, they might be crucial).

So once you've checked the first six or seven words in every sentence, check the last five or six as well. If those words are not the most important, complex, or weighty, revise so that they are. Look especially at the ends of sentences that introduce paragraphs or even sections.

17.6 SPIT AND POLISH

We've focused on those issues of sentence style relevant to writing research reports, and on principles of diagnosis and revision that help us make prose as readable as possible. There are other principles—sentence length, the right choice of words, concision, and so on. But those are issues pertinent to writing of all kinds and are addressed by many books. And, of course, readability alone is not enough. After you revise your style, you still have to check your grammar, spelling, and punctuation. Then you have to make sure that you have observed the accepted conventions for representing numbers, proper names, foreign words, and so on. Though important, those matters fall outside the purview of this book.

Our advice about revision may seem overly detailed, but if you revise in steps, it's not difficult to follow. The first step is the most important: as you draft, remember to forget these steps (except for this one about remembering). Your first job is to draft something to revise. You will never do that if you keep asking yourself whether you should have just used a verb or a noun. If you don't have time to look at every sentence, start with passages where you found it hard to explain your ideas. When you struggle to write about confusing content, your sentences tend toward confusion as well.

For Clarity and Flow

To diagnose:

1. Highlight the first five or six words in every sentence. Ignore short introductory phrases such as *At first, For the most part,* and so on.

2. Run your eye down the page, checking whether you highlighted a consistent set of related words. The words that begin a series of sentences need not be identical, but they should name people or concepts that your readers will see are clearly related. If not, revise.

3. Check the highlighted words in each sentence. They should include a subject that names a character and a verb that names an important action. If not, revise.

To revise:

1. Identify your main characters, real or conceptual. Make them the subjects of verbs.

2. Look for nouns ending in *-tion, -ment, -ence,* and so on. If they are the subjects of verbs, turn them into verbs.

3. Make sure that each sentence begins with familiar information, preferably a character you have mentioned before.

For Emphasis

To diagnose:

1. Underline the last four or five words in every sentence.

2. You should have underlined

   - technical-sounding words that you are using for the first time

   - the newest, most complex information

   - information that is most emphatic

   - concepts that the next several sentences will develop

3. If you do not see that information there, revise: put those words last in the sentence.

PART V

Some Last Considerations

The Ethics of Research

In the last few hundred pages, we've offered a lot of practical advice, but almost as much preaching about creating social contracts with your readers, projecting an ethos that will encourage their trust, guarding against biases in collecting and reporting evidence, avoiding plagiarism, and so on. Now we want to share with you the underlying ethical issues that shape our advice, hoping that when you close this book, you'll give them more thought.

Everything we've said about research reflects our belief that it is a profoundly *social* activity that connects you both to those who will use your research and to those who might benefit—or suffer—from that use. But it also connects you and your readers to everyone whose research you used and beyond them to everyone whose research they used. To understand our responsibility to those in that network, now and in the future, we have to move beyond mere technique to think about the ethics of civil communication.

We start with two broad conceptions of the word *ethics*: the forging of bonds that create a community and the moral choices we face when we act in that community. The term *ethical* comes from the Greek *ethos*, meaning either a community's shared *customs* or an individual's *character*, good or bad. So far, we have focused on the community-building aspects of research, the bonds we create with our readers and our sources. But as does any social activity, research challenges us to define our individual ethical principles and then to make choices that honor or violate them.

At first glance, a purely academic researcher seems on relatively safe ethical ground—we are less tempted to sacrifice principle for gain than, say, a Wall Street analyst evaluating a stock that her firm wants her to push on investors, or a scientist paid by a drug company to "prove" that a product is safe (regardless of whether it works). No teacher will pay you to write a report supporting her views, and you probably won't have occasion to fake results to gain fame—like the American researcher who became famous (and powerful) for discovering an HIV virus, when he had in fact "borrowed" it from a laboratory in France.

Even so, you will face such choices from the very beginning of your project. Some are the obvious *Thou shalt nots*:

- Ethical researchers do not plagiarize or claim credit for the results of others.

- They do not misreport sources, invent data, or fake results.

- They do not submit data whose accuracy they don't trust, unless they say so.

- They do not conceal objections that they cannot rebut.

- They do not caricature or distort opposing views.

- They do not destroy data or conceal sources important for those who follow.

We apply these principles easily enough to obvious cases: the biologist who used india ink to fake "genetic" marks on his mice, the Enron accountants and their auditors at Arthur Andersen who shredded source documents, the government political advisers who erase e-mails, or the student who submits a paper purchased on the Internet.

More challenging are those occasions when ethical principles take us beyond any simple moral *Do not* to what we should affirmatively *Do*. When we think about ethical choices in that way, we move beyond simple conflicts between our own self-interest and the honest pursuit of truth, or between what we want for ourselves and what is good for or at least not harmful to others. If reporting research is genuinely a collaborative effort between readers and writers to find the best solution to shared problems, then the challenge is to find ways to create ethical partnerships to make ethical choices (what we traditionally call *character*) that can help build ethical communities.

Such a challenge raises more questions than we can answer here. Some of those questions have answers that we all agree on; others are controversial. The three of us answer some of them differently. But one thing we agree on is that research offers every researcher an ethical invitation that, when not just dutifully accepted but *embraced*, can serve the best interests of both researchers and their readers.

- When you create, however briefly, a community of shared understanding and interest, you set a standard for your work higher than any you could set for yourself alone.

- When you explain to others why your research *should* change their understanding and beliefs, you must examine not only your own understanding and interests, but your responsibility to them if you convince them to change theirs.

- When you acknowledge your readers' alternative views, including their strongest objections and reservations, you move closer not just to more reliable knowledge, better understanding, and sounder beliefs, but to honoring the dignity and human needs of your readers.

In other words, when you do research and report it as a conversation among equals working toward greater knowledge and better understanding, the ethical demands you place on yourself should redound to the benefit of all—even when we cannot all agree on a common good. When you decline that conversation, you risk harming yourself and possibly those who depend on your work.

It is this concern for the integrity of the common work of a community that underscores why researchers condemn plagiarism so strongly. Plagiarism is theft, but of more than words. By not acknowledging a source, the plagiarist steals the modest recognition that honest researchers should receive, the respect that a researcher spends a lifetime struggling to earn. And that weakens the community as a whole, by reducing the value of research to those who follow.

That is true in all research communities, including the undergraduate classroom. The student plagiarist steals not only from his sources, but from his colleagues by making their work seem lesser by comparison to what was bought or stolen. When such intellectual thievery becomes common, the community grows suspicious, then distrustful, then cynical—*Everyone does it. I'll fall behind if I don't.* Teachers must then worry as much about not being tricked as about teaching and learning. What's worse, the plagiarist compromises her own education and so steals from the larger society that devotes its resources to training her and her generation to do reliable work later, work that the community will depend on.

In short, when you report your research ethically, you join a community in a search for some common good. When you respect sources, preserve and acknowledge data that run against your results, assert claims only as strongly as warranted, acknowledge the limits of your certainty, and meet all the other ethical obligations on your report, you move beyond gaining a grade or other material goods—you earn the larger benefit that comes from creating a bond with your readers. You discover that research focused on the best interests of others is also in your own.

A Postscript for Teachers

In this postscript we want to make explicit what has been implicit throughout. We hope you will join in an effort to improve the national "research scene." Too many teachers of undergraduates say, *I've given up teaching the research paper.* Colleagues tell us that the ones they get are boring patchworks, that students aren't up to the task, that in any event the hard-copy research paper is an relic of pre-digital days, even that no one but ivory-tower academics does research anymore.

We think otherwise, of course. We think doing research is the best way to learn to read and think critically. And we know for a fact that the vast majority of our students will have careers in which, if they do not do their own research, they will have to evaluate and depend on the research of others. We also know that most of that research will be in written form, even if it happens to be delivered online. And we can think of no way to prepare for that responsibility better than doing research of one's own.

We wrote this book for those who agree, and believe—or will at least consider—two propositions:

- Students learn to do research well and report it clearly when they take the perspective of their readers and of the community whose values and practices define competent research and its reporting.

• They learn to manage an important part of that mental and social process when they understand how a few key formal features of their reports influence how their readers read and judge them.

These two propositions, we believe, are closely related. By understanding the complementary processes of reading and writing, students plan, perform, and report their research better. They can use the features that readers expect to guide themselves through not only the process of drafting, but all the stages of their project. And by understanding what their readers look for in a report, they learn to read the reports of others more critically. The two processes, reading and writing, are mutually supporting.

THE RISKS AND LIMITATIONS OF IMPOSING FORMAL RULES

Emphasizing formal matters, though, carries a risk, especially with new researchers. It is easy to trivialize formal structures into empty drills. Those who teach dancers only to hit their marks or pianists only to find the right keys deprive students of the deepest pleasures of dance and music. Those who teach research as if it were merely learning the proper forms for footnotes and bibliography deprive their students of the pleasures of discovery, driving them to join those countless students turned off by Gradgrind formulae, students who might otherwise have blessed the world with their own good research.

If students are shown how to approach them in the right spirit, the features of an argument become not empty forms to be mindlessly filled, but answers to questions that encourage hard thinking. They help students recognize what is important in the relationship between a researcher, her sources, her disciplinary colleagues and readers—a crucial prerequisite to creative and original research.

Forms empty of meaning encourage empty imitation, especially when teachers fail to create in their classrooms a rhetorical context that dramatizes for students their social role as researchers, even if at first only in simulation or role-playing. No textbook can fully create that context, because it requires a class experience that only imaginative teachers can orchestrate.

Only a teacher, understanding his unique students, can devise assignments that create situations whose social dynamic gives point and purpose to research and whose expectations students can recognize and understand. The less experience students have, the more social support teachers must provide before their students can use formal structures in productive ways.

ON ASSIGNMENT SCENARIOS: CREATING A GROUND FOR CURIOSITY

Teachers have found many ways to construct research assignments that give students that necessary support. The most successful have these features:

1. **Good assignments establish outcomes beyond a product to be evaluated.** Good teachers ask students to raise a question or problem that at least *they* want to resolve, and to support that resolution with reliable and relevant evidence. Good research assignments then ask students to translate that private interest into a public one, so that they can experience, or at least imagine, readers who need the understanding that only they can provide.

The best assignments ask students to write for those who actually need to know or understand something better. Those readers might be a transient community of researchers that a problem creates, as when students do their research for a client outside of class. A senior design class, for example, might address a problem of a local company or civic organization; a music class might write program notes; a history class might investigate the origins of some part of their university or an institution in their local community.

Less experienced students might write for their classmates, but they might also write for students in another class who could actually use the information that a beginning researcher could provide. They might do preliminary research for those senior design students or for students in a graduate seminar; or they might even write reports back to students still in high school.

Next best are assignments that simulate such situations, in which students assume that other students or a client or even other researchers have a problem that the student researcher can resolve. Even in large classes, students can work in small groups whose members serve as readers with interests that beginning researchers can reasonably address.

2. **Good assignments help students learn about their readers.** Most students have trouble imagining readers whom they have never met and whose situation they have never experienced. Biology students with no knowledge or experience working with a government agency will be unlikely to write a plausible report that meets the concerns of a state EPA administrator. But teachers can help by urging students to imagine those distant readers. Alternatively, they can turn the class into its own audience by letting students decide what problems need solving, what questions need answering. If students can define the problems they're interested in, they will make the best possible readers for one another's research.

3. **Good assignments create scenarios that are rich in contextual information.** When students write to resolve the problems of readers known and accessible to them, the assignment presents a scenario rich in detail. Students can investigate, interrogate, and analyze the situation for as long as time and ingenuity allow.

But when it's not practical to locate the project in a real context, the assignment should create as much of that context as possible. It is seldom possible to anticipate everything students need to know about such a scenario, so it is important to make analysis and discussion of it a part of the writing process. Only when students are working in a social context do they have meaningful choices and good reasons to make them. Only then are those choices rhetorically significant. And only when writers can make rhetorically significant choices will they understand that at the heart of every real writing project is the anticipation of their readers' responses. When students have no choices because their project has no rhetorical "scene" and so is only a mechanical drill, doing research and writing it up become merely make-work—for you as much as for them.

Again we stress the importance of lively discussion among the students, either in class, if the class is small enough, or in subgroups if the class is large.

4. Good assignments provide interim readers. Few professional researchers call a report finished before they have solicited responses, something students need even more. Encourage students to solicit early responses from colleagues, friends, family, even from you. Getting responses is easier if you build opportunities into the assignment itself. Other students can play this role reasonably well, but not if they think that their task is just "editing"— which for them often means rearranging a sentence here and fixing a misspelling there. Have student responders work through some of the steps in chapters 14–17; you can even create teams of responders, each with responsibility for specific features of the text. Those who provide interim responses must participate in the scenario as imagined readers.

5. As with any real project, good assignments give students time and a schedule of interim deadlines. Research is messy, so it does no good to march students through it lockstep: (1) Select topic, (2) state thesis, (3) write outline, (4) collect bibliography, (5) read and take notes, (6) write report. That caricatures real research. But students need some framework, a schedule of tasks that helps them monitor their progress. They need time for false starts and blind alleys, for revision and reconsideration. They need interim deadlines and stages for sharing and criticizing their progress. Those stages can reflect the various sequences outlined in this book.

RECOGNIZING AND TOLERATING THE INEVITABLE MESSINESS OF LEARNING

Students also seriously—sometimes desperately—need other kinds of support, especially recognition of what can be expected of them and tolerance for the predictable missteps of even experienced researchers. Beginners behave in awkward ways, taking suggestions and principles as inflexible rules that they apply mechanically. They work through a topic to a question to the online catalog to a few Web sites marching on and on to a feeble conclusion, not because they lack imagination or creativity, but because they are struggling to acquire a skill that to them is surpassingly strange. Such awkwardness is an inevitable stage in learning any skill. It passes, but too often only after they have moved on to other classes.

We urge you not to be troubled when a whole class of beginning students produces reports that look alike. We three have had to learn to be patient with students, as we wait for the delayed gratification that comes when the learners arrive at genuine originality—knowing it will likely come when we are no longer there to see it.

We try to assure students that even if they do not solve their problem, they succeed if they can pose it in a way that convinces us that it is new—at least to them—and arguably *needs* a solution. Proving that there is a problem to be solved often requires more research and more critical ability than solving it, certainly more than one in which a student can ask a simple question and answer it.

We know that some students use research assignments simply to gather information on a topic, to review a field just to gain control over it. To them, the demand for a significant problem seems artificial. You can only ask them to imagine that they are writing for a reader who is intelligent and possibly interested in their topic but does not have the time to do any research, a reader who is, indeed, in the circumstance they are in.

Finally, different students stand in different relations to the research practices you teach. Advanced students should strive toward the full quality of your own disciplinary practices. But few beginners are yet committed to any research community or to the values that underlie everything in this book. Some will make that commitment early, but most will not. Some never will.

In sum: To teach research well, we teachers must adapt the steps we've outlined here to fit the particular circumstances and needs of the individuals before us in class. We can only hope that students at all levels learn these steps, learn to identify them in other writing projects, and then attempt them on their own. Maybe then they can move toward the kind of sound research and reasoned decision making that our society so badly needs but too seldom gets.

Appendix
BIBLIOGRAPHICAL RESOURCES

There is a large literature on finding and presenting information, only some of which can be listed here. For a larger and more current selection, consult the Library of Congress catalog and commercial Web sites that provide customer reviews of books. If there is no date listed for an item, the publication appears annually. Sources available online or as a CD-ROM (in addition to or in place of traditional print formats) are so indicated. Online sources for which no URL is given are readily available from multiple online databases.

This list is divided as follows:

For most of those areas, six kinds of resources are listed:

1. specialized dictionaries that offer short essays defining concepts in a field

2. general and specialized encyclopedias that offer more extensive overviews of a topic

3. guides to finding resources in different fields and using their methodologies

4. bibliographies, abstracts, and indexes that list past and current publications in different fields

5. writing manuals for different fields

6. style manuals that describe required features of citations in different fields

INTERNET DATABASES (BIBLIOGRAPHIES AND INDEXES)
General

ArticleFirst. Dublin, OH: OCLC, 1990–. http://oclc.org/.

The Booklist. Chicago: American Library Association. 1969–. http://www.ala.org/booklist/.

ClasePeriodica. Mexico, D.F.: UNAM, 2003–. http://oclc.org.

Digital Dissertations. Ann Arbor, MI: UMI, [19—]–. http://wwwlib.umi.com/dissertations/.

Electronic Resources Review. Bradford, UK: MCB University Press, 1997–2000. http://www.emeraldinsight.com/1364-5137.htm.

ERIC. Educational Resources Information Center. Ipswich, MA: EBSCO Pub., 1994–; Bethesda, MD: Cambridge Scientific Abstracts, 1998–. http://www.lib.umt.edu/laser/cdalpo.htm.

Essay and General Literature. Bronx, NY: H. W. Wilson, 1900–. http://wilson-web2.hwwilson.com.

FirstSearch Dissertations. Ann Arbor, MI: University Microfilms. http://wwwlib.umi.com/dissertations/.

FRANCIS. Institut de l'information scientifique et technique (France); Getty Information Institute; Research Libraries Group. Mountain View, CA: Research Libraries Group, 1984–. http://connectsciences.inist.fr/internes/oldi/baseSearch.php.

General Reference Center Gold. Farmington Hills, MI: Gale Group, 1999–. http://infotrac.galegroup.com/.

InfoTrac OneFile. Farmington Hills, MI: Gale Group. http://web5.infotrac.galegroup.com/itw/infomark.

ISI Web of Knowledge. Philadelphia: Institute for Scientific Information, 2000–. http://isinet.com/webofknowledge.

LexisNexis Academic Universe. Dayton, OH: LexisNexis. http://web.lexis-nexis.com/universe/.

Library Literature and Information Science Full Text. Bronx, NY: H. W. Wilson, 1900–. http://wilsonweb2.hwwilson.com.

Periodicals Index Online. ProQuest Information and Learning Company, 1990–. http://pio.chadwyck.co.uk/home.do.

ProQuest Research Library. Ann Arbor, MI: ProQuest Information and Learning, 1998–. http://proquest.umi.com/pqdweb?RQT=306&DBld=4138#sform.

Wilson Omnifile Full Text. Mega edition. Bronx, NY: H. W. Wilson, 1990–. http://hwwilsonweb.com.

WorldCat. Dublin, OH: Online Computer Library Center. http://www.oclc.org/ worldcat/.

Humanities

Arts and Humanities Search. Philadelphia: Institute for Scientific Information; Dublin, OH: OCLC, 1990–. http://oclc.org.

Bibliography of the History of Art. Santa Monica, CA: J. Paul Getty Trust; Vandoeuvre-lès-Nancy, France: Centre national de la recherche scientifique, 1990–. http://www.eureka.rig.org.

History Resource Center U.S. Farmington Hills, MI: Gale Group, ca. 2000–. http://www.galenet.com/servlet/HistRC.

Humanities Full Text. Bronx, NY: H. W. Wilson, 1990–. http://hwwilsonweb.com/.

Social Sciences

Anthropological Literature. Cambridge, MA: Tozzer Library, Harvard University, 1984–. telnet://cobalt.rig.org.

LawDesk. http://lawlibrary.ucdavis.edu/lawlib/august02/0095.html.

On-Line Index to Indian Social Science Journals and Press Clippings Files. New Delhi: ISID. http://isidev.nic.in/odb.html.

PAISArchive. Public Affairs Information Service. Dublin, OH: OCLC, 2004–. http://www.oclc.org.

PAIS International. Public Affairs Information Service. Norwood, MA: SilverPlatter International, 1900–. http://www.bowdoin.edu/dept/library/erl/spirs/pais.

Political Science Resources on the Web. Ann Arbor, MI: Document Center, University of Michigan, 1996–. http://www.lib.umich.edu/govdocs/polisci.html.

PsycARTICLES. Washington, DC: American Psychological Association, 2001–. http://psycinfo.com/library/fulltext.cfm.

PsycINFO. American Psychological Association. New York: Ovid Technologies, 1900–. http://www.apa.org/psycinfo/.

Social Sciences Abstracts. Bronx, NY: H. W. Wilson, 1997–. http://www.oclc.org.

Social Sciences Citation Index with Abstracts. Philadelphia: Institute for Scientific Information, ca. 1992–. http://www.isinet.com/products/citation/ssci/.

Sociological Abstracts. Sociological Abstracts, Inc. Dublin, OH: OCLC, 1990–. http://www.oclc.com.

Natural Sciences

AGRICOLA (AGRICultural OnLine Access). Beltsville, MD: The Library, 1970–. http://purl.access.gpo.gov/GPO/LPS1292.

Applied Science and Technology Abstracts. Bronx, NY: H. W. Wilson; Dublin, OH: OCLC, 1983–. http://www.oclc.org.

ISI Web of Science. Philadelphia: Institute for Scientific Information, ca. 1998–. http://isiknowledge.com.

PubSCIENCE United States. Washington, DC: U.S. Dept. of Energy, Office of Scientific and Technical Information, 1999–2002. http://purl.access.gpo.gov/ GPO/LP3399.

Science Citation Index. Philadelphia: Institute for Scientific Information, ca. 1988–. http://isi01.isiknowledge.com/portal.cgi/wos.

Web of Science. Philadelphia: Institute for Scientific Information, 1998–. http:// isiknowledge.com, http://www.webofscience.com/.

PRINT AND ELECTRONIC RESOURCES
General

1. Bowman, John S., ed. *The Cambridge Dictionary of American Biography.* Cambridge: Cambridge University Press, 1995.

1. Garraty, John A., and Mark C. Carnes, eds. *American National Biography.* New York: Oxford University Press, 1999.

1. Matthew, H. C. G., and Brian Howard Harrison, eds. *Oxford Dictionary of National Biography, in Association with the British Academy: From the Earliest Times to the Year 2000.* New York: Oxford University Press, 2004. Also at http://www .oxforddnb.com.

2. Jackson, Kenneth T., Karen Markoe, and Arnie Markoe, eds. *The Scribner Encyclopedia of American Lives.* 6 vols. covering 1981–2002. New York: Charles Scribner's Sons, 1998–ca. 2004.

2. Lagassé, Paul, ed. *The Columbia Encyclopedia.* 6th ed. New York: Columbia University Press, 2000. Also at http://www.bartleby.com/65/.

2. *New Encyclopaedia Britannica.* 15th ed. 32 vols. Chicago: Encyclopaedia Britannica, 2005. Also at http://www.eb.com.

3. Balay, Robert, ed. *Guide to Reference Books.* 11th ed. Chicago: American Library Association, 1996.

3. Hacker, Diana, and Barbara Fister. *Research and Documentation in the Electronic Age.* 3rd ed. Boston: Bedford/St. Martin's, 2002. Also at http://www .dianahacker.com/resdoc/.

3. Kane, Eileen, and Mary O'Reilly-de Brún. *Doing Your Own Research.* New York: Marion Boyars, 2001.

3. Lipson, Charles. *Doing Honest Work in College: How to Prepare Citations, Avoid Plagiarism, and Achieve Real Academic Success.* 2nd ed. Chicago: University of Chicago Press, 2008.

3. Mann, Thomas. *Oxford Guide to Library Research.* 3rd ed. New York: Oxford University Press, 2005.

3. Preece, Roy A. *Starting Research: An Introduction to Academic Research and Dissertation Writing.* London: Continuum, 2000.

3. Rowely, Jennifer, and John Farrow. *Organizing Knowledge: An Introduction to Managing Access to Information.* 3rd ed. Aldershot, Hampshire, UK: Gower, 2000.

3. Sears, Jean L., and Marilyn K. Moody. *Using Governmental Information Sources: Electronic and Print.* 3rd ed. Phoenix: Oryx Press, 2001.

3. Whiteley, Sandra, ed. *The American Library Association Guide to Information Access: A Complete Handbook and Directory.* New York: Random House, 1994.

4. *Alternative Press Index.* College Park, MD: Alternative Press Centre, 1969.

4. *Bibliographic Index.* New York: H. W. Wilson. Also at http://hwwilsonweb .com.

4. *Book Review Index.* Detroit: Gale Research, 1965–.

4. *Book Review Index: A Master Cumulation.* Detroit: Gale Research, 1980–.

4. *Books in Print.* New Providence, NJ: R. R. Bowker. Also at http://www.booksinprint.com/bip.

4. Brigham, Clarence S. *History and Bibliography of American Newspapers, 1690–1820.* 2 vols. Westport, CT: Greenwood Press, 1976.

4. *Conference Papers Index.* Louisville, KY: Data Courier, 1978–.

4. *Current Book Review Citations* in English. New York: H. W. Wilson, 1976–82.

4. *Current Book Review Citations* in multiple languages. Bronx, NY: H. W. Wilson, 1976–82.

4. Fanning, C. E., Margaret Jackson, Mary Katharine Reely, and Mertice May James. *Book Review Digest. Annual Cumulation.* New York: H. W. Wilson, 1905–.

4. Farber, Evan Ira, and Ruth Matteson Blackmore, eds. *Combined Retrospective Index to Book Reviews in Scholarly Journals, 1886–1974.* Arlington, VA: Carrollton Press, 1979–.

4. Gregory, Winifred, ed. *American Newspapers 1821–1936: A Union List of Files Available in the United States and Canada.* New York: H. W. Wilson, 1937.

4. *Kirkus Reviews.* New York: Kirkus Service, 1991–.

4. *Library of Congress Subject Catalog.* Washington, DC: Library of Congress. Also at http://catalog.loc.gov/.

4. *National Newspaper Index.* Menlo Park, CA: Information Access. Also online from multiple sources.

4. *Newspapers in Microform.* Ann Arbor, MI: University Microfilms International.

4. *New York Times Index.* New York: New York Times.

4. *Periodical Abstracts and General Periodicals. Research II.* Ann Arbor, MI: University Microfilms International. 1990s–.

4. Poole, William Frederick, and William Isaac Fletcher. *Poole's Index to Periodical Literature.* Rev. ed. Gloucester, MA: Peter Smith, 1970.

4. *Popular Periodical Index.* Camden, NJ: Rutgers University.

4. *ProQuest Digital Dissertations.* Ann Arbor, MI: University Microfilms International. Also at http://wwwlib.umi.com/dissertations/.

4. *Readers' Guide to Periodical Literature.* New York: H. W. Wilson. Also at http://hwwilsonweb.com/.

4. *Reference Books Bulletin.* Chicago: American Library Association, 1984–.

4. *Serials in Microform.* Ann Arbor, MI: University Microfilms International.

4. *Serials Review.* San Diego: Pergamon, 1975–. Also by subscription through ScienceDirect.

4. *Subject Guide to Books in Print.* New York: R. R. Bowker. Also at http://www.booksinprint.com/bip/.

4. *Wall Street Journal Index.* New York: Dow Jones. Also at http://www.il.proquest.com/products/pt-product-WSJ.shtml.

5. Bolker, Joan, ed. *Writing Your Dissertation in Fifteen Minutes a Day: A Guide to Starting, Revising, and Finishing Your Doctoral Thesis.* New York: Henry Holt, 1998.

5. Miller, Jane E. *The Chicago Guide to Writing about Numbers.* Chicago: University of Chicago Press, 2004.

5. Sternberg, David Joel. *How to Complete and Survive a Doctoral Dissertation.* New York: St. Martin's Griffin, 1981.

5. Strunk, William, and E. B. White. *The Elements of Style.* 4th ed. New York: Longman, 2004.

5. Williams, Joseph M. *Style: Toward Clarity and Grace.* Chicago: University of Chicago Press, 1990.

6. *The Chicago Manual of Style.* 15th ed. Chicago: University of Chicago Press, 2003.

Visual Representation of Data (Tables, Figures, etc.)

2. Harris, Robert L. *Information Graphics: A Comprehensive Illustrated Reference.* New York: Oxford University Press, 2000.

3. Cleveland, William S. *The Elements of Graphing Data.* 2nd ed. Summit, NJ: Hobart Press, 1994.

3. ———. *Visualizing Data.* Summit, NJ: AT&T Bell Laboratories, 1993.

3. Monmonier, Mark. *Mapping It Out: Expository Cartography for the Humanities and Social Sciences.* Chicago: University of Chicago Press, 1993.

3. Tufte, Edward R. *Envisioning Information.* Cheshire, CT: Graphics Press, 1990.

3. ———. *Visual and Statistical Thinking: Displays of Evidence for Decision Making.* Cheshire, CT: Graphics Press, 1997.

3. ———. *The Visual Display of Quantitative Information.* Cheshire, CT: Graphics Press, 1983.

3. Wainer, Howard. *Visual Revelations: Graphical Tales of Fate and Deception from Napoleon Bonaparte to Ross Perot.* New York: Copernicus, Springer-Verlag, 1997.

5. Briscoe, Mary Helen. *Preparing Scientific Illustrations: A Guide to Better Posters, Presentations, and Publications.* 2nd ed. New York: Springer-Verlag, 1996.

5. Kosslyn, Stephen M. *Elements of Graph Design.* New York: W. H. Freeman, 1994.

5. National Institutes of Health, Division of Research Services, Medical Arts and Photography Branch. *Graphics User Guide.* Bethesda, MD: The Branch, 1986?.

5. Nicol, Adelheid A. M., and Penny M. Pexman. *Presenting Your Findings: A Practical Guide for Creating Tables.* Washington, DC: American Psychological Association, 1999.

5. Robbins, Naomi B. *Creating More Effective Graphs.* New York: John Wiley & Sons, 2004.

5. Ross, Ted. *The Art of Music Engraving and Processing: A Complete Manual, Reference, and Text Book on Preparing Music for Reproduction and Print.* Miami: Hansen Books, 1970.

5. Zweifel, Frances W. *A Handbook of Biological Illustration.* 2nd ed. Chicago: University of Chicago Press, 1988.

6. CBE Scientific Illustration Committee. *Illustrating Science: Standards for Publication.* Bethesda, MD: Council of Biology Editors, 1988.

Posters

Corbin, Nancy C. "The Well-Dressed Poster Board." In *A Mission to Communicate: Proceedings, 32nd International Technical Communication Conference, May 19–22, 1985, Houston, Texas, VC 26–29*. Washington, DC: Society for Technical Communication, 1985.

Dubois, Betty Lou. "Poster Sessions at Biomedical Meetings: Design and Presentation." *English for Special Purposes Journal* 4, no. 1 (1985): 37–48.

Esposito, Mona, Kaye Marshall, and Fredericka L. Stoller. "Poster Sessions by Experts." In *New Ways in Content-Based Instruction*, edited by Donna M. Brinton and Peter Master, 115–18. Alexandria, VA: Teachers of English to Speakers of Other Languages, 1997.

George Mason University, Department of Biology. "A Guide to Writing in the Biological Sciences: The Poster Session." http://classweb.gmu.edu/biologyresources/writingguide/Poster.htm.

Griffith, George W. "Poster Sessions: One-to-One Technical Communication." In *Proceedings: 28th International Technical Communication Conference, May 20–23, 1981, Pittsburgh, PA, G26–G27*. Pittsburgh: Society for Technical Writing, 1981.

Larkin, Greg. "Storyboarding: A Concrete Way to Generate Effective Visuals." *Journal of Technical Writing and Communication* 26, no. 3 (1996): 273–90.

Rice University, Cain Project in Engineering and Professional Communication. "Designing Scientific and Engineering Posters." http://www.owlnet.rice.edu/~cainproj/ih_posters.html.

Shalom, Celia. "Established and Evolving Spoken Research Process Genres: Plenary Lecture and Poster Session Discussions at Academic Conferences." *English for Specific Purposes Journal* 12, no. 1 (1993): 37–50.

Stanford University, Visual Art Services. "Posters Templates." http://stanford.edu/dept/VAS/posters/poster_temps.html.

University of California, Davis, Nutrition Department. "Poster Printer." http://teaching.ucdavis.edu/poster/template.htm.

White, J. T. "Technical Poster Fabrication." In *Proceedings: 28th International Technical Communication Conference, May 20–23, 1981, Pittsburgh, PA, G64–G65*. Pittsburgh: Society for Technical Writing, 1981.

Humanities
General

1. Murphy, Bruce, ed. *Benet's Reader's Encyclopedia*. 4th ed. New York: HarperCollins, 1996.

3. Kirkham, Sandi. *How to Find Information in the Humanities*. London: Library Association, 1989.

4. *American Humanities Index*. Troy, NY: Whitston.

4. *Arts and Humanities Citation Index*. Philadelphia: Institute for Scientific Information, 1976–.

4. *Arts and Humanities Index*. Philadelphia: Institute for Scientific Information. Also at http://www.isiknowledge.com.

4. Blazek, Ron, and Elizabeth Smith Aversa. *The Humanities: A Selective Guide to Information Sources.* 5th ed. Englewood, CO: Libraries Unlimited, 2000. Also at http://www.netlibrary.com.

4. *British Humanities Index.* London: Library Association; Bethesda, MD: Cambridge Scientific Abstracts.

4. Harzfeld, Lois A. *Periodical Indexes in the Social Sciences and Humanities: A Subject Guide.* Microform. Metuchen, NJ: Scarecrow Press, 1978.

4. *Humanities Index.* New York: H. W. Wilson, 1974. Also at http://hwwilsonweb.com.

4. *Index to Book Reviews in the Humanities.* Williamston, MI: P. Thomson, 1960–90.

4. *Index to Social Sciences and Humanities Proceedings.* Philadelphia: Institute for Scientific Information, 1979–.

4. Walford, Albert J., Anthony Chalcraft, Ray Prytherch, and Stephen Willis, eds. *Walford's Guide to Reference Material.* Vol. 3, *Generalia, Language and Literature, The Arts.* 7th ed. London: Library Association, 1998.

5. Northey, Margot, and Maurice Legris. *Making Sense in the Humanities: A Student's Guide to Writing and Style.* Toronto: Oxford University Press, 1990.

Art

1. Chilvers, Ian, and Harold Osborne, eds. *The Oxford Dictionary of Art.* 3rd ed. Oxford: Oxford University Press, 2004. Also at http://www.oxfordreference.com.

1. Myers, Bernard L., and Trewin Copplestone, eds. *The Macmillan Encyclopedia of Art.* Rev. ed. London: Macmillan, 1981.

1. Myers, Bernard S., and Shirley D. Myers, eds. *McGraw-Hill Dictionary of Art.* 5 vols. New York: McGraw-Hill, 1969.

2. Myers, Bernard S., ed. *Encyclopedia of World Art.* 17 vols. New York: McGraw-Hill, 1987.

3. Arntzen, Etta, and Robert Rainwater. *Guide to the Literature of Art History.* Chicago: American Library Association, 1980.

3. Jones, Lois Swan. *Art Information and the Internet: How to Find It, How to Use It.* Phoenix: Oryx Press, 1999.

3. ———. *Art Information: Research Methods and Resources.* 3rd ed. Dubuque, IA: Kendall/Hunt, 1990.

3. Marmor, Max, and Alex Ross. *Guide to the Literature of Art History 2.* Chicago: American Library Association, 2005.

3. Minor, Vernon Hyde. *Art History's History.* 2nd ed. Upper Saddle River, NJ: Prentice Hall, 2001.

4. *Art Abstracts.* Bronx, NY: H. W. Wilson, 1984–. Also at http//wilsonweb2.hwwilson.com.

4. *Art Index.* New York: H. W. Wilson. Also at http://hwwilsonweb.com.

4. *Art Index Retrospective.* Bronx, NY: H. W. Wilson, 1997–. Also at http://wilsonweb2.hwwilson.com.

5. Barnet, Sylvan. *A Short Guide to Writing about Art.* 8th ed. New York: Pearson Longman, 2005.

History

1. Cook, Chris. *A Dictionary of Historical Terms.* 3rd ed. Houndmills, UK: Macmillan, 1998.

1. Ritter, Harry. *Dictionary of Concepts in History.* Westport, CT: Greenwood Press, 1986.

2. Breisach, Ernst. *Historiography: Ancient, Medieval, and Modern.* 2nd ed. Chicago: University of Chicago Press, 1994.

3. Benjamin, Jules R. *A Student's Guide to History.* 9th ed. Boston: Bedford/St. Martin's, 2004.

3. Brundage, Anthony. *Going to the Sources: A Guide to Historical Research and Writing.* 3rd ed. Wheeling, IL: Harlan Davidson, 2002.

3. Frick, Elizabeth. *History: Illustrated Search Strategy and Sources.* 2nd ed. Ann Arbor, MI: Pierian Press, 1995.

3. Fritze, Ronald H., Brian E. Coutts, and Louis Andrew Vyhnanek. *Reference Sources in History: An Introductory Guide.* 2nd ed. Santa Barbara, CA: ABC-Clio, 2004.

3. Higginbotham, Evelyn Brooks, Leon F. Litwack, and Darlene Clark Hine. *The Harvard Guide to African-American History.* Cambridge, MA: Harvard University Press, 2001.

3. Kyvig, David E., and Myron A. Marty. *Nearby History: Exploring the Past Around You.* 2nd ed. Walnut Creek, CA: AltaMira Press, 2000.

3. Prucha, Francis Paul. *Handbook for Research in American History: A Guide to Bibliographies and Other Reference Works.* 2nd ed. Lincoln: University of Nebraska Press, 1994.

4. *America: History and Life.* Santa Barbara, CA: ABC-Clio. Also at http://serials.abc-clio.com.

4. Blazek, Ron, and Anna H. Perrault. *United States History: A Selective Guide to Information Sources.* Englewood, CO: Libraries Unlimited, 1994. Also at http://www.netlibrary.com.

4. Danky, James Philip, and Maureen E. Hady. *African-American Newspapers and Periodicals: A National Bibliography.* Cambridge, MA: Harvard University Press, 1998.

4. *Historical Abstracts.* Santa Barbara, CA: ABC-Clio. Also at http://serials.abc-clio.com.

4. Kinnel, Susan K., ed. *Historiography: An Annotated Bibliography of Journal Articles, Books, and Dissertations.* 2 vols. Santa Barbara, CA: ABC-Clio, 1987.

4. Mott, Frank Luther. *A History of American Magazines.* 5 vols. Cambridge, MA: Belknap Press of Harvard University Press, 1930–68.

5. Barzun, Jacques, and Henry F. Graff. *The Modern Researcher.* 6th ed. Belmont, CA: Thomson/Wadsworth, 2004.

5. Marius, Richard, and Melvin E. Page. *A Short Guide to Writing about History.* 5th ed. New York: Pearson Longman, 2005.

Literary Studies

1. Abrams, M. H. *A Glossary of Literary Terms.* 8th ed. Boston: Thomson/Wadsworth, 2005.

1. Baldick, Chris, ed. *The Concise Oxford Dictionary of Literary Terms.* 2nd ed. Oxford: Oxford University Press, 2001.

1. Brogan, Terry V. F., ed. *The New Princeton Handbook of Poetic Terms.* Princeton, NJ: Princeton University Press, 1994.

1. Groden, Michael, Martin Kreiswirth, and Imre Szeman, eds. *The Johns Hopkins Guide to Literary Theory and Criticism.* 2nd ed. Baltimore: Johns Hopkins University Press, 2005.

1. Preminger, Alex, and Terry V. F. Brogan, eds. *The New Princeton Encyclopedia of Poetry and Poetics.* Princeton, NJ: Princeton University Press, 1993.

2. Drabble, Margaret, ed. *The Oxford Companion to English Literature.* 6th ed. New York: Oxford University Press, 2000. Also at http://www.oxfordreference.com.

2. Hart, James David, and Phillip W. Leininger, eds. *The Oxford Companion to American Literature.* 6th ed. New York: Oxford University Press, 1995. Also at http://www.oxfordreference.com.

2. Lentricchia, Frank, and Thomas McLaughlin, eds. *Critical Terms for Literary Study.* 2nd ed. Chicago: University of Chicago Press, 1995.

2. Parini, Jay, ed. *The Oxford Encyclopedia of American Literature.* 4 vols. New York: Oxford University Press, 2004.

2. Ward, Sir Adolphus William, A. R. Waller, William Peterfield Trent, John Erskine, Stuart Pratt Sherman, and Carl Van Doren. *The Cambridge History of English and American Literature: An Encyclopedia in Eighteen Volumes.* New York: G. P. Putnam's Sons, 1907–21. Also at http://www.bartleby.com/cambridge/.

3. Altick, Richard Daniel, and John J. Fenstermaker. *The Art of Literary Research.* 4th ed. New York: Norton, 1993.

3. Harner, James L. *Literary Research Guide: An Annotated Listing of Reference Sources in English Literary Studies.* 4th ed. New York: Modern Language Association of America, 2002.

3. Klarer, Mario. *An Introduction to Literary Studies.* 2nd ed. London: Routledge, 2004.

3. Vitale, Philip H. *Basic Tools of Research: An Annotated Guide for Students of English.* 3rd ed., rev. and enl. New York: Barron's Educational Series, 1975.

4. *Abstracts of English Studies.* Boulder, CO: National Council of Teachers of English, 1958–.

4. Blanck, Jacob, Virginia L. Smyers, and Michael Winship. *Bibliography of American Literature.* 9 vols. New Haven, CT: Yale University Press, 1955–91. Also at http://lion.chadwyck.co.uk/.

4. *Index of American Periodical Verse.* Metuchen, NJ: Scarecrow Press, 1971–.

4. *MLA International Bibliography of Books and Articles on the Modern Languages and Literature.* New York: Modern Language Association of America. Also online from multiple sources.

5. Barnet, Sylvan, and William E. Cain. *A Short Guide to Writing about Literature.* 10th ed. New York: Longman Pearson, 2005.

5. Griffith, Kelley. *Writing Essays about Literature: A Guide and Style Sheet.* 7th ed. Boston: Heinle & Heinle, 2005.

6. Gibaldi, Joseph. *MLA Handbook for Writers of Research Papers*. 6th ed. New York: Modern Language Association of America, 2003.

Music

1. Randel, Don Michael, ed. *The Harvard Dictionary of Music*. 4th ed. Cambridge: Belknap Press of Harvard University Press, 2003.

1. Sadie, Stanley, and John Tyrrell, eds. *The New Grove Dictionary of Music and Musicians*. 2nd ed. 29 vols. New York: Grove, 2001. Also at http://www.grovemusic.com.

2. Netti, Bruno, Ruth M. Stone, James Porter, and Timothy Rice, eds. *The Garland Encyclopedia of World Music*. 10 vols. New York: Garland, 2002.

2. Sadie, Stanley, ed. *The Norton/Grove Concise Encyclopedia of Music*. Rev. and enl. ed. New York: W. W. Norton, 1994.

3. Brockman, William S. *Music: A Guide to the Reference Literature*. Littleton, CO: Libraries Unlimited, 1987.

3. Duckles, Vincent H., Ida Reed, and Michael A. Keller, eds. *Music Reference and Research Materials: An Annotated Bibliography*. 5th ed. New York: Schirmer Books, 1997.

4. *The Music Index*. Detroit: Information Service. Also at http://www.hppmusicindex.com.

4. *RILM Abstracts of Music Literature*. New York: RILM. Also online from multiple sources.

5. Druesedow, John E., Jr. *Library Research Guide to Music: Illustrated Search Strategy and Sources*. Ann Arbor, MI: Pierian Press, 1982.

5. Herbert, Trevor. *Music in Words: A Short Guide to Researching and Writing about Music*. London: Associated Board of the Royal Schools of Music, 2001.

5. Wingell, Richard. *Writing about Music: An Introductory Guide*. 3rd ed. Upper Saddle River, NJ: Prentice Hall, 2002.

6. Bellman, Jonathan. *A Short Guide to Writing about Music*. New York: Longman, 2000.

6. Holoman, D. Kern. *Writing about Music: A Style Sheet from the Editors of 19th Century Music*. Berkeley: University of California Press, 1988. Also at http://www.netlibrary.com.

Philosophy

1. Blackburn, Simon. *The Oxford Dictionary of Philosophy*. 2nd ed. Oxford: Oxford University Press, 2005. Also at http://www.oxfordreference.com.

2. Edwards, Paul. *The Encyclopedia of Philosophy*. 8 vols. New York: Simon & Schuster Macmillan, 1996.

2. Parkinson, George H. R. *The Handbook of Western Philosophy*. New York: Macmillan, 1988.

2. Urmson, J. O., and Jonathan Rée, eds. *The Concise Encyclopedia of Western Philosophy and Philosophers*. 3rd ed. London: Routledge, 2005.

3. List, Charles J., and Stephen H. Plum. *Library Research Guide to Philosophy*. Ann Arbor, MI: Pierian Press, 1990.

4. *The Philosopher's Index*. Bowling Green, OH: Philosopher's Information Center. Also at http://www.ovid.com/site/catalog/DataBase/.

5. Martinich, Aloysius. *Philosophical Writing: An Introduction*. 3rd ed. Malden, MA: Blackwell, 2005.

5. Watson, Richard A. *Writing Philosophy: A Guide to Professional Writing and Publishing*. Carbondale: Southern Illinois University Press, 1992. Also at http://www.netlibrary.com.

Social Sciences
General

1. Calhoun, Craig, ed. *Dictionary of the Social Sciences*. New York: Oxford University Press, 2002. Also at http://www.oxfordreference.com.

1. *Statistical Abstract of the United States*. Washington, DC: U.S. Census Bureau. Also at http://www.census.gov/statab/www/.

2. Sills, David, ed. *International Encyclopedia of the Social Sciences*. 19 vols. New York: Macmillan, 1991.

3. Herron, Nancy L. *The Social Sciences: A Cross-Disciplinary Guide to Selected Sources*. 3rd ed. Englewood, CO: Libraries Unlimited, 2002.

3. Light, Richard J., and David B. Pillemer. *Summing Up: The Science of Reviewing Research*. Cambridge, MA: Harvard University Press, 1984.

3. Øyen, Else, ed. *Comparative Methodology: Theory and Practice in International Social Research*. London: Sage, 1990.

4. *Bibliography of Social Science Research and Writings on American Indians*. Compiled by Russell Thornton and Mary K Grasmick. Minneapolis: Center for Urban and Regional Affairs, University of Minnesota, 1979.

4. *Book Review Index to Social Science Periodicals*. Ann Arbor, MI: Pierian Press, 1964–70.

4. *CommSearch*. Annandale, VA: Speech Communication Association, 1995–.

4. *C.R.I.S.: The Combined Retrospective Index Set to Journals in Sociology, 1895–1974*. Compiled by Annadel N. Wile and Arnold Jaffe. Washington, DC: Carrollton Press, 1978.

4. *Current Contents: Social and Behavioral Sciences*. Philadelphia: Institute for Scientific Information, 1974–.

4. *Document Retrieval Index*. U.S. Dept. of Justice, Law Enforcement Assistance Administration, National Institute of Law Enforcement and Criminal Justice, 1979–. Microfiche.

4. Grossmann, Jorge. *Indice general de publicaciones periódicas latinoamericanas: Humanidades y ciencias sociales; Index to Latin American Periodicals: Humanities and Social Sciences*. Metuchen, NJ: Scarecrow Press, 1961–70.

4. Harzfeld, Lois A. *Periodical Indexes in the Social Sciences and Humanities: A Subject Guide*. Metuchen, NJ: Scarecrow Press, 1978.

4. *Index of African Social Science Periodical Articles*. Dakar: Council for the Development of Economic and Social Research in Africa, ca. 1989–.

4. *Index to Social Sciences and Humanities Proceedings*. Philadelphia: Institute for Scientific Information, 1979–.

4. *PAIS International*. New York: SilverPlatter Information; OCLC Public Affairs Information Service, 1900s–.

4. *PAIS International in Print*. New York: OCLC Public Affairs Information Service, 1991–.

4. *Social Sciences Citation Index*. Philadelphia: Institute for Scientific Information, 1969–.

4. *Social Sciences Index*. New York: H. W. Wilson. Also at http://hwwilsonweb .com.

4. Walford, A. J., Alan Day, and Michael Walsh, eds. *Walford's Guide to Reference Material*. Vol. 2, *Social and Historical Sciences, Philosophy, and Religion*. 8th ed. London: Library Association, 2000.

5. Becker, Howard S. *Writing for Social Scientists: How to Start and Finish Your Thesis, Book, or Article*. Chicago: University of Chicago Press, 1986.

5. Bell, Judith. *Doing Your Research Project: A Guide for First-Time Researchers in Education, Health, and Social Science*. 4th ed. Maidenhead, UK: Open University Press, 2005.

5. Krathwohl, David R. *How to Prepare a Research Proposal: Guidelines for Funding and Dissertations in the Social and Behavioral Sciences*. 3rd ed. Syracuse, NY: Syracuse University Press, 1988.

5. Northey, Margot, Lorne Tepperman, and James Russell. *Making Sense: Social Sciences; A Student's Guide to Research and Writing*. Updated 2nd ed. Ontario: Oxford University Press, 2005.

Anthropology

1. Barfield, Thomas J., ed. *The Dictionary of Anthropology*. Oxford: Blackwell, 2000. Also at http://www.netlibrary.com.

1. Winthrop, Robert H. *Dictionary of Concepts in Cultural Anthropology*. New York: Greenwood Press, 1991.

2. Barnard, Alan, and Jonathan Spencer, eds. *Encyclopedia of Social and Cultural Anthropology*. London: Routledge, 2004.

2. Ember, Melvin, Carol R. Ember, and Ian A. Skoggard, eds. *Encyclopedia of World Cultures: Supplement*. New York: Gale Group/Thomson Learning, 2002.

2. Ingold, Tim, ed. *Companion Encyclopedia of Anthropology: Humanity, Culture, and Social Life*. New ed. London: Routledge, 2002.

2. Levinson, David, ed. *Encyclopedia of World Cultures*. 10 vols. Boston: G. K. Hall, 1996.

2. Levinson, David, and Melvin Ember, eds. *Encyclopedia of Cultural Anthropology*. 4 vols. New York: Henry Holt, 1996.

3. Bernard, H. Russell, ed. *Handbook of Methods in Cultural Anthropology*. Walnut Creek, CA: AltaMira Press, 2000.

3. ———. *Research Methods in Anthropology: Qualitative and Quantitative Approaches*. 4th ed. Lanham, MD: AltaMira Press, 2005.

3. *Current Topics in Anthropology: Theory, Methods, and Content*. 8 vols. Reading, MA: Addison-Wesley, 1971–.

3. Glenn, James R. *Guide to the National Anthropological Archives, Smithsonian Institution.* Rev. and enl. ed. Washington, DC: National Anthropological Archives, 1996.

3. Poggie, John J., Jr., Billie R. DeWalt, and William W. Dressler, eds. *Anthropological Research: Process and Application.* Albany: State University of New York Press, 1992. Also at http://www.netlibrary.com.

4. *Abstracts in Anthropology.* Amityville, NY: Baywood.

4. *Annual Review of Anthropology.* Palo Alto, CA: Annual Reviews. Also online from multiple sources.

Business

1. Friedman, Jack P. *Dictionary of Business Terms.* 3rd ed. Hauppauge, NY: Barron's Educational Series, 2000. Also at http://www.netlibrary.com.

1. Link, Albert N. *Link's International Dictionary of Business Economics.* Chicago: Probus, 1993.

1. Nisberg, Jay N. *The Random House Dictionary of Business Terms.* New York: Random House, 1992.

1. Wiechmann, Jack G., and Laurence Urdang, eds. *NTC's Dictionary of Advertising.* 2nd ed. Lincolnwood, IL: National Textbook, 1993.

2. Folsom, W. Davis, and Rick Boulware. *Encyclopedia of American Business.* New York: Facts on File, 2004.

2. *The Lifestyle Market Analyst: A Reference Guide for Consumer Market Analysis.* Wilmette, IL: Standard Rate & Data Service.

2. McDonough, John, and Karen Egolf, eds. *The Advertising Age Encyclopedia of Advertising.* 3 vols. New York: Fitzroy Dearborn, 2003.

2. Vernon, Mark. *Business: The Key Concepts.* New York: Routledge, 2002. Also at http://www.netlibrary.com.

2. Warner, Malcolm, and John P. Kotter, eds. *International Encyclopedia of Business and Management.* 2nd ed. 8 vols. London: Thomson Learning, 2002.

3. Amor, Louise, ed. *The Online Manual: A Practical Guide to Business Databases.* 6th ed. Oxford: Learned Information, 1997.

3. Daniells, Lorna M. *Business Information Sources.* 3rd ed. Berkeley: University of California Press, 1993.

3. Kervin, John B. *Methods for Business Research.* New York: HarperCollins, 1992.

3. Moss, Rita W., and Diane Wheeler Strauss. *Strauss's Handbook of Business Information: A Guide for Librarians, Students, and Researchers.* 2nd ed. Westport, CT: Libraries Unlimited, 2004.

3. Sekaran, Uma. *Research Methods for Business: A Skill Building Approach.* 4th ed. New York: John Wiley & Sons, 2003.

3. Woy, James B., ed. *Encyclopedia of Business Information Sources.* 19th ed. Farmington Hills, MI: Gale Group, 2004.

4. *Business Periodicals Index.* New York: H. W. Wilson. Also at http://hwwilsonweb .com.

5. Farrell, Thomas J., and Charlotte Donabedian. *Writing the Business Research Paper: A Complete Guide.* Durham, NC: Carolina Academic Press, 1991.

6. Vetter, William. *Business Law, Legal Research, and Writing: Handbook.* Needham Heights, MA: Ginn Press, 1991.

Communication, Journalism, and Media Studies

1. Miller, Toby, ed. *Television: Critical Concepts in Media and Cultural Studies.* London: Routledge, 2003.

1. Newton, Harry. *Newton's Telecom Dictionary: Covering Telecommunications, Networking, Information Technology, the Internet, the Web, Computing, Wireless, and Fiber.* 21st ed. San Francisco: CMP Books, 2005.

1. Watson, James, and Anne Hill. *A Dictionary of Communication and Media Studies.* 4th ed. London: Arnold, 1997.

1. Weik, Martin H. *Communications Standard Dictionary.* 3rd ed. New York: Chapman & Hall, 1996.

1. Weiner, Richard. *Webster's New World Dictionary of Media and Communications.* Rev. and updated ed. New York: Macmillan, 1996.

2. Barnouw, Erik, ed. *International Encyclopedia of Communications.* 4 vols. New York: Oxford University Press, 1989.

2. Johnston, Donald H., ed. *Encyclopedia of International Media and Communications.* 4 vols. San Diego, CA: Academic Press, 2003.

2. Jones, Steve, ed. *Encyclopedia of New Media: An Essential Reference to Communication and Technology.* Thousand Oaks, CA: Sage, 2003.

2. Paneth, Donald. *The Encyclopedia of American Journalism.* New York: Facts on File, 1983.

2. Stern, Jane, and Michael Stern. *Jane and Michael Stern's Encyclopedia of Pop Culture: An A to Z Guide of Who's Who and What's What, from Aerobics and Bubble Gum to Valley of the Dolls and Moon Unit Zappa.* New York: HarperPerennial, 1992.

3. Clark, Vivienne, James Baker, and Eileen Lewis Key. *Concepts and Skills for Media Studies.* London: Hodder & Stoughton, 2003.

3. Stokes, Jane. *How to Do Media and Cultural Studies.* London: Sage, 2003.

3. Storey, John. *Cultural Studies and the Study of Popular Culture: Theories and Methods.* 2nd ed. Athens: University of Georgia Press, 2003.

4. Block, Eleanor S., and James K. Bracken. *Communication and the Mass Media: A Guide to the Reference Literature.* Englewood, CO: Libraries Unlimited, 1991.

4. Blum, Eleanor, and Frances Goins Wilhoit. *Mass Media Bibliography: An Annotated Guide to Books and Journals for Research and Reference.* 3rd ed. Urbana: University of Illinois Press, 1990.

4. Cates, Jo A. *Journalism: A Guide to the Reference Literature.* 3rd ed. Westport, CT: Libraries Unlimited, 2004.

4. *CD Review.* Hancock, NH: WGE, 1989–96.

4. *Communications Abstracts.* Los Angeles: Dept. of Journalism, University of California, Los Angeles.

4. *Film Review Annual.* Englewood, NJ: J. S. Ozer, 1981–.

4. Matlon, Ronald J., and Sylvia P. Ortiz, eds. *Index to Journals in Communication Studies through 1995.* Annadale, VA: National Communication Association, 1997.

4. *Media Review Digest.* Ann Arbor, MI: Pierian Press, 1974–.

4. *New York Theatre Critics' Reviews.* New York: Critics' Theatre Reviews, 1943–95.

4. *New York Times Directory of the Film.* New York: Arno Press, 1971–.

4. *Records in Review.* Great Barrington, MA: Wyeth Press, 1957–81.

4. Sterling, Christopher H., James K. Bracken, and Susan M. Hill, eds. *Mass Communications Research Resources: An Annotated Guide.* Mahwah, NJ: Erlbaum, 1998.

6. Goldstein, Norm, ed. *Stylebook and Briefing on Media Law.* 40th ed. New York: Associated Press, 2005.

Economics

1. Pearce, David W., ed. *MIT Dictionary of Modern Economics.* 4th ed. Cambridge, MA: MIT Press, 1992.

2. Eatwell, John, Murray Milgate, Peter K. Newman, and Sir Robert Harry Inglis Palgrave, eds. *The New Palgrave: A Dictionary of Economics.* 4 vols. New York: Palgrave, 2004.

2. Greenwald, Douglas, ed. *The McGraw-Hill Encyclopedia of Economics.* 2nd ed. New York: McGraw-Hill, 1994.

2. Mokyr, Joel, ed. *The Oxford Encyclopedia of Economic History.* 5 vols. Oxford: Oxford University Press, 2003.

3. Fletcher, John, ed. *Information Sources in Economics.* 2nd ed. London: Butterworths, 1984.

3. Johnson, Glenn L. *Research Methodology for Economists: Philosophy and Practice.* New York: Macmillan, 1986.

4. *Journal of Economic Literature.* Nashville, TN: American Economic Association. Also at http://www.jstor.org.

5. McCloskey, Donald N. *The Writing of Economics.* New York: Macmillan, 1987.

5. Thomson, William. *A Guide for the Young Economist.* Cambridge, MA: MIT Press, 2001.

Education

1. Barrow, Robin, and Geoffrey Milburn. *A Critical Dictionary of Educational Concepts: An Appraisal of Selected Ideas and Issues in Educational Theory and Practice.* 2nd ed. New York: Teacher's College Press, 1990.

1. Collins, John Williams, and Nancy P. O'Brien, eds. *The Greenwood Dictionary of Education.* Westport, CT: Greenwood, 2003.

1. Gordon, Peter, and Dennis Lawton. *Dictionary of British Education.* 3rd ed. London: Woburn Press, 2003.

2. Alkin, Marvin C., ed. *Encyclopedia of Educational Research.* 6th ed. 4 vols. New York: Macmillan, 1992.

2. Guthrie, James W., ed. *Encyclopedia of Education*. 2nd ed. 8 vols. New York: Macmillan Reference USA, 2003. Also at http://www.netlibrary.com.

2. Husen, Torsten, and T. Neville Postlethwaite, eds. *The International Encyclopedia of Education*. 2nd ed. 12 vols. Oxford: Pergamon, 1994.

2. Levinson, David L., Peter W. Cookson, and Alan R. Sadovnik, eds. *Education and Sociology: An Encyclopedia*. New York: RoutledgeFalmer, 2002.

2. Unger, Harlow G. *Encyclopedia of American Education*. 2nd ed. 3 vols. New York: Facts on File, 2001.

3. Bausell, R. Barker. *Advanced Research Methodology: An Annotated Guide to Sources*. Metuchen, NJ: Scarecrow Press, 1991.

3. Keeves, John P., ed. *Educational Research, Methodology, and Measurement: An International Handbook*. 2nd ed. New York: Pergamon, 1997.

3. Tuckman, Bruce W. *Conducting Educational Research*. 5th ed. Fort Worth, TX: Harcourt Brace, 1999.

4. *Education Index*. New York: H. W. Wilson. Also at http://hwwilsonweb.com.

4. *The ERIC Database*. Lanham, MD: Educational Resources Information Center. Also at http://www.eric.ed.gov/.

4. O'Brien, Nancy P. *Education: A Guide to Reference and Information Sources*. 2nd ed. Englewood, CO: Libraries Unlimited, 2000. Also at http://www.netlibrary.com.

5. Carver, Ronald P. *Writing a Publishable Research Report: In Education, Psychology, and Related Disciplines*. Springfield, IL: C. C. Thomas, 1984.

Geography

1. Witherick, M. E., Simon Ross, and John Small. *A Modern Dictionary of Geography*. 4th ed. London: Arnold, 2001.

2. Dunbar, Gary S. *Modern Geography: An Encyclopedic Survey*. New York: Garland, 1991.

2. McCoy, John, ed. *Geo-Data: The World Geographic Encyclopedia*. 3rd ed. Detroit: Thomson-Gale, 2003. Also at www.netlibrary.com.

2. Parker, Sybil P., ed. *World Geographical Encyclopedia*. 5 vols. New York: McGraw-Hill, 1995.

3. Walford, Nigel. *Geographical Data Analysis*. New York: John Wiley & Sons, 1995.

4. Conzen, Michael P., Thomas A. Rumney, and Graeme Wynn. *A Scholar's Guide to Geographical Writing on the American and Canadian Past*. Chicago: University of Chicago Press, 1993.

4. *Current Geographical Publications*. New York: American Geographical Society of New York.

4. *Geographical Abstracts*. Norwich, UK: Geo Abstracts.

4. Okuno, Takashi. *A World Bibliography of Geographical Bibliographies*. Japan: Institute of Geoscience, University of Tsukuba, 1992.

5. Durrenberger, Robert W., John K. Wright, and Elizabeth T. Platt. *Geographical Research and Writing*. New York: Crowell, 1985.

5. Northey, Margot, and David B. Knight. *Making Sense: A Student's Guide to Research and Writing: Geography and Environmental Sciences.* 2nd updated ed. Ontario: Oxford University Press, 2005.

Law

1. Curzon, L. B. *Dictionary of Law.* 6th ed. Harlow, UK: Pearson Education Limited, 2002.

1. Garner, Bryan A., and Henry C. Black, eds. *Black's Law Dictionary.* 8th ed. St. Paul, MN: Thomson/West, 2004.

1. Martin, Elizabeth A., ed. *A Dictionary of Law.* 5th ed. Oxford: Oxford University Press, 2003. Also at http://www.oxfordreference.com.

2. Baker, Brian L., and Patrick J. Petit, eds. *Encyclopedia of Legal Information Sources.* 2nd ed. Detroit: Gale Research, 1993.

2. *Corpus Juris Secundum.* St. Paul, MN: West.

2. Hall, Kermit, and David Scott Clark, eds. *The Oxford Companion to American Law.* New York: Oxford University Press, 2002. Also at http://www.oxford reference.com.

2. Lehman, Jeffrey, and Shirelle Phelps. *West's Encyclopedia of American Law.* 2nd ed. 13 vols. Detroit: Thomson/Gale, 2005. Also online from multiple sources.

3. Campbell, Enid Mona, Lee Poh-York, and Joycey G. Tooher. *Legal Research: Materials and Methods.* 4th ed. North Ryde, Australia: LBC Information Services, 1996.

3. Long, Judy A. *Legal Research Using the Internet.* Albany, NY: West Legal Studies/Thomson Learning, 2000. Also at http://www.netlibrary.com.

4. *Current Index to Legal Periodicals.* Seattle: M. G. Gallagher Law Library and Washington Law Review. Also at http://lib.law.washington.edu/cilp/cilp.html.

4. *Current Law Index: Multiple Access to Legal Periodicals.* Farmington Hills, MI: Gale Group, 2001.

4. *Index to Legal Periodicals and Books.* New York: H. W. Wilson. Also at http://hwwilsonweb.

5. Bast, Carol M., and Margie Hawkins. *Foundations of Legal Research and Writing.* 2nd ed. Albany, NY: West/Thomson Learning, 2002.

5. Garner, Bryan A. *The Elements of Legal Style.* 2nd ed. New York: Oxford University Press, 2002.

6. *The Bluebook: A Uniform System of Citation.* 18th ed. Cambridge, MA: Harvard Law Review Association, 2005.

Political Science

1. Robertson, David. *A Dictionary of Modern Politics.* 4th ed. London: Europa, 2005.

2. *The Almanac of American Politics.* Washington, DC: National Journal. Also at http://nationaljournal.com/members/almanac.

2. Hawkesworth, Mary E., and Maurice Kogan, eds. *Encyclopedia of Government and Politics.* 2nd ed. 2 vols. London: Routledge, 2004.

2. Lal, Shiv, ed. *International Encyclopedia of Politics and Laws.* 17 vols. New Delhi: Election Archives, 1987.

2. Miller, David, ed. *The Blackwell Encyclopaedia of Political Thought.* Oxford: Blackwell, 1998. Also at http://www.netlibrary.com.

3. Green, Stephen W., and Douglas J. Ernest, eds. *Information Sources in Political Science.* 5th ed. Santa Barbara, CA: ABC-Clio, 2005.

3. Johnson, Janet Buttolph, and H. T. Reynolds. *Political Science Research Methods.* 5th ed. Washington, DC: Congressional Quarterly Press, 2005.

4. *ABC PolSci.* Santa Barbara, CA: ABC-Clio.

4. *PAIS International Journals Indexed.* New York: Public Affairs Information Service.

4. *United States Political Science Documents.* Pittsburgh: University of Pittsburgh, University Center for International Studies, 1975–91.

4. Wynkoop, Sally. *Subject Guide to Government Reference Books.* Littleton, CO: Libraries Unlimited, 1972.

5. Biddle, Arthur W., Kenneth M. Holland, and Toby Fulwiler. *Writer's Guide: Political Science.* Lexington, MA: D. C. Heath, 1987.

5. Lovell, David W., and Rhonda Moore. *Essay Writing and Style Guide for Politics and the Social Sciences.* Sydney: Australasian Political Studies Association, 1992.

5. Schmidt, Diane E. *Writing in Political Science: A Practical Guide.* 3rd ed. New York: Pearson Longman, 2005.

5. Scott, Gregory M., and Stephen M. Garrison. *The Political Science Student Writer's Manual.* 5th ed. Upper Saddle River, NJ: Pearson/Prentice Hall, 2004.

6. American Political Science Association. *Style Manual for Political Science.* Rev. ed. Washington, DC: American Political Science Association, 2001.

Psychology

1. Colman, Andrew M. *Oxford Dictionary of Psychology.* Oxford: Oxford University Press, 2003. Also at http://www.oxfordreference.com.

1. Eysenck, Michael, ed. *The Blackwell Dictionary of Cognitive Psychology.* Oxford: Blackwell, 1997.

1. Hayes, Nicky, and Peter Stratton. *A Student's Dictionary of Psychology.* 4th ed. London: Arnold, 2003.

1. Wolman, Benjamin B., ed. *Dictionary of Behavioral Science.* 2nd ed. San Diego, CA: Academic Press, 1989.

2. Colman, Andrew M., ed. *Companion Encyclopedia of Psychology.* 2 vols. London: Routledge, 1997.

2. Craighead, W. Edward, Charles B. Nemeroff, and Raymond J. Corsini, eds. *The Corsini Encyclopedia of Psychology and Behavioral Science.* 3rd ed. 4 vols. New York: Wiley, 2002.

2. Kazdin, Alan E., ed. *Encyclopedia of Psychology.* 8 vols. Washington, DC: American Psychological Association; Oxford: Oxford University Press, 2000.

3. Breakwell, Glynis M., Sean Hammond, and Chris Fife-Schaw. *Research Methods in Psychology.* 2nd ed. London: Sage, 2004.

3. Elmes, David G., Barry H. Kantowitz, and Henry L. Roediger III. *Research Methods in Psychology*. 8th ed. Belmont, CA: Wadsworth, 2005.

3. Reed, Jeffrey G., and Pam M. Baxter. *Library Use: A Handbook for Psychology*. 3rd ed. Washington, DC: American Psychological Association, 2003.

3. Shaughnessy, John J., Eugene B. Zechmeister, and Jeanne S. Zechmeister. *Research Methods in Psychology*. 7th ed. Boston: McGraw-Hill, 2005.

3. Wilson, Christopher. *Research Methods in Psychology: An Introductory Laboratory Manual*. Dubuque, IA: Kendall-Hunt, 1990.

4. *Annual Review of Psychology*. Palo Alto, CA: Annual Reviews. Also at http://arjournals.annualreviews.org.

4. *Compact Cambridge MEDLINE*. Bethesda, MD: NLM by Cambridge Scientific Abstracts. Also at http://www.ncbi.nlm.nih.gov/entrez/query.fcgi/.

4. *NASPSPA Abstracts*. Champaign, IL: Human Kinetics.

4. *PsycINFO*. Washington, DC: American Psychological Association. Also online from multiple sources.

4. *The Web of Science Citation Databases*. Philadelphia: Institute for Scientific Information. Also at http://isiknowledge.com.

5. Solomon, Paul R. *A Student's Guide to Research Report Writing in Psychology*. Glenview, IL: Scott, Foresman, 1985.

5. Sternberg, R. J. *The Psychologist's Companion: A Guide to Scientific Writing for Students and Researchers*. 4th ed. Cambridge: Cambridge University Press, 2003.

6. *Publication Manual of the American Psychological Association*. 5th ed. Washington, DC: American Psychological Association, 2003.

Religion

1. Bowker, John, ed. *The Concise Oxford Dictionary of World Religions*. Oxford: Oxford University Press, 2000. Also at http://www.oxfordreference.com.

1. Pye, Michael, ed. *Continuum Dictionary of Religion*. New York: Continuum, 1994.

2. Jones, Lindsay, ed. *Encyclopedia of Religion*. 15 vols. Detroit: Macmillan Reference USA, 2005.

2. Routledge Encyclopedias of Religion and Society (series). New York: Routledge.

3. Kennedy, J. *Library Research Guide to Religion and Theology: Illustrated Search Strategy and Sources*. 2nd ed., rev. Ann Arbor, MI: Pierian, 1984.

4. Brown, David, and Richard Swinbourne. *A Selective Bibliography of the Philosophy of Religion*. Rev. ed. Oxford: Sub-Faculty of Philosophy, 1995.

4. Chinvamu, Salms. *An Annotated Bibliography on Religion*. Malawi: Malawi Library Association, 1993.

4. *Guide to Social Science and Religion in Periodical Literature*. Flint, MI: National Library of Religious Periodicals, 1970–88.

4. *Index to Book Reviews in Religion*. Chicago: American Theological Library Association. Also at http://www.ovid.com.

4. *Islamic Book Review Index*. Berlin: Adiyok, 1982–.

4. O'Brien, Betty A., and Elmer J. O'Brien, eds. *Religion Index Two: Festschriften, 1960–1969.* Chicago: American Theological Library Association, 1980. Also at http://www.ovid.com.

4. *Religion Index One: Periodicals.* Chicago: American Theological Library Association, 1977–.

4. *Religion Index Two: Multi-Author Works.* Chicago: American Theological Library Association. Also at http://www.ovid.com.

Sociology

1. Abercrombie, Nicholas, Stephen Hill, and Bryan S. Turner. *The Penguin Dictionary of Sociology.* 4th ed. London: Penguin, 2000.

1. Johnson, Allan G. *The Blackwell Dictionary of Sociology: A User's Guide to Sociological Language.* 2nd ed. Oxford: Blackwell, 2002.

1. Scott, John, and Marshall Gordon, eds. *A Dictionary of Sociology.* 3rd ed. New York: Oxford University Press, 2005.

2. Beckert, Jens, and Milan Zafirovksi, eds. *Encyclopedia of Economic Sociology.* London: Routledge, 2005.

2. Borgatta, Edgar F., ed. *Encyclopedia of Sociology.* 2nd ed. 5 vols. New York: Macmillan Reference USA, 2000.

2. Levinson, David L., Peter W. Cookson, and Alan R. Sadovnik, eds. *Education and Sociology: An Encyclopedia.* New York: RoutledgeFalmer, 2002.

2. Ritzer, George, ed. *Encyclopedia of Social Theory.* 2 vols. Thousand Oaks, CA: Sage, 2005.

2. Smelser, N., ed. *Handbook of Sociology.* Newbury Park, CA: Sage, 1988.

3. Aby, Stephen H., James Nalen, and Lori Fielding, eds. *Sociology: A Guide to Reference and Information Sources.* 3rd ed. Westport, CT: Libraries Unlimited, 2005.

3. Lieberson, Stanley. *Making It Count: The Improvement of Social Research and Theory.* Berkeley: University of California Press, 1987.

4. *Annual Review of Sociology.* Palo Alto, CA: Annual Reviews. Also at http://www.jstor.org and at http://arjournals.annualreviews.org/loi/soc/.

4. *Applied Social Sciences Index and Abstracts (ASSIA).* Bethesda, MD: Cambridge Scientific Abstracts. Also at http://www.csa.

4. *Social Science Research.* San Diego, CA: Academic Press. Also at http://www.sciencedirect.com.

4. *Sociological Abstracts.* Bethesda, MD: Sociological Abstracts. Also at http://www.csa.com.

5. Sociology Writing Group. *A Guide to Writing Sociology Papers.* 5th ed. New York: Worth, 2001.

5. Tomovic, Vladislav A., ed. *Definitions in Sociology: Convergence, Conflict, and Alternative Vocabularies: A Manual for Writers of Term Papers, Research Reports, and Theses.* St. Catharines, ON: Diliton, 1979.

Women's Studies

1. Bataille, Gretchen M., and Laurie Lisa, eds. *Native American Women: A Biographical Dictionary.* 2nd ed. New York: Routledge, 2001.

1. Mills, Jane. *Womanwords: A Dictionary of Words about Women.* New York: Henry Holt, 1993.

1. Salem, Dorothy C., ed. *African American Women: A Biographical Dictionary.* New York: Garland, 1993.

1. Uglow, Jennifer S., Frances Hinton, and Maggy Hendry, eds. *The Northeastern Dictionary of Women's Biography.* 3rd ed. Boston: Northeastern University Press, 1999.

2. Hine, Darlene Clark, Elsa Barkley Brown, and Rosalyn Terborg-Penn, eds. *Black Women in America: An Historical Encyclopedia.* 2 vols. Bloomington: Indiana University Press, 1994.

2. Kramarae, Cheris, and Dale Spender, eds. *Routledge International Encyclopedia of Women: Global Women's Issues and Knowledge.* 4 vols. New York: Routledge, 2000.

2. Tierney, Helen, ed. *Women's Studies Encyclopedia.* Rev. and expanded ed. 3 vols. Westport, CT: Greenwood Press, 1999. Also at http://www.gem.greenwood.com/.

2. Willard, Frances E., and Mary A. Livermore, eds. *American Women: Fifteen Hundred Biographies with Over 1,400 Portraits.* Rev. ed. 2 vols. Detroit: Gale Research, 1973.

3. Atkinson, Steven D., and Judith Hudson. *Women Online: Research in Women's Studies Using Online Databases.* New York: Haworth, 1990.

3. Carter, Sarah, and Maureen Ritchie. *Women's Studies: A Guide to Information Sources.* London: Mansell, 1990.

3. Searing, Susan E. *Introduction to Library Research in Women's Studies.* Boulder, CO: Westview Press, 1985.

4. *Studies on Women and Gender Abstracts.* Oxfordshire, UK: Carfax. Also at http://www.tandf.co.uk/swa/.

4. *Women Studies Abstracts.* Rush, NY: Rush.

4. *Women's Review of Books.* Wellesley, MA: Wellesley College Center for Research on Women, 1983–2004.

4. *Women's Studies International.* Baltimore: National Information Services Corp. Also at http://www.nisc.com.

Natural Sciences
General

1. *McGraw-Hill Dictionary of Scientific and Technical Terms.* 6th ed. New York: McGraw-Hill, 2003. Also at http://www.accessscience.com.

1. Morris, Christopher, ed. *Academic Press Dictionary of Science and Technology.* San Diego, CA: Academic Press, 1992.

1. Porter, Ray, and Marilyn Bailey Ogilvie, eds. *The Biographical Dictionary of Scientists.* 3rd ed. 2 vols. New York: Oxford University Press, 2000.

1. *Science Navigator.* New York: McGraw-Hill, 1998. CD-ROM, version 4.0.

1. Walker, Peter M. B., ed. *Chambers Dictionary of Science and Technology.* London: Chambers, 2000.

2. Heilbron, J. L., ed. *The Oxford Companion to the History of Modern Science.* Oxford: Oxford University Press, 2003. Also at http://www.oxfordreference.com.

2. *McGraw-Hill Encyclopedia of Science and Technology.* 9th ed. New York: McGraw-Hill, 2002. Also at http://www.accessscience.com.

2. *Nature Encyclopedia: An A–Z Guide to Life on Earth.* New York: Oxford University Press, 2001.

2. *Van Nostrand's Scientific Encyclopedia.* 9th ed. New York: Wiley-Interscience, 2002.

3. *Directory of Technical and Scientific Directories: A World Bibliographic Guide to Medical, Agricultural, Industrial, and Natural Science Directories.* 6th ed. Phoenix: Oryx Press, 1989.

3. Hurt, Charlie Deuel. *Information Sources in Science and Technology.* 3rd ed. Englewood, CO: Libraries Unlimited, 1998. Also at http://www.netlibrary.com.

3. Nielsen, Harry A. *Methods of Natural Science: An Introduction.* Englewood Cliffs, NJ: Prentice-Hall, 1967.

4. *Applied Science and Technology Index.* New York: H. W. Wilson. Also at http://hwwilsonweb.com.

4. *British Technology Index.* London: Library Association, 1962–80.

4. *Compumath Citation Index.* Philadelphia: Institute for Scientific Information, 1981–.

4. Fanning, C. E., Margaret Jackdon, Mary Katharine Reely, and Mertice May James. *Book Review Digest: Annual Cumulation.* New York: H. W. Wilson, 1905–.

4. *General Science Index.* New York: H. W. Wilson, 1978–. Also at http://hwwilsonweb.com.

4. *Genetics Citation Index: Experimental Citation Indexes to Genetics with Special Emphasis on Human Genetics.* Comp. Eugene Garfield and Irving H. Sher. Philadelphia: Institute for Scientific Information, 1963.

4. *Index to Scientific Reviews: An International Interdisciplinary Index to the Review Literature of Science, Medicine, Agriculture, Technology, and the Behavioral Sciences.* Philadelphia: Institute for Scientific Information, 1974.

4. *ISI Web of Science: Science Citation Index.* Philadelphia: Institute for Scientific Information. Also at http://www.isiknowledge.com.

4. *Science and Technology Annual Reference Review.* Phoenix: Oryx Press, ca. 1989–.

4. *Science Citation Index.* Philadelphia: Institute for Scientific Information, 1961–.

4. *Technical Book Review Index.* New York: Special Libraries Association, 1935–. Available on microfilm and microfiche from University Microfilms.

5. Booth, Vernon. *Communicating in Science: Writing a Scientific Paper and Speaking at Scientific Meetings.* 2nd ed. Cambridge: Cambridge University Press, 1993.

5. Gilpin, Andrea A., and Patricia Patchet-Golubev. *A Guide to Writing in the Sciences.* Toronto: University of Toronto Press, 2000.

5. Valiela, Ivan. *Doing Science: Design, Analysis, and Communication of Scientific Research.* Oxford: Oxford University Press, 2001.

5. Wilson, Anthony, et al. *Handbook of Science Communication.* Bristol: Institute of Physics Pub., 1998. Also at http://www.netlibrary.com.

6. Rubens, Phillip, ed. *Science and Technical Writing: A Manual of Style.* 2nd ed. New York: Routledge, 2001. Also at http://www.netlibrary.com.

Biology

1. *A Dictionary of Biology.* 5th ed. Oxford: Oxford University Press, 2004. Also at http://www.oxfordreference.com.

1. Allaby, Michael, ed. *The Oxford Dictionary of Natural History.* Oxford: Oxford University Press, 1985.

1. Lawrence, Eleanor, ed. *Henderson's Dictionary of Biology.* 13th ed. Harlow, UK: Prentice Hall, 2005.

1. Singleton, Paul, and Diana Sainsbury. *Dictionary of Microbiology and Molecular Biology.* 3rd ed. New York: Wiley, 2001.

1. Smith, Anthony D., ed. *Oxford Dictionary of Biochemistry and Molecular Biology.* Rev. ed. Oxford: Oxford University Press, 2003.

2. *Biology Encyclopedia.* New York: HarperCollins, 1991. Videodisc.

2. Creighton, Thomas E., ed. *Encyclopedia of Molecular Biology.* 4 vols. New York: John Wiley & Sons, 1999.

2. Dulbecco, Renato, ed. *Encyclopedia of Human Biology.* 2nd ed. 9 vols. San Diego, CA: Academic Press, 1997.

2. Eldredge, Niles, ed. *Life on Earth: An Encyclopedia of Biodiversity, Ecology, and Evolution.* 2 vols. Santa Barbara, CA: ABC-Clio, 2002.

2. Hall, Brian Keith, and Wendy M. Olson, eds. *Keywords and Concepts in Evolutionary Developmental Biology.* Cambridge, MA: Harvard University Press, 2003.

2. Pagel, Mark D., ed. *Encyclopedia of Evolution.* 2 vols. Oxford: Oxford University Press, 2002.

3. Boorkman, Jo Anne, Jeffrey T. Huber, and Fred W. Roper. *Introduction to Reference Sources in the Health Sciences.* 4th ed. New York: Neal-Schuman, 2004.

3. Wyatt, H. V., ed. *Information Sources in the Life Sciences.* 4th ed. London: Bowker-Saur, 1997.

4. *Biological Abstracts.* Philadelphia: BioSciences Information Service of Biological Abstracts. Also at http://www.ovid.com.

4. *Biological and Agricultural Index.* New York: H. W. Wilson. Also at http://hwwilsonweb.com.

4. *Environment Sciences and Pollution Management.* Bethesda, MD: Cambridge Scientific Abstracts. Also at http://www.csa.com.

4. *Genetics Citation Index; Experimental Citation Indexes to Genetics with Special Emphasis on Human Genetics.* Comp. Eugene Garfield and Irving H. Sher. Philadelphia: Institute for Scientific Information, 1963.

5. McMillan, Victoria E. *Writing Papers in the Biological Sciences.* 3rd ed. Boston: Bedford/St. Martin's, 2001.

6. Council of Science Editors. *Scientific Style and Format: The CSE Manual for Authors, Editors, and Publishers.* 7th ed. Reston, VA: Rockefeller University Press, 2006.

Chemistry

1. Hawley, Gessner Goodrich, and Richard J. Lewis Sr. *Hawley's Condensed Chemical Dictionary.* 14th ed. New York: Wiley, 2002.

2. Kroschwitz, Jacqueline, and Arza Seidel, eds. *Kirk-Othmer Encyclopedia of Chemical Technology.* 5th ed. Hoboken, NJ: Wiley-Interscience, 2004.

2. Lide, David R. *CRC Handbook of Chemistry and Physics*. 86th ed. Boca Raton, FL: CRC Press, 2005.

2. Meyers, Robert A., ed. *Encyclopedia of Physical Science and Technology*. 3rd ed. 18 vols. San Diego, CA: Academic Press, 2002. Also at http://www.sciencedirect.com.

3. Leslie, Davies. *Efficiency in Research, Development, and Production: The Statistical Design and Analysis of Chemical Experiments*. Cambridge: Royal Society of Chemistry, 1993.

3. Wiggins, Gary. *Chemical Information Sources*. New York: McGraw-Hill, 1991.

4. *ACS Publications*. Columbus, OH: American Chemical Society. Also at http://pubs.acs.org.

4. *Chemical Abstracts*. Columbus, OH: American Chemical Society. Also at http://www.cas.org.

4. *Composite Index for CRC Handbooks*. 3rd ed. 3 vols. Boca Raton, FL: CRC Press, 1991.

4. *CrossFire Beilstein*. San Leandro, CA: MDL Information Systems. Also at http://www.beilstein.com/products/xfire/.

4. *ScienceDirect*. New York: Elsevier Science. Also at http://www.sciencedirect.com/.

5. Beall, Herbert, and John Trimbur. *A Short Guide to Writing about Chemistry*. 2nd ed. New York: Longman, 2001.

5. Ebel, Hans Friedrich, Claus Bliefert, and William E. Russey. *The Art of Scientific Writing: From Student Reports to Professional Publications in Chemistry and Related Fields*. 2nd ed. Weinheim, Germany: Wiley-VCH, 2004.

5. Schoenfeld, Robert. *The Chemist's English, with "Say It in English, Please!"* 3rd rev. ed. New York: Wiley-VCH, 2001.

6. Coghill, Anne M., and Lorrin R. Garson, eds. *The ACS Style Guide: Effective Communication of Scientific Information*. 3rd ed. Washington, DC: American Chemical Society, 2006.

Computer Sciences

1. Gattiker, Urs E. *The Information Security Dictionary: Defining the Terms that Define Security for E-Business, Internet, Information, and Wireless Technology*. Boston: Kluwer Academic, 2004.

1. LaPlante, Phillip A. *Dictionary of Computer Science, Engineering, and Technology*. Boca Raton, FL: CRC Press, 2001.

1. Pfaffenberger, Bryan. *Webster's New World Computer Dictionary*. 10th ed. Indianapolis: Wiley, 2003.

1. *Random House Concise Dictionary of Science and Computers*. New York: Random House Reference, 2004.

1. South, David W. *The Computer and Information Science and Technology Abbreviations and Acronyms Dictionary*. Boca Raton, FL: CRC Press, 1994.

2. Henderson, Harry. *Encyclopedia of Computer Science and Technology*. New York: Facts on File, 2003.

2. Marins, Brigham, ed. *World of Computer Science.* 2 vols. Detroit: Gale Group/Thomson Learning, 2002.

2. Reilly, Edwin D., Anthony Ralston, and David Hemmendinger, eds. *Encyclopedia of Computer Science.* 4th ed. Chichester, UK: Wiley, 2003.

3. Ardis, Susan B., and Jean A. Poland. *A Guide to the Literature of Electrical and Electronics Engineering.* Littleton, CO: Libraries Unlimited, 1987.

4. Cibbarelli, Pamela R. *Directory of Library Automation Software, Systems, and Services.* Medford, NJ: Information Today, 2006.

5. Eckstein, C. J. *Style Manual for Use in Computer-Based Instruction.* Brooks Air Force Base, TX: Air Force Human Resources Laboratory, Air Force Systems Command, 1990.

Geology and Earth Sciences

1. Clark, John O. E., and Stella Stiegeler, eds. *The Facts on File Dictionary of Earth Science.* New York: Facts on File, 2000.

1. Jackson, Julia A., and Robert Latimer Bates, eds. *Glossary of Geology.* 4th ed. Alexandria, VA: American Geological Institute, 1997.

1. *McGraw-Hill Dictionary of Geology and Mineralogy.* 2nd ed. New York: McGraw-Hill, 2003.

2. Bishop, Arthur C., Alan R. Woolley, and William R. Hamilton. *Cambridge Guide to Minerals, Rocks, and Fossils.* Rev. ed. Cambridge: Cambridge University Press, 2001.

2. Bowes, Donald R., ed. *The Encyclopedia of Igneous and Metamorphic Petrology.* New York: Van Nostrand Reinhold, 1989.

2. Dasch, E. Julius, ed. *Macmillan Encyclopedia of Earth Sciences.* 2 vols. New York: Macmillan Reference USA, 1996.

2. Good, Gregory A., ed. *Sciences of the Earth: An Encyclopedia of Events, People, and Phenomena.* 2 vols. New York: Garland, 1998.

2. Hancock, Paul L., and Brian J. Skinner, eds. *The Oxford Companion to the Earth.* Oxford: Oxford University Press, 2000. Also at http://www.oxfordreference.com.

2. Nierenberg, William A., ed. *Encyclopedia of Earth System Science.* 4 vols. San Diego, CA: Academic Press, 1992.

2. Selley, Richard C., L. R. M. Cocks, and I. R. Plimer, eds. *Encyclopedia of Geology.* 5 vols. Amsterdam: Elsevier Academic, 2005.

2. Seyfert, Carl K., ed. *The Encyclopedia of Structural Geology and Plate Tectonics.* New York: Van Nostrand Reinhold, 1987.

2. Singer, Ronald, ed. *Encyclopedia of Paleontology.* 2 vols. Chicago: Fitzroy Dearborn, 1999.

2. Steele, John H., S. A. Thorpe, and Karl K. Turekian, eds. *Encyclopedia of Ocean Sciences.* 6 vols. San Diego, CA: Academic Press, 2001. Also at http://www.sciencedirect.com/science/referenceworks/.

4. *Bibliography and Index of Geology.* Alexandria, VA: American Geological Institute. Also at http://georef.cos.com/.

4. *Geobase.* New York: Elsevier Science. Also online from multiple sources.

4. Wood, David N., Joan E. Hardy, and Anthony P. Harvey. *Information Sources in the Earth Sciences.* 2nd ed. London: Bowker-Saur, 1989.

5. Bates, Robert L., Marla D. Adkins-Heljeson, and Rex C. Buchanan, eds. *Geowriting: A Guide to Writing, Editing, and Printing in Earth Science.* Rev. 5th ed. Alexandria, VA: American Geological Institute, 2004.

5. Dunn, J., et al. *Organization and Content of a Typical Geologic Report.* Rev. ed. Arvada, CO: American Institute of Professional Geologists, 1993.

Mathematics

1. Borowski, E. J., and J. M. Borwein, eds. *Collins Dictionary: Mathematics.* 2nd ed. Glasgow: HarperCollins, 2002.

1. James, Robert Clarke, and Glenn James. *Mathematics Dictionary.* 5th ed. New York: Van Nostrand Reinhold, 1992.

1. Schwartzman, Steven. *The Words of Mathematics: An Etymological Dictionary of Mathematical Terms Used in English.* Washington, DC: Mathematical Association of America, 1994.

2. Darling, David J. *The Universal Book of Mathematics: From Abracadabra to Zeno's Paradoxes.* Hoboken, NJ: Wiley, 2004.

2. Ito, Kiyosi, ed. *Encyclopedic Dictionary of Mathematics.* 2nd ed. 2 vols. Cambridge, MA: MIT Press, 1993.

2. Weisstein, Eric W. *CRC Concise Encyclopedia of Mathematics.* 2nd ed. Boca Raton, FL: Chapman & Hall/CRC, 2003.

3. Pemberton, John E. *How to Find Out in Mathematics: A Guide to Sources of Information.* 2nd rev. ed. Oxford: Pergamon, 1969.

4. *East European Scientific Abstracts.* Arlington, VA: Joint Publications Research Service.

4. *Mathematical Reviews: 50th Anniversary Celebration.* Providence, RI: American Mathematical Society, 1990.

4. *MathSci.* Providence, RI: American Mathematical Society. Also at http://www.ams.org/mathscinet/.

5. *A Manual for Authors of Mathematical Papers.* Rev. ed. Providence, RI: American Mathematical Society, 1990.

5. Miller, Jane E. *The Chicago Guide to Writing about Multivariate Analysis.* Chicago: University of Chicago Press, 2005.

Physics

1. Basu, Dipak, ed. *Dictionary of Pure and Applied Physics.* Boca Raton, FL: CRC Press, 2001.

1. Isaacs, Alan, ed. *A Dictionary of Physics.* 4th ed. Oxford: Oxford University Press, 2000.

1. Sube, Ralf. *Dictionary: Physics Basic Terms; English-German.* Berlin: A. Hatier, 1994.

1. Thewlis, James. *Concise Dictionary of Physics and Related Subjects.* 2nd ed. rev. and enl. Oxford: Pergamon, 1979.

2. Lerner, Rita G., and George L. Trigg, eds. *Encyclopedia of Physics*. 3rd ed. Weinheim, Germany: Wiley-VCH, 2005.

2. *McGraw-Hill Concise Encyclopedia of Physics*. New York: McGraw-Hill, 2005.

2. Meyers, Robert A., ed. *Encyclopedia of Modern Physics*. San Diego, CA: Academic Press, 1990.

2. Trigg, George L., ed. *Encyclopedia of Applied Physics*. Weinheim, Germany: Wiley-VCH, 2004.

2. Woan, Graham. *The Cambridge Handbook of Physics Formulas*. Cambridge: Cambridge University Press, 2000.

3. Shaw, Dennis F. *Information Sources in Physics*. 3rd ed. London: Bowker-Saur, 1994.

4. *American Institute of Physics Journals*. College Park, MD: AIP. Also at http://www.aip.org/ojs/service.html.

4. *Astronomy and Astrophysics Abstracts*. Berlin: Springer-Verlag.

4. *Current Physics Index*. New York: American Institute of Physics. Also at http://ojps.aip.org/spinweb/.

4. *IEEE Xplore*. New York: Institute of Electrical and Electronics Engineers. Also at http://www.ieee.org/ieeexplore/.

4. *Inspec*. Stevenage, UK: Institution of Electrical Engineers. Also at http://www.iee.org/Publish/INSPEC/.

4. *Institute of Physics Electronic Journals*. London: IOP. Also at http://www.iop.org/EJ/.

4. *Physics Abstracts*. London: Institution of Electrical Engineers.

5. Katz, Michael J. *Elements of the Scientific Paper*. New Haven, CT: Yale University Press, 1985.

6. American Institute of Physics. *AIP Style Manual*. 4th ed. New York: American Institute of Physics, 1990. Also at http://www.aip.org/pubservs/style/4thed/toc.html.

Index